How to Use
MICROSOFT ACCESS

How to Use MICROSOFT ACCESS

ERIC STONE

Illustrated by
CHERIE PLUMLEE COMPUTER GRAPHICS & ILLUSTRATION

Ziff-Davis Press
Emeryville, California

Copy Editor	Kate Hoffman
Technical Reviewer	Mark Hall
Project Coordinator	Barbara Dahl
Proofreader	Carol Burbo
Cover Illustration	Dave Feasey and Cherie Plumlee Computer Graphics & Illustration
Cover Design	Carrie English
Book Design	Dennis Gallagher/Visual Strategies, San Francisco
Screen Graphics Editors	Dan Brodnitz and Cat Haglund
Technical Illustration	Cherie Plumlee Computer Graphics & Illustration
Word Processing	Howard Blechman
Page Layout	Tony Jonick
Indexer	Carol Burbo

Ziff-Davis Press books are produced on a Macintosh computer system with the following applications: FrameMaker®, Microsoft® Word, QuarkXPress®, Adobe Illustrator®, Adobe Photoshop®, Adobe Streamline™, MacLink® *Plus*, Aldus® FreeHand™, Collage Plus™.

If you have comments or questions or would like to receive a free catalog, call or write:
Ziff-Davis Press
5903 Christie Avenue
Emeryville, CA 94608
1-800-688-0448

ISBN 1-56276-223-0

Manufactured in the United States of America
10 9 8 7 6 5 4 3 2 1

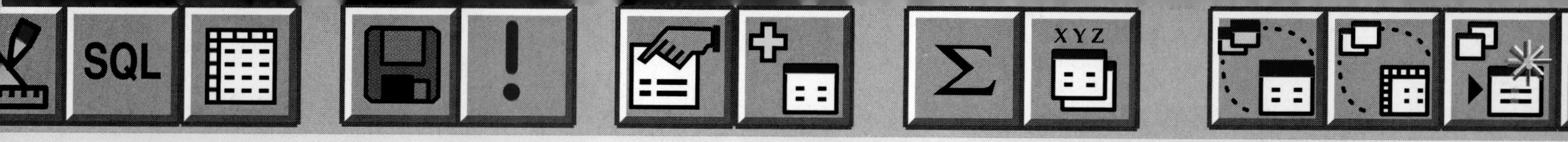

TABLE OF CONTENTS

Introduction x

CHAPTER 1

WHAT IS A DATABASE MANAGEMENT SYSTEM? 1

What Can a Database Management System Do? 2

Microsoft Access Is Your Database Management System 4

CHAPTER 2

WHAT ARE DOS AND WINDOWS? 7

How to Start Windows from DOS 8

How to Start a Program from Program Manager 10

How to Use the Mouse in Windows 12

How to Use the Keyboard in Windows 14

How to Talk to a Dialog Box 16

CHAPTER 3

WELCOME TO MICROSOFT ACCESS 19

How to Get Started in Microsoft Access 20

The Most Important Microsoft Access Terms and Concepts 22

How to Start a New Database 24

How to Open a Database from Disk 26

CHAPTER 4

DESIGNING TABLES 29

How to Start a New Table 30

How to Define Fields in a New Table 32

How to Name, Save, and Close a Table 34

How to Exit Microsoft Access 36

CHAPTER 5

BUILDING AND IMPROVING TABLES 39

How to Open and View a Table 40

How to Enter Data in a Table 42

How to Change the Contents of a Table 44

How to Change the Design of a Table 46

How to Print a Table 48

CHAPTER 6

WORKING WITH LARGE TABLES 51

How to Find Data 52

How to Sort a Table 54

CHAPTER 7

RESCUE 57

How to Undo an Action 58

How to Get Help from Microsoft Access 60

TRY IT! 62

CHAPTER 8

PULLING INFORMATION FROM A TABLE 67

How to Start a New Query 68

How to Specify What Fields a Query Will Display 70

How to Specify What Records a Query Will Display 72

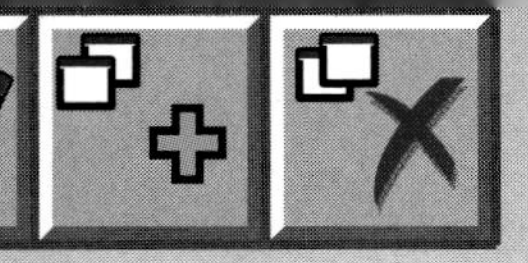      

How to Name, Save, and Close a Query 74

How to Run a Query 76

CHAPTER 9

IMPROVING QUERIES 79

How to Correct and Improve a Query 80

How to Perform a Calculation in a Query 82

TRY IT! 84

CHAPTER 10

CREATING FORMS 89

How to Start a New Form 90

How to Name, Save, and Close a Form 92

CHAPTER 11

USING FORMS 95

How to View Records in a Form 96

How to Edit Data in a Form 98

How to Enter Records in a Form 100

How to Sort Records in a Form 102

How to Display Only Selected Records in a Form 104

CHAPTER 12

CREATING REPORTS 107

How to Start a Report 108

How to Select a Report Type 110

How to Specify the Contents and Look of a Report 112

How to Name, Save, and Close a Report 114

CHAPTER 13

USING AND IMPROVING REPORTS 117

How to Preview a Report 118

How to Print a Report 120

How to Change the Appearance of a Report 122

How to Change the Contents of a Report 124

TRY IT! 126

CHAPTER 14

SHORTCUTS 131

The Toolbars 132

The Most Useful Keyboard Techniques 134

APPENDIX

INSTALLATION 137

Tips on Installing Microsoft Access 138

Index 140

ACKNOWLEDGMENTS

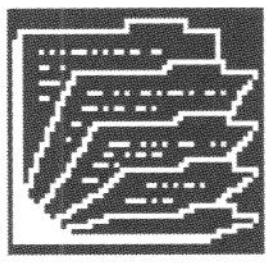

For supplying this book's uniquely graphical character, I offer a laurel and a hearty handshake to Dan Brodnitz, Carrie English, Dennis Gallagher, Tony Jonick, and Cherie Plumlee. The fact that this book teaches effectively (and looks great!) is due substantially to their efforts.

Credit for the fact that this book speaks the truth—and without deviating too much from the norms of modern English—goes to Carol Burbo, Mark Hall, Kate Hoffman, and Barbara Dahl.

Valuable behind-the-scenes insight and support came from Elisabeth Beller, Howard Blechman, Charles Cowens, Cat Haglund, Cheryl Holzaepfel, Cori Pansarasa, Joe Schneider, and Simon Tonner.

Finally, my sincerest thanks go to Valerie Haynes Perry and Ron White for their early inspiration and guidance, and to Tracy Van Hoof of Microsoft Corporation for her timely support.

INTRODUCTION

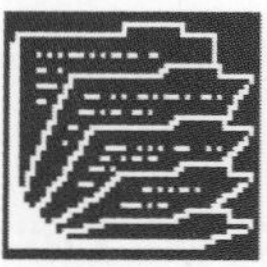

How to Use Microsoft Access is perfect for most people who own Microsoft Access, version 2.0. Why? Because most people just want to get their software to work so they can manage business data and print nice-looking reports without a lot of hassle. They don't turn cartwheels over the latest software features. They don't need hotshot shortcuts just yet. They are not looking to print works of art. They're beginning users with little or no computer experience, and maybe they're just a little bit skittish about learning a new program.

Is that you?

If so, you're sure to appreciate the concise, graphical approach of *How to Use Microsoft Access.* This tested and proven format, designed here at Ziff-Davis Press, puts database operations right before your eyes, step by step, task by task. When done reading, you will be a comfortable, confident user of the most important features Microsoft Access offers.

Each chapter of this book presents up to five related topics. Because each topic spans two facing pages, everything you need to know about a topic is in front of you at one time. Just follow the numbered steps around the pages, reading the text and looking at the pictures.

Flip through the pages of this book and then accept my promise: It's really as easy as it looks!

Colorful, realistic examples are included to help you understand each Microsoft Access feature. You may wish to type and work with the sample data as you learn, but doing so is not at all mandatory. If you want to stay focused on your own work and use this book as a reference, you will find it well suited for that purpose.

Even experienced computer users stumble into unfamiliar territory now and then. Read the "Tip Sheet" accompanying each topic to learn more about the occasional pitfall or quirky feature.

You will find special sections called "Try It" at strategic spots in this book. A Try It section is a hands-on exercise that gives you valuable practice with the database management skills you've acquired to that point. As you read a Try It section, be sure to follow each step at your computer.

To get the most out of this book, read it in sequence. However, if you have any experience with Microsoft Windows, Microsoft Access, or database management in general, you may already be familiar with the information in the first few chapters. Feel free to skip or skim such material.

I am eager to know your reactions to this book. Please mail any comments and suggestions for future editions to:

Eric Stone
Ziff-Davis Press
5903 Christie Avenue
Emeryville, CA 94608

Welcome aboard.

CHAPTER 1

What Is a Database Management System?

A computerized *database management system* helps you store, change, find, and present information.

What kind of information? Typically it's business information: personnel data, client lists, transaction records, inventories, and so on. But database management software can help you organize almost any kind of information. Historians, stamp collectors, gourmet cooks—anyone who has to keep track of data can do so efficiently on a personal computer with a database management system.

Imagine the data needs of some of the larger companies you do business with, such as banks and airlines. These businesses maintain information about millions of customers, transactions, employees, and inventory items. Given the obvious complexity of these information systems, it should not surprise you that database planning and management have become important specialties in today's business world. But you do not need any special skills to profit considerably from database management software.

Your personal computer wasn't built with the ability to manage databases—or to do much of anything else. Just as a CD player needs discs to play music, a computer needs *programs* to tell it what to do. Database management systems are programs that enable you to manage data on your computer. Your computer may also run other programs such as word processors, spreadsheets, and games.

This book teaches you how to use the Microsoft Access database management system, produced by Microsoft Corporation of Redmond, Washington.

What Can a Database Management System Do?

Database management systems vary in their capabilities, but they all have the same basic functions illustrated here. As you read further, you will discover how Microsoft Access handles each of these important functions.

TIP SHEET

- **It's worthwhile to know what database management systems in general do, but no doubt you're eager to learn what *Microsoft Access* can do and how to get it up and running. Relax. The rest of this book covers just that.**
- **Perhaps you have used another database management system such as dBASE and are now switching to Microsoft Access. You'll find that modern database management systems can all do pretty much the same things. The difference lies in how easy each task is, and you'll find that Microsoft Access is, overall, one of the easiest database management systems to use.**

1. Database management systems let you store and change *tables* of related data. All the data you enter in Microsoft Access is stored in one or more tables.

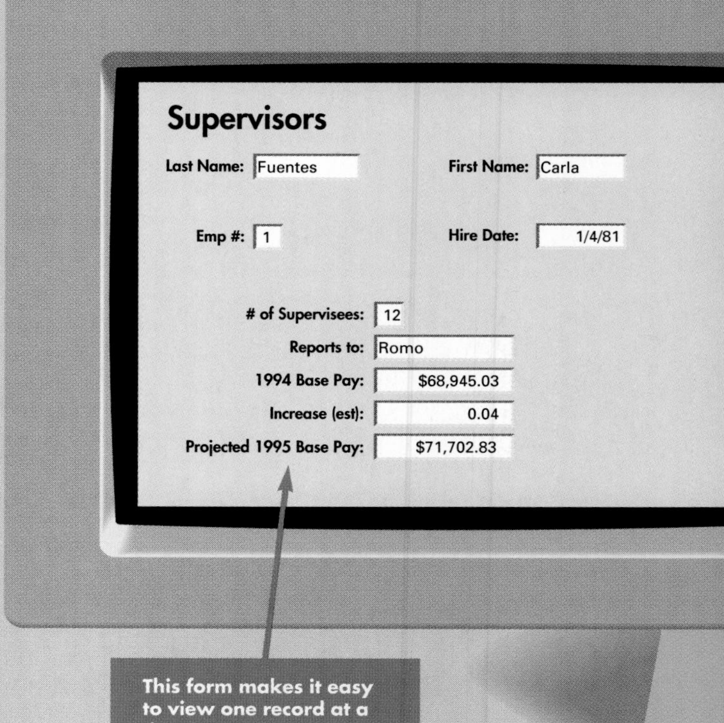

This form makes it easy to view one record at a time (step 5).

5. A *form* is an optional way to look at, enter, and change data in a table. While tables force you to examine many records at a time, forms let you concentrate on individual records in a way that is far easier on the eyes.

2 A *field* is a category of information, and a *record* is all the information relating to a single entity (such as one person or one product). For example, in the table on this page, the fields include Last Name, Hire Date, 1994 Base Pay, and several others. The table contains nine records: Carla Fuentes's record, Jay Rothstein's record, and so on.

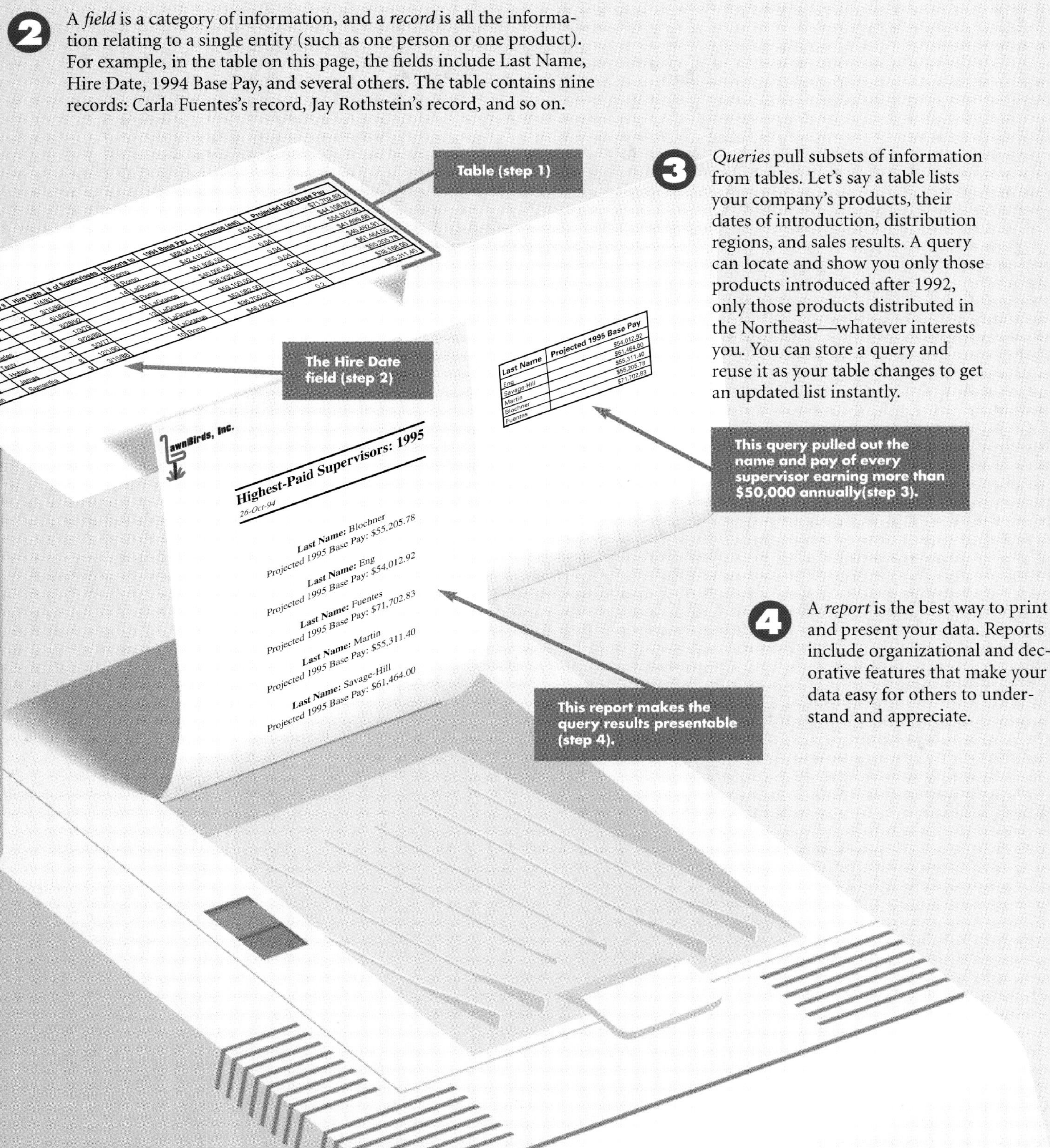

3 *Queries* pull subsets of information from tables. Let's say a table lists your company's products, their dates of introduction, distribution regions, and sales results. A query can locate and show you only those products introduced after 1992, only those products distributed in the Northeast—whatever interests you. You can store a query and reuse it as your table changes to get an updated list instantly.

4 A *report* is the best way to print and present your data. Reports include organizational and decorative features that make your data easy for others to understand and appreciate.

Microsoft Access Is Your Database Management System

Microsoft Access is a product—a brand, if you will. Just as there is a variety of similar soft drinks on the market, so there are many database management systems. While some are excellent, none is plainly superior—although, as with soft drinks, people tend to have their preferences. You may have heard of other database management systems such as Paradox and dBASE. These products compete with Microsoft Access for the hearts and dollars of people involved in database management. Manufacturers are forever beefing up their database management systems with new features and greater speed to win over more users.

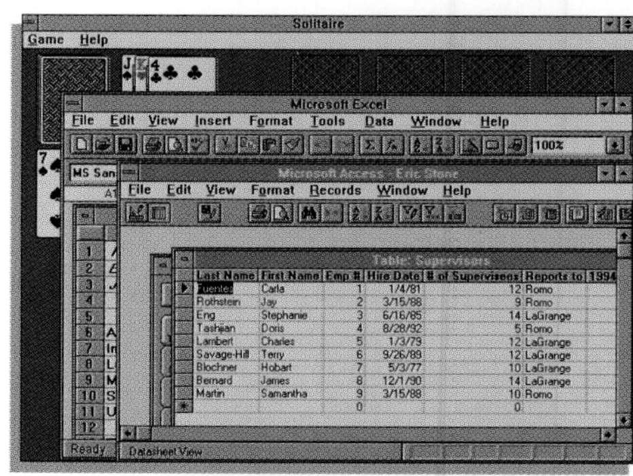

2 Microsoft Access is based on Microsoft Windows, a program that controls, among other things, the "look" of your computer screen. The Microsoft Access *interface* (the way you give instructions to it and receive information from it) is similar to that of many other Windows-based programs, including some you may already use.

1 Microsoft Access is not built into your computer; you buy it and install it. It might *seem* like Microsoft Access was built into your computer if someone else installed it on the computer's hard disk for you, or if you use a copy that's installed on your office network.

TIP SHEET

- **This book is about version 2.0 of Microsoft Access, released in early 1994. Unless you have version 2.0, you cannot be sure that everything you read in this book applies to you. Check your Microsoft Access packaging to verify the version number if you're not sure of it.**
- **Chapter 2 of this book is for first-time computer users or first-time Windows users. If you can start Microsoft Windows, use the mouse, select commands from a menu, and make selections in a dialog box, skip ahead to Chapter 3. If you can't do all these things (or if you don't even know what they mean!), Chapter 2 is just for you.**

❸ Microsoft Access is quite well regarded. Many database experts—and ordinary users, too—consider it the finest of the small crop of database management systems for Windows. You'll be using a product that earned the respect of the computing community almost immediately upon its introduction.

❹ What makes Microsoft Access such a standout? Well, it has lots of useful features, plenty of convenient shortcuts, and a stockpile of powerful customization tools for expert users and programmers. But most users would answer in less tangible terms: "It's easy," or "It feels right." As a beginner, you're apt to take a quick liking to Microsoft Access not because of what it can do but because you feel comfortable using it.

❺ Microsoft Access is a database management system, and it sports the same basic features as other modern database management systems. Like the others, it helps you store, change, find, and present information. You may have heard about fancy Microsoft Access features such as those that let you place pictures in reports. While impressive, these are not the features most people use frequently.

CHAPTER 2

What Are DOS and Windows?

DOS and Windows are programs that enable you to run all the programs you really *want* to run: your database management system (Microsoft Access), your word processor, your games, and so on.

DOS, short for *disk operating system,* moves information to and from the disks in your computer. Without an operating system, your computer cannot do anything useful for you. You cannot run a program like Microsoft Access unless you tell DOS to copy it temporarily from the disk into *random-access memory* (RAM), a temporary holding place. Likewise, you cannot electronically store and later reuse your data unless you have DOS copy it from RAM onto a disk.

Windows can simplify your role in directing these and many other tasks on your computer. It also provides a consistent and fairly appealing backdrop for Windows-based programs such as Microsoft Access. Windows-based programs look comfortingly similar on the screen, and there are many similarities in the ways you work with them. If you've used any Windows-based program, certain Microsoft Access operations will be familiar to you.

You never need to "start" DOS; it is running whenever you are using your computer. Windows, on the other hand, need not be running as you use your computer. But Windows *must* be running before you can start Microsoft Access or any other Windows-based program. This chapter helps you start and run Windows.

How to Start Windows from DOS

The heart and soul of DOS, at least from the user's viewpoint, is the *DOS prompt*. This is where DOS asks you for information and you provide it. By typing *commands* at the DOS prompt, you can run programs, check the contents of your disks, reset the time on your computer's internal clock, and much more. For now, the only DOS command you absolutely must know is the one that starts Windows.

1. Switch on your computer. You may need to flick switches on several components of your computer system, including the main box containing the hard disk and the floppy-disk drives, the monitor (screen), and the printer. Give the computer a minute or so to go through its wake-up ritual. When it's ready to accept information from you, it will ask you for the information or display the DOS prompt.

TIP SHEET

- **Your computer may be set up to bypass the DOS prompt and start Windows automatically. If Windows has started, you'll see the words *Program Manager* somewhere on the screen. In this case, you can skip steps 4 and 5.**
- **Some computers automatically run the *DOS Shell,* an interface designed to make DOS operations easier, upon start-up. If your computer is running the DOS Shell, you'll see the words *MS-DOS Shell* across the top of the screen. Hold down the Alt key as you type** fx **to exit the DOS Shell and face the DOS prompt. Then proceed with step 4.**
- **Your office computer specialist may have set up a *custom menu* that appears in place of the DOS prompt. This menu should contain an entry for *Windows* (or possibly *Microsoft Windows* or *Windows 3.1* or a similar variation). To start Windows, you probably have to press the Down Arrow key until the Windows entry is highlighted, and then press Enter. However, you may have to consult with your office computer specialist to learn how the custom menu works.**

2 Type in any information the computer asks for, and then press the Enter key. Some computers ask for the date and time. If your computer is on a network—a setup where personal computers in an office are hooked together to share information—it may ask you for your name and password. (Your office's network administrator can help you with this step.)

3 After providing any initial information your computer needs, you see the DOS prompt. This is the way DOS asks you to give it a command. The most common DOS prompt looks like *C:\>* but it can vary. For example, the prompt may be gussied up with special characters such as brackets or even with a message, as in *C:\DOS> — Type a command, please.* You can easily start Windows no matter how the DOS prompt looks.

4 Type **win** and press the Enter key. On most computers, this command starts Windows. After a few seconds, you'll see the words *Program Manager* somewhere on the screen, indicating that Windows is now running. Skip the next step if this step worked fine.

5 If step 4 produced a message such as *Bad command or file name*, try typing **c:\windows\win** and pressing Enter. If that fails, try **d:\windows\win**. Still can't start Windows? Well, the possible reasons and solutions are too many to enumerate here, but a computer-savvy colleague should be able to help you in short order. Or call Microsoft technical support, which fields questions like yours routinely.

How to Start a Program from Program Manager

Program Manager is a Windows-based program that comes with Windows. Its role is to make it easy to start *other* programs, including Microsoft Access. Program Manager opens when you start Windows and remains open as long as Windows is running. The large screen to the right shows how Program Manager might look when you start Windows. Then again, Windows is highly customizable, so your starting screen may look quite different.

TIP SHEET

- **To open a program group window using the keyboard, press the Alt key once, type** w **to pull down the Window menu, and type the number next to the program group you want to open. To start a program using the keyboard, open its program group, use the arrow keys to highlight the name of the program, and press Enter.**
- **Under Windows, you can have more than one program running at a time. After starting one program, press Alt+Esc (hold down Alt, press and release Esc, and release Alt) to return to Program Manager. Then find and start the next program. Use the Alt+Esc key combination to switch among all your open programs.**
- **To close a document window, double-click on the *Control Menu box* in its upper-right corner. You can close an application window the same way, but that has the effect of shutting down the program. Closing the Program Manager application window closes Windows and returns you to DOS.**

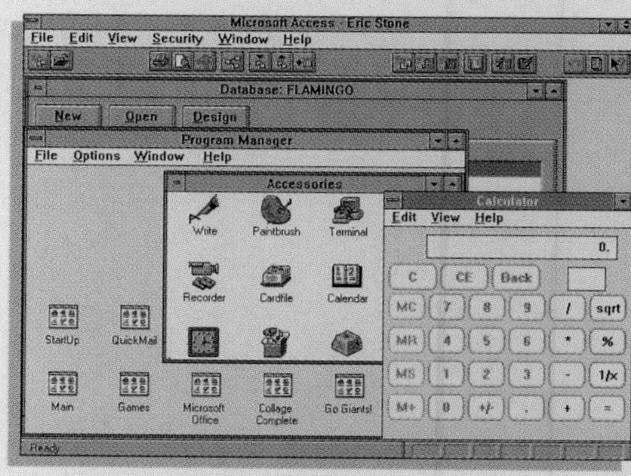

1 A *window* is simply an on-screen box containing information. Like most Windows-based programs, Program Manager has an *application window* and multiple *document windows.* In this screen, five windows are wholly or partially visible. (Microsoft Access, Calculator, and Program Manager are application windows, and Database: FLAMINGO and Accessories are document windows.)

5 When you want to start a program, first open the program group containing its program item. To open a program group such as Accessories, roll the mouse until the arrow points to the group name or icon, and then *double-click* (click the left mouse button twice in rapid succession).

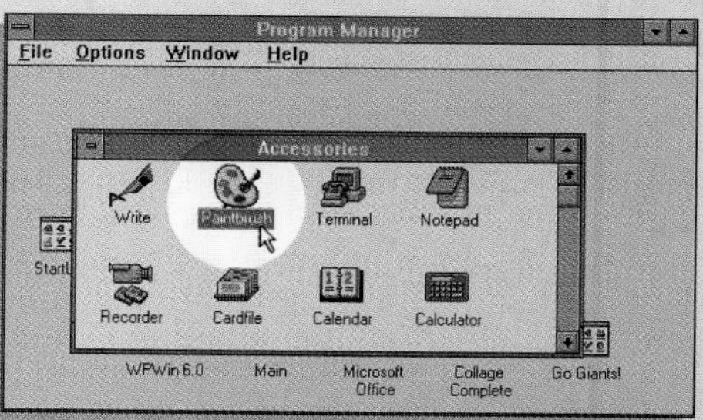

6 Then, to start a program such as Paintbrush, locate its program item in the program group window, roll the mouse to point to the program name or icon, and double-click.

2 An application window contains a program's *title bar,* which displays the program name—in this case, Program Manager. You issue commands from a program's *menu bar.* The application window for Program Manager also contains icons representing *program groups,* collections of related programs that you can run.

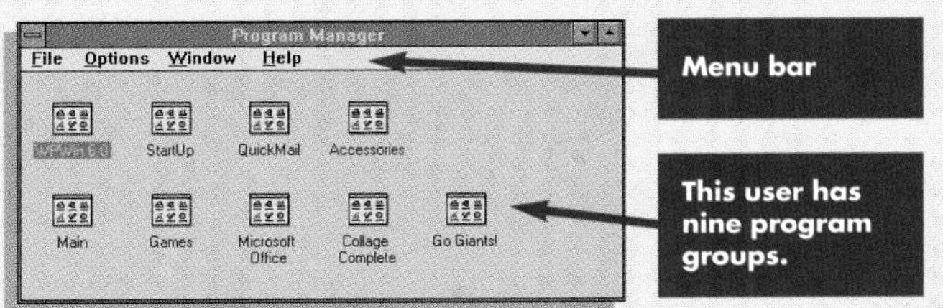

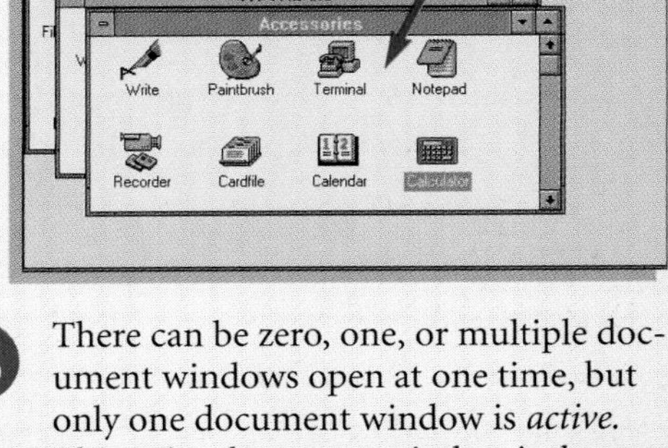

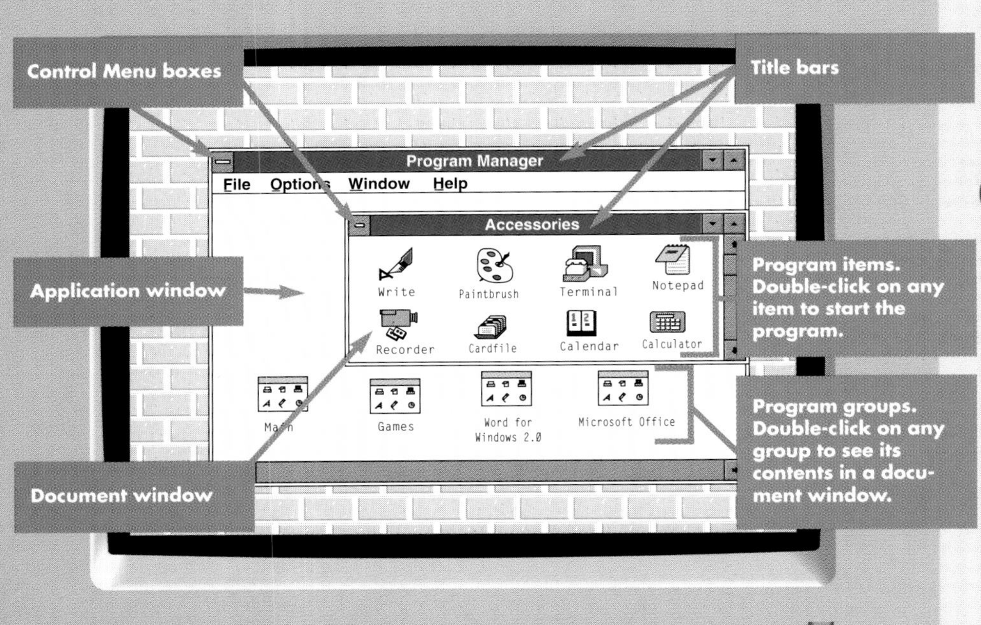

3 There can be zero, one, or multiple document windows open at one time, but only one document window is *active.* The active document window is the one that will be affected by commands you issue. The title bar of each document window contains the document name, and the title bar of the active document window is highlighted.

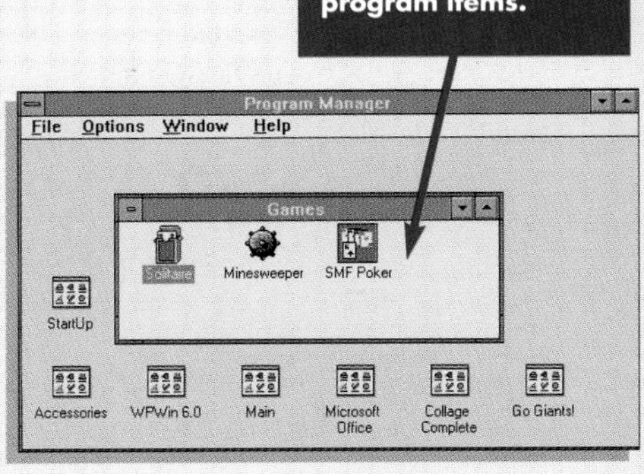

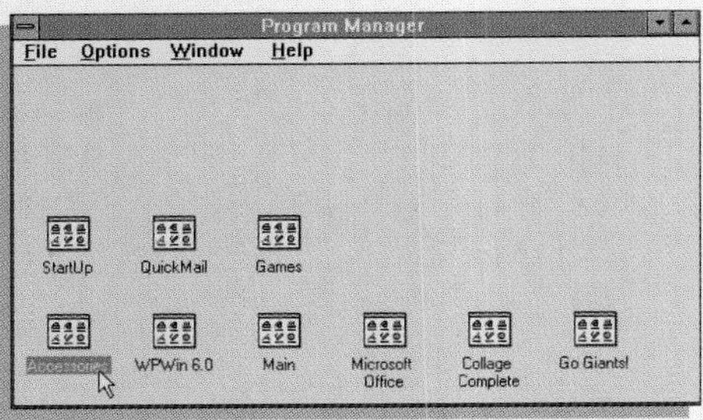

4 Generally, a document window contains a document. In Program Manager, however, document windows contain *program items,* little icons representing the programs within a program group. The fact that the window is called a "document window" is a quirk of Windows terminology. For clarity, many people refer to document windows in Program Manager as *program group windows.*

How to Use the Mouse in Windows

An *input device* is a means of giving instructions to the computer. You're probably familiar with the keyboard as the most common input device. A *mouse,* so named for its hunched-over appearance and taillike cable, is a hand-held input device also used routinely in Windows. Although it's possible to get by without a mouse and do all your work from the keyboard, it's not too wise. The Windows interface was designed with the mouse in mind. Keyboard alternatives can be awkward—and it's not always easy to find out what they are. Take a few minutes to learn the major mouse moves, and you'll be rewarded with smoother computing.

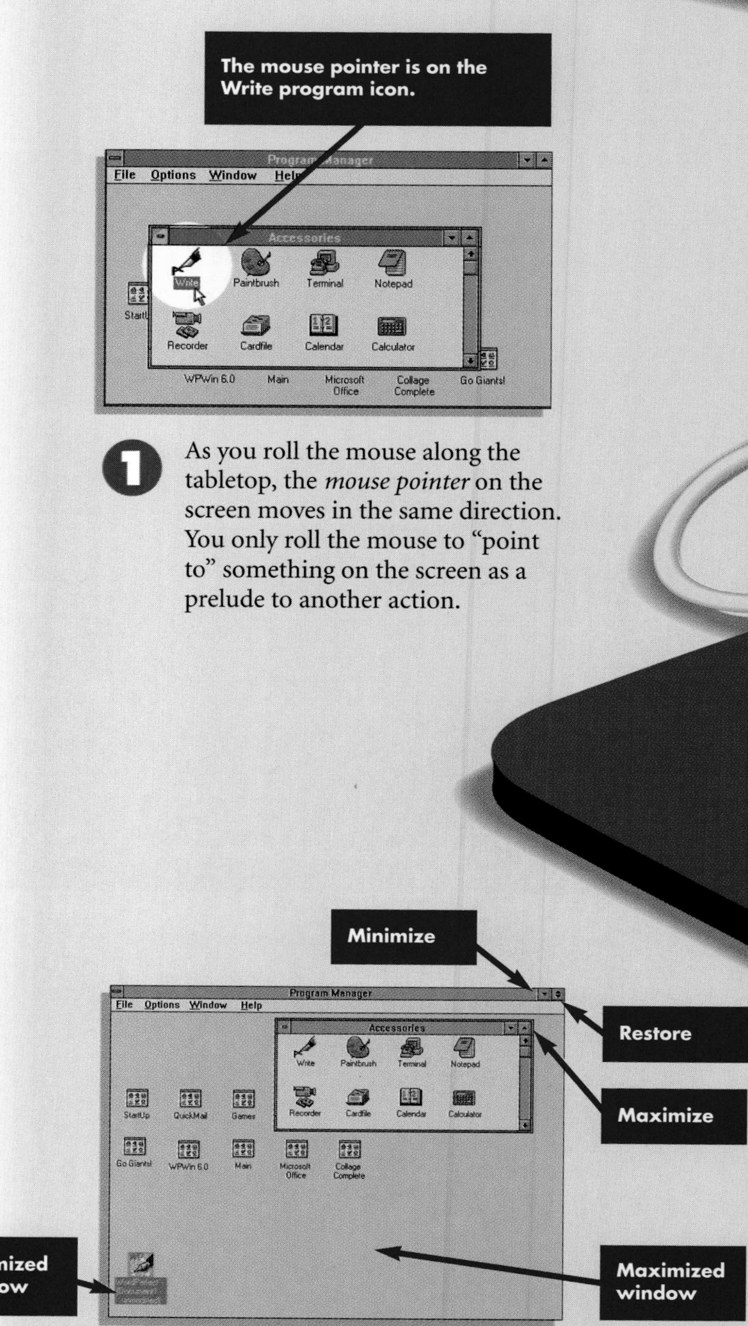

1 As you roll the mouse along the tabletop, the *mouse pointer* on the screen moves in the same direction. You only roll the mouse to "point to" something on the screen as a prelude to another action.

6 To *maximize* a window (enlarge it so an application window fills the screen or so a document window fills its application window), click on its maximize button. To *restore* a maximized window to its original size, click on its restore button. To *minimize* a window so it's merely an icon with a title, click on its minimize button. To restore a minimized window to its original size, double-click on its title or icon.

TIP SHEET

- **Unless instructed otherwise, use the *left* mouse button. The other mouse buttons are used so infrequently in Windows that when they are used, you're always told about it specifically.**
- **Some mice have two buttons, and others have three. The right mouse button is used infrequently, and the middle button on the three-button mouse is almost never used.**
- **For keyboard alternatives to the scroll bars and the maximize/minimize/restore buttons, turn the page.**

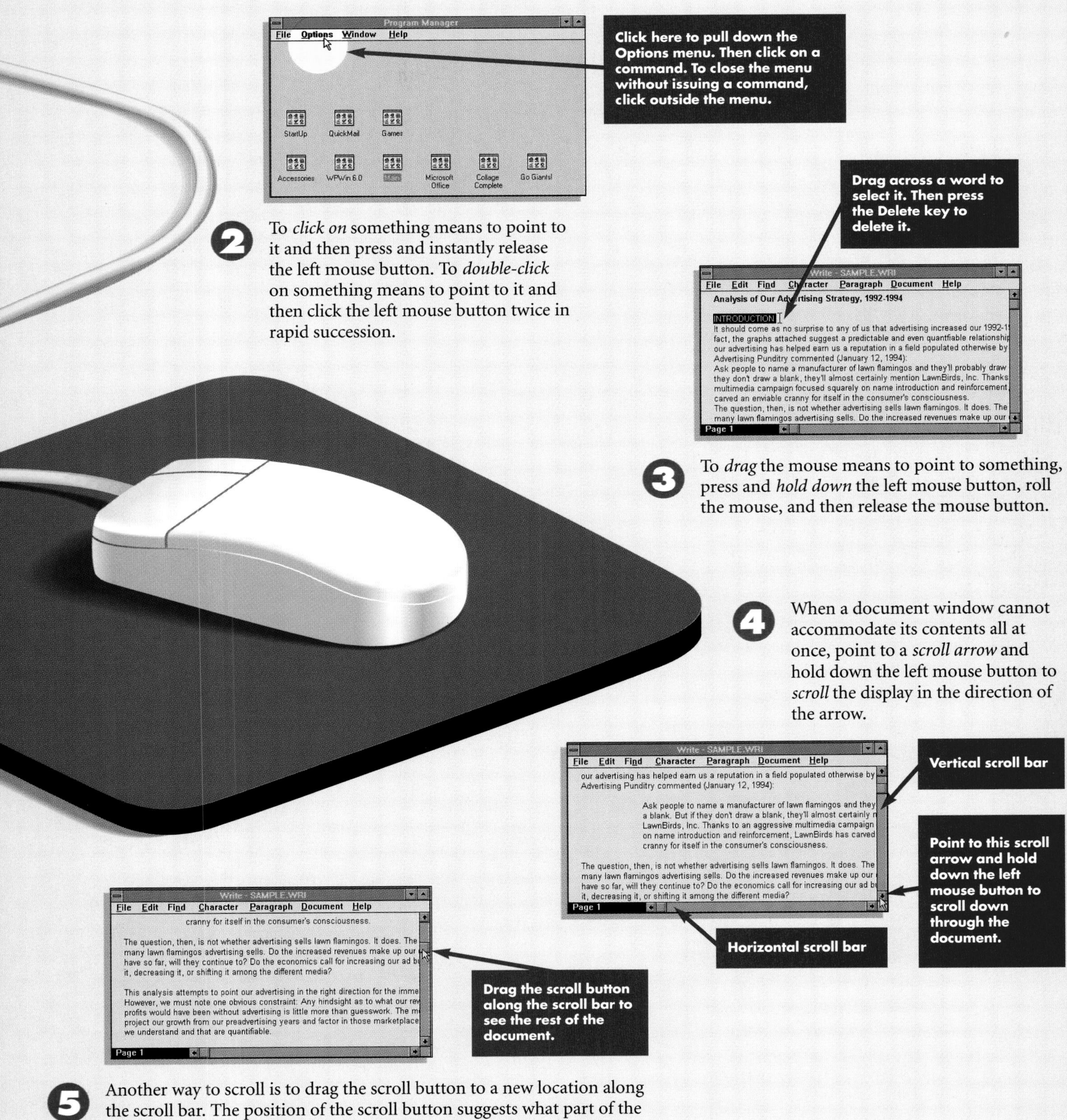

2 To *click on* something means to point to it and then press and instantly release the left mouse button. To *double-click* on something means to point to it and then click the left mouse button twice in rapid succession.

3 To *drag* the mouse means to point to something, press and *hold down* the left mouse button, roll the mouse, and then release the mouse button.

4 When a document window cannot accommodate its contents all at once, point to a *scroll arrow* and hold down the left mouse button to *scroll* the display in the direction of the arrow.

5 Another way to scroll is to drag the scroll button to a new location along the scroll bar. The position of the scroll button suggests what part of the contents you are viewing. For example, when the scroll button is about one-third of the way down the vertical scroll bar in a document window, you are one-third of the way from the top of the window contents.

How to Use the Keyboard in Windows

In Windows and in most Windows-based programs, you don't have to use the keyboard for much of anything—except, of course, to type text. But if you type quite a bit, you may be interested in optional ways to issue commands, move through documents, and perform other common actions without having to reach for the mouse. The more experience you get in a Windows-based program, the more likely you'll hanker for keyboard alternatives to the mouse actions you perform most often. Even if you're a true mouse-o-phile, you should be aware of the major keyboard techniques in case your mouse ever malfunctions.

TIP SHEET

- **In many programs, the PgUp and PgDn keys scroll the window contents in large increments, Ctrl+Home moves to the top of the window contents, and Ctrl+End moves to the bottom.**
- **Your function keys may be across the top of the keyboard or along the left side. Function keys along the side are easier for touch typists to reach and may make it worthwhile to memorize some keyboard shortcuts in your favorite programs.**

1. The Shift, Alt, and Ctrl keys always work in combination with other keys. No doubt you know that pressing the Shift key along with a letter key types a capital letter. The other available combinations vary by program.

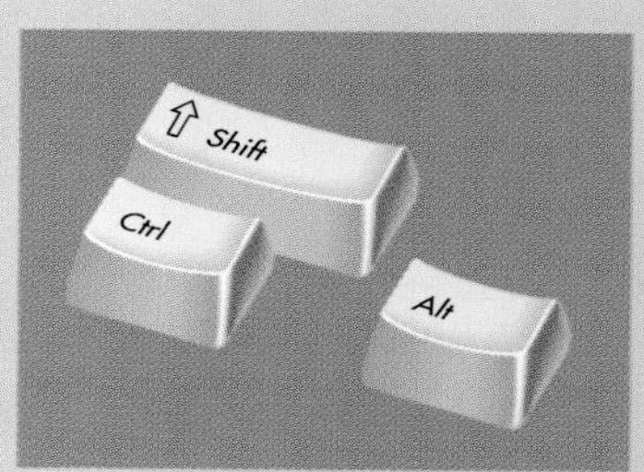

6. Not surprisingly, the Escape key (Esc on most keyboards) lets you slam the door on possible hazards. If you pull down a menu but decide not to issue a command, press Escape twice to deactivate the menu bar. If you issue a command and a dialog box appears (see next page) but you don't want to proceed, press Escape to close the dialog box.

2 Most often, Shift, Alt, and Ctrl combine with the *function keys*, labeled F1 through F10 or F12, as an alternative way to issue a command. For example, in most Windows programs, pressing Alt+F4 (holding down Alt, pressing and releasing F4, and releasing Alt) closes the program. The function keys can also work alone.

3 When you don't want to reach for the mouse to scroll through the contents of a window, use the Up, Down, Left, and Right arrow keys instead. If the arrows on the numeric keypad don't work, press the Num Lock key and they should work fine.

Control menu of the Accessories document window

4 To maximize, minimize, restore, or close a window, first open its Control menu. Press Alt+spacebar to open the Control menu of an application window; press Alt+hyphen to open the Control menu of a document window. Use the Down Arrow key to highlight the command you want: Maximize, Minimize, Restore, or Close. Then press Enter.

Type the underlined character to issue the command.

5 To pull down a menu from the menu bar, press Alt and then type the underlined character in the menu name. Then, to issue a command from the menu, type the underlined character in the command name.

How to Talk to a Dialog Box

A *dialog box* is where you give Windows (or a Windows-based program) the information it needs to carry out a command you have issued. Say you issue a command called Print, a command found on the File menu of most programs. Before doing any printing, the program may present a dialog box to ask you how much of the window contents to print, how many copies to print, what printer to print it on, and so forth. Once you answer, the Print command takes effect. The name *dialog box* is just slightly misleading. In a human dialog, the participants take turns speaking. In a computerized dialog, the program asks all its questions at once, and then you give all your answers. It's more like a questionnaire than a dialog.

TIP SHEET

- **To choose a dialog box option from the keyboard, hold down Alt and press the underlined character in the option name. If the dialog box lacks underlined characters, press Tab to move from option to option. Then press the spacebar to mark or clear a check box; use the arrow keys to mark the desired radio button within a group; or press the Down Arrow key to drop down a list, press the down arrow to highlight your choice, and press Tab.**
- **If you need to see what's behind a dialog box, move the box by dragging its title bar.**
- **To close a dialog box without issuing the command, click on the Cancel button (available in most dialog boxes), double-click on the dialog box's Control Menu box, or press Escape.**

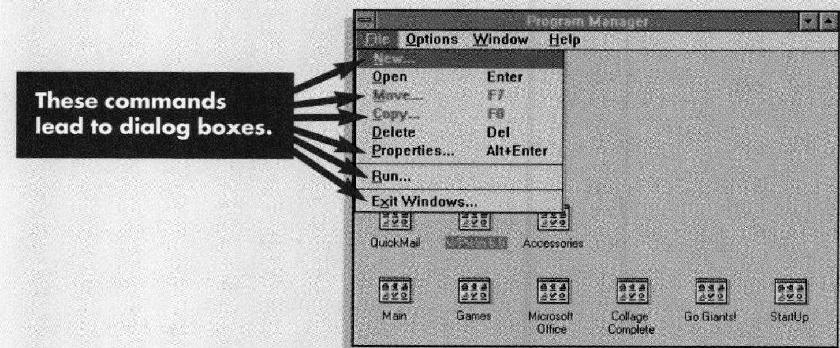

1 In Windows menus, the presence of three dots after a command name means that a dialog box will appear when you issue the command.

OK

6 When you've provided all the information requested, issue the command by clicking on the button labeled OK or on another appropriately named button. (The button name might be Print or Find or something else related to the command.)

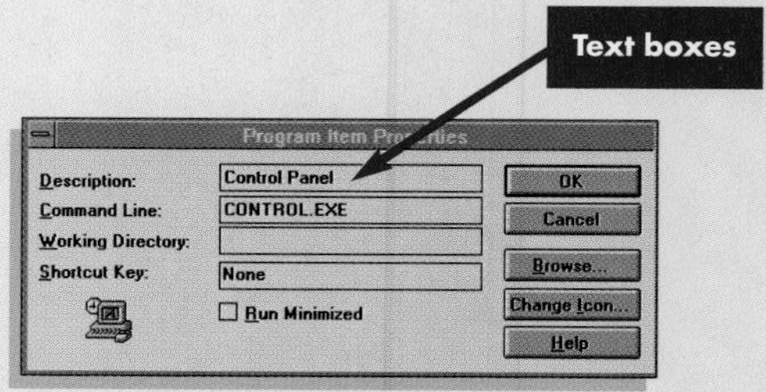

5 To change the entry in a *text box,* first click anywhere in the box. Then use the arrow keys to position the cursor, use the Backspace and Delete keys to delete text as needed, and type new text from the keyboard.

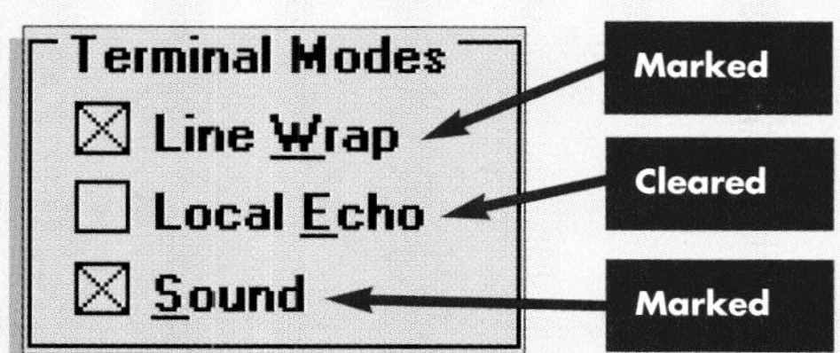

2 One way to answer a question in a dialog box is to mark or clear a square *check box.* Click in an empty check box to mark it and accept the option; click in a marked check box to clear it and reject the option.

3 Sometimes options are grouped in *radio buttons.* In such a group, you can select only one option at a time. Select an option by clicking in the round button; the previously selected button is cleared. It's just like the station-selector buttons on old-time car radios—hence the name.

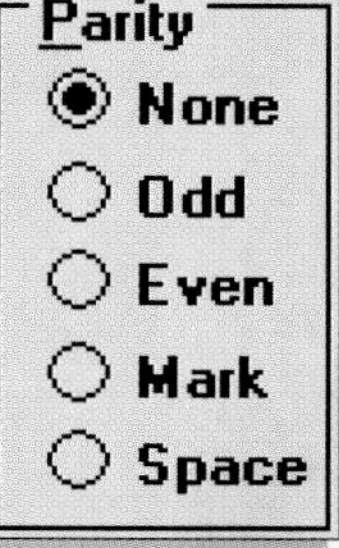

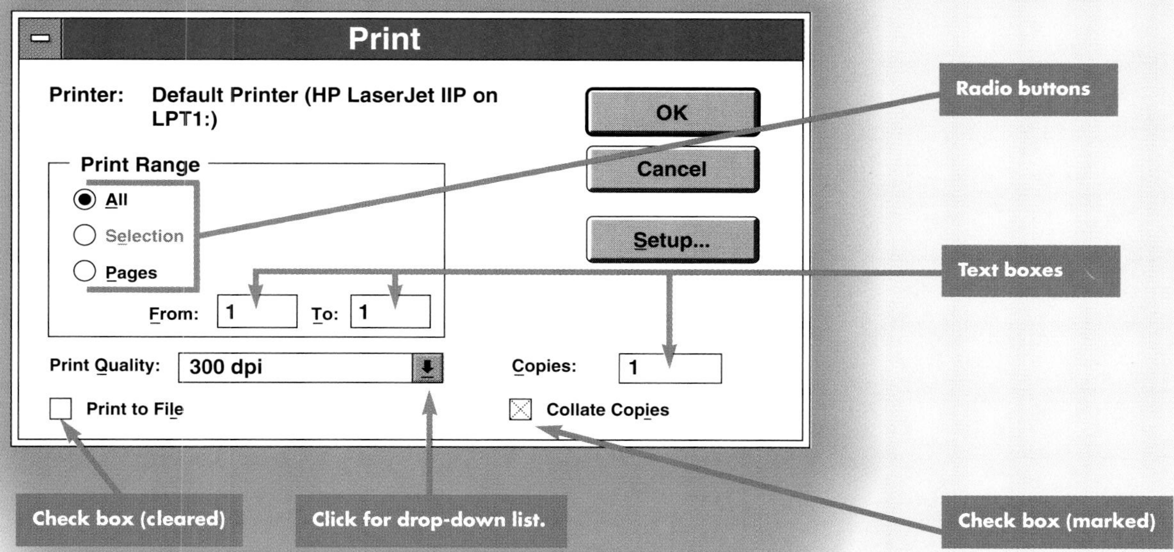

4 A downward-pointing *drop-down arrow* with a horizontal line below it means you can click on the arrow to see a *drop-down list* of options. When you spot the option you need, click on it.

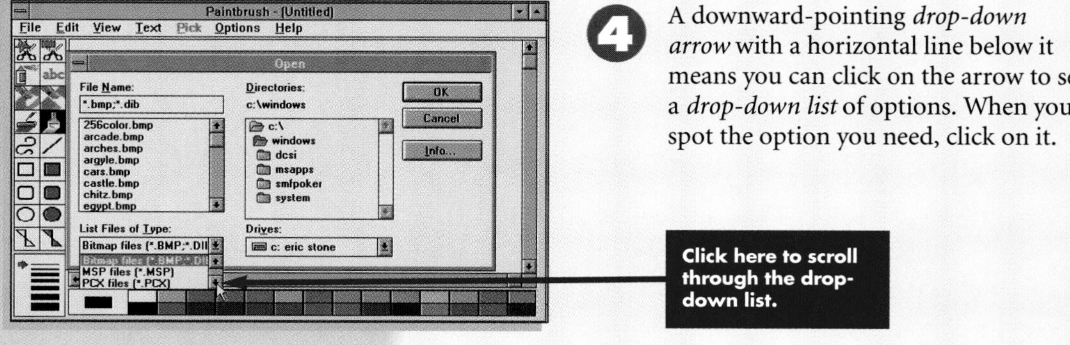

CHAPTER 3

Welcome to Microsoft Access

In this chapter you'll fire up Microsoft Access and start touring its most basic features.

This chapter—and, in fact, the whole book—will describe Microsoft Access as most people see and use it. Why only "most" people? Well, Microsoft Access is a highly customizable program. If you are in an office where many people work with the same data, a computer administrator or consultant may have equipped Microsoft Access with special on-screen tools suited to your situation. He or she may also have set up Microsoft Access to start with a database already open. In such cases, your Microsoft Access opening screen won't exactly match the one you see on the next page.

In addition, your job responsibilities affect the way you use Microsoft Access. For example, you may only be working with data supplied by others, in which case you will never need to build a table as described in Chapter 5.

Regardless, you should not worry about discrepancies between what you see in this book and on your computer screen, or between the way you eventually use Microsoft Access and the techniques described in this book. Differences in the appearance of your Microsoft Access screen are likely to be inconsequential—and whoever is responsible for them will surely be happy to explain them to you. What's more, this book is designed to allow you to skip topics that do not apply to your work; you don't have to read the chapters sequentially to understand later topics.

How to Get Started in Microsoft Access

When you start Microsoft Access, the program does not know what type of work you want to do. Do you want to work with existing data or enter new data? Examine query results? Print a report? There are so many possibilities that Microsoft Access does not even take a guess at your intentions. It presents an application window that is essentially blank—and no document window at all. But the application window is not *completely* blank. It contains several tools and informational areas with which you should familiarize yourself. Relax and take some time to get your bearings!

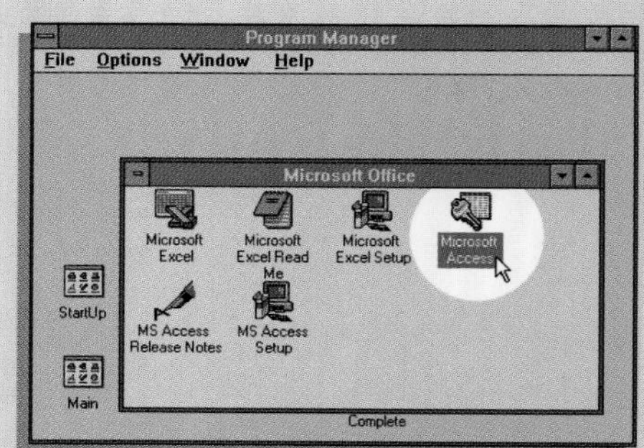

1. To start Microsoft Access, first start Windows. Then open the program group containing Microsoft Access and double-click on the Microsoft Access icon. (See Chapter 2 for help with these operations.)

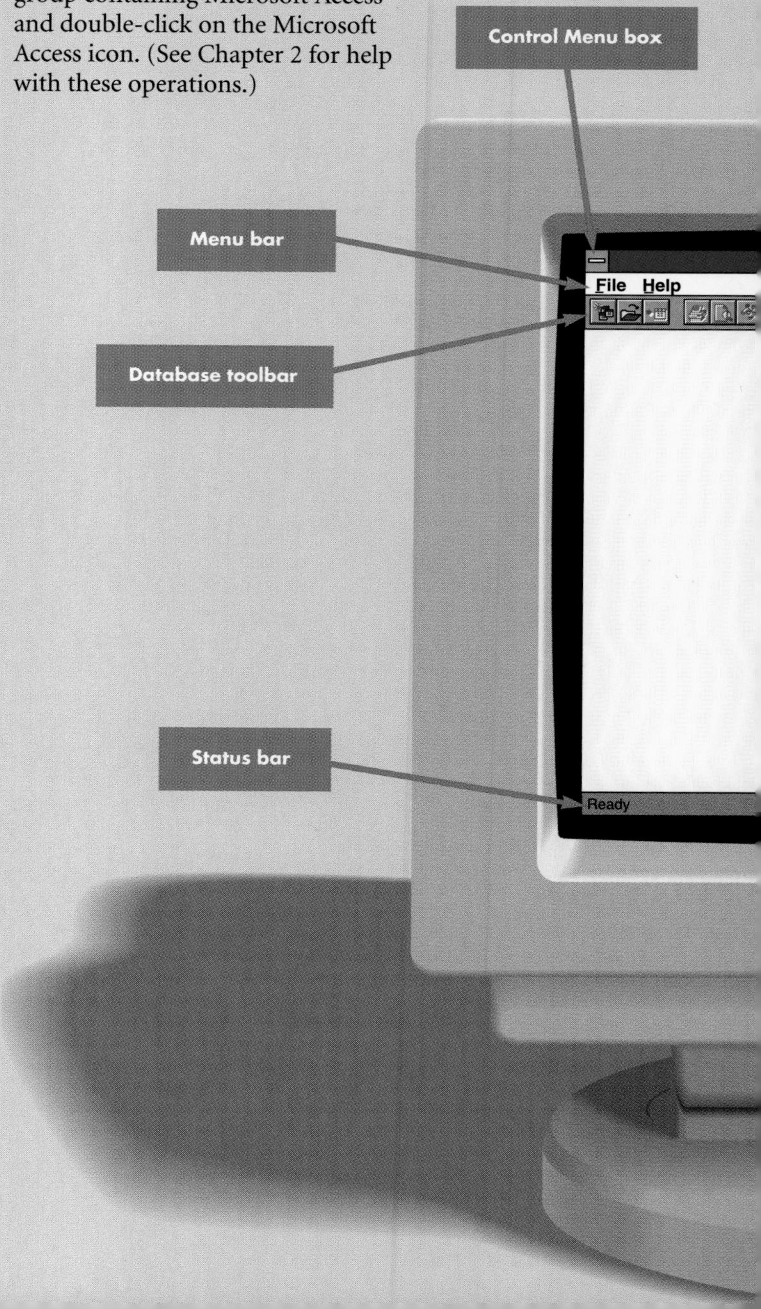

Control Menu box

Menu bar

Database toolbar

Status bar

File Help

Ready

TIP SHEET

- **If you cannot find the Microsoft Access icon in Program Manager (step 1), start the program this way: Click on the File command in the menu bar, and then click on the Run command. In the Run dialog box, type** c:\access\msaccess **and click on the OK button.**
- **You may observe that menu commands and toolbar tools are sometimes dimmed. This means that the command or tool is temporarily unavailable. Generally a command or tool is unavailable because it wouldn't make sense to use it at the moment. For example, the Database toolbar contains a tool that looks like a printer. This tool prints the table, query results, form, or report you are working with. Because you are not working with data yet, there is nothing to print, and the tool is temporarily dimmed.**

2 A blank application window appears, as shown below. It may or may not be maximized (set to fill the entire screen). If the window is not maximized, you may wish to maximize it by clicking on the maximize button—the upward-pointing arrow in the top-right corner of the window. (An already-maximized window has no maximize button.) That way, your screen can show more information—and will more closely match the pictures in this book.

3 The Microsoft Access menu bar initially contains only two menus, but as you work with data, more menus will appear. To experiment, you can click on a menu name to pull down the menu and see what commands are available. A command name followed by three dots leads to a dialog box (see Chapter 2). A command name followed by an arrow leads to another menu. Click outside the pulled-down menu to close it without issuing a command.

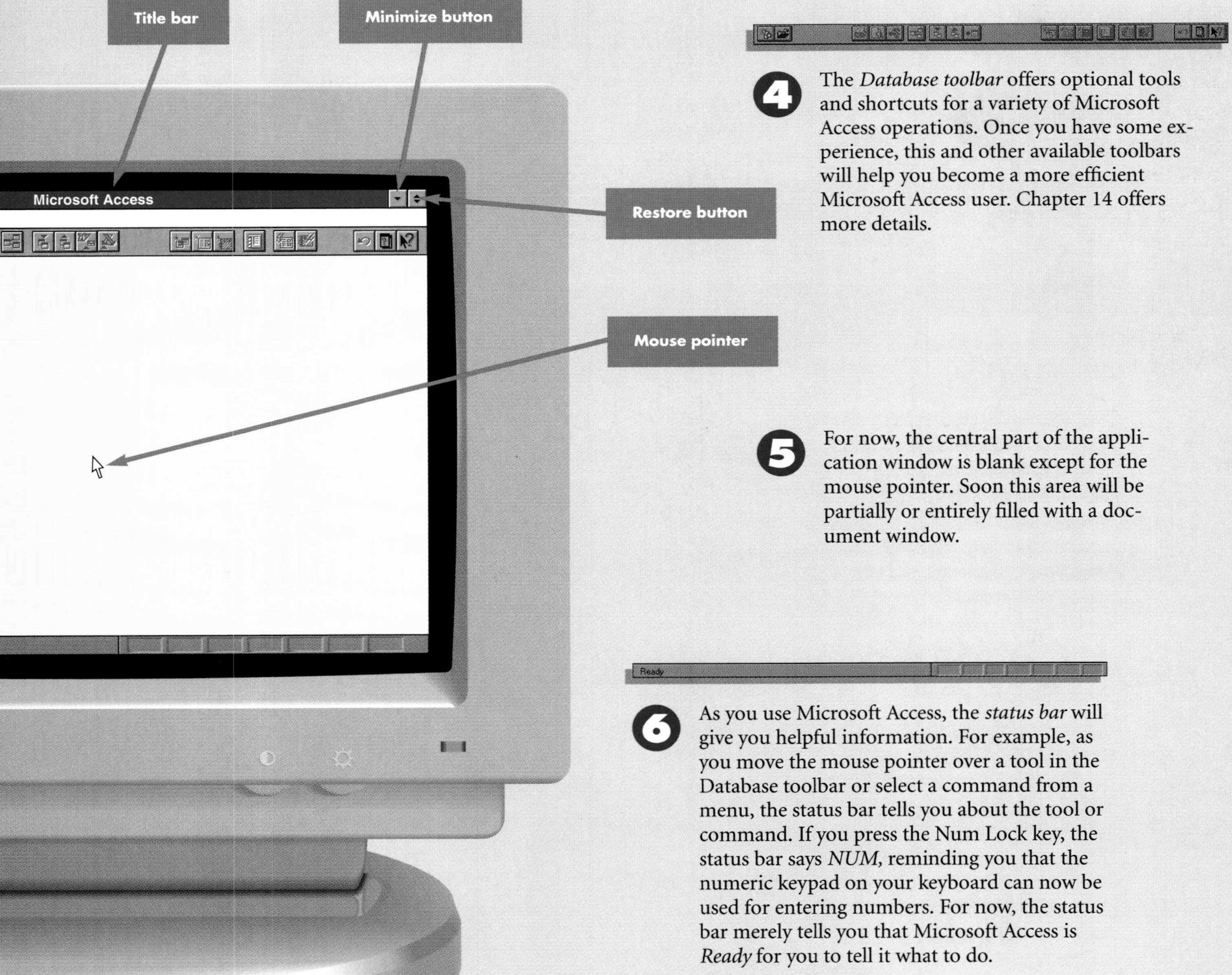

4 The *Database toolbar* offers optional tools and shortcuts for a variety of Microsoft Access operations. Once you have some experience, this and other available toolbars will help you become a more efficient Microsoft Access user. Chapter 14 offers more details.

5 For now, the central part of the application window is blank except for the mouse pointer. Soon this area will be partially or entirely filled with a document window.

6 As you use Microsoft Access, the *status bar* will give you helpful information. For example, as you move the mouse pointer over a tool in the Database toolbar or select a command from a menu, the status bar tells you about the tool or command. If you press the Num Lock key, the status bar says *NUM,* reminding you that the numeric keypad on your keyboard can now be used for entering numbers. For now, the status bar merely tells you that Microsoft Access is *Ready* for you to tell it what to do.

The Most Important Microsoft Access Terms and Concepts

Chapter 1 introduced several database terms, including *field, record, report, form,* and *query.* These are general database terms that apply to almost any database management system. But Microsoft Access has its own terminology and its own ways of looking at data. Here you'll learn the few terms and concepts that every efficient Microsoft Access user should know.

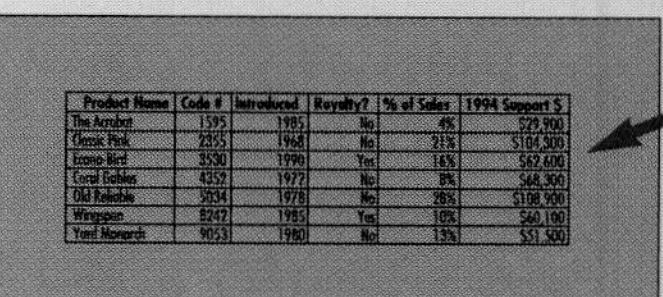

1 You might think of a single table (fields and records) as a "database," but in Microsoft Access, a database includes much more.

5 If you have used other software such as a word processor, you may be familiar with the concept of *files.* In a word processor, each document is stored on disk as a file. But in Microsoft Access, an entire database is stored together as a file.

TIP SHEET

- **If you work or hang out with computer junkies, you may have heard phrases like "object-oriented programming" and thought that *object* (step 3) is a technical term. And, in fact, it is. But that is of no consequence to you as a beginning user of Microsoft Access. It is enough to know that an object is any table or tool that makes up a database—and you need to know this much only because Access sometimes uses the word *object* in messages and dialog boxes.**
- **A good reason to know about views (step 4) is that occasionally you may select a command by mistake and wind up in an unfamiliar view. For example, it is possible to look at a query in SQL view, which is meaningful only to programmers. If you ever find yourself in this situation, simply click on View in the Microsoft Access menu bar and then click on a more familiar view.**

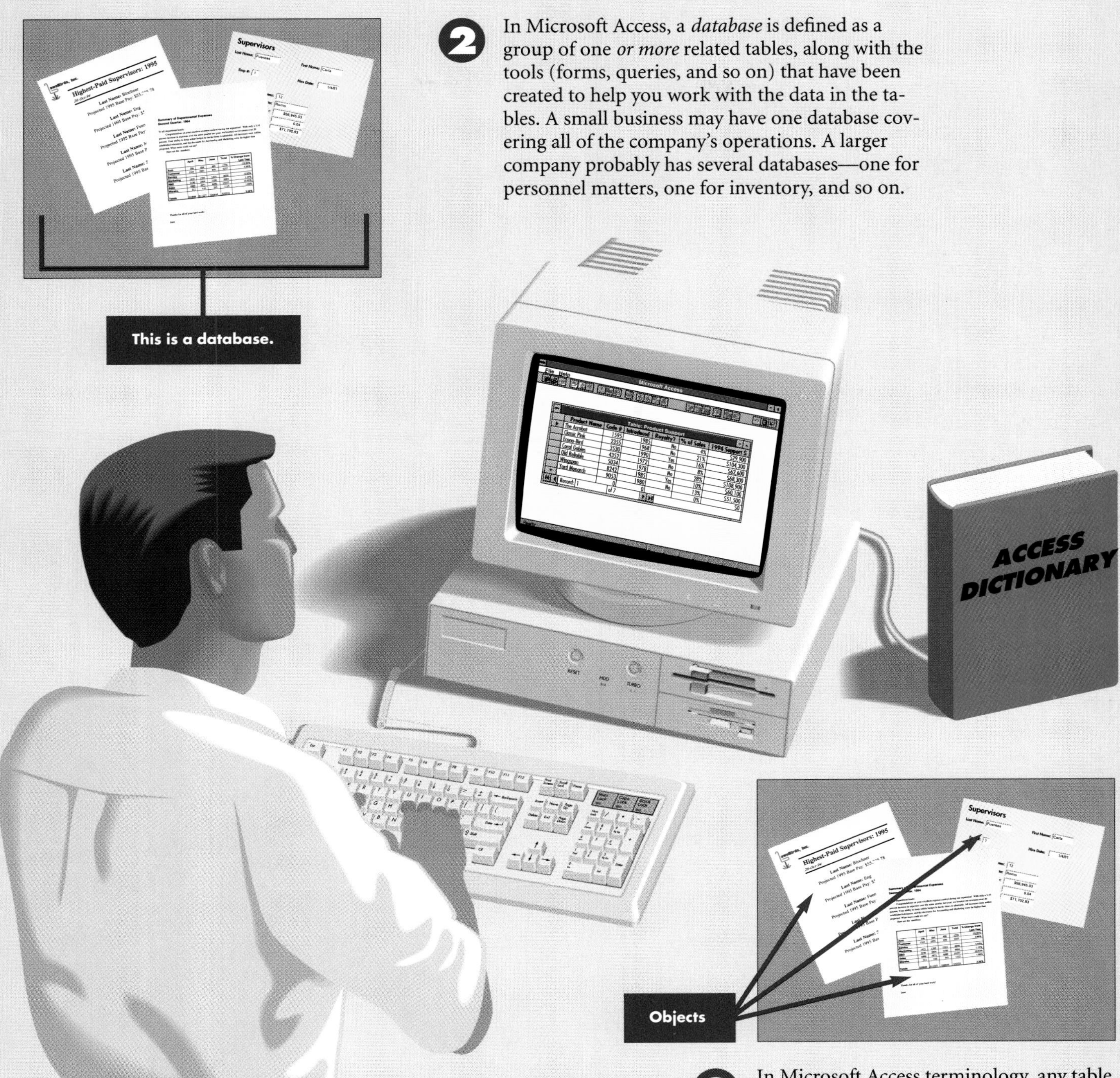

2 In Microsoft Access, a *database* is defined as a group of one *or more* related tables, along with the tools (forms, queries, and so on) that have been created to help you work with the data in the tables. A small business may have one database covering all of the company's operations. A larger company probably has several databases—one for personnel matters, one for inventory, and so on.

3 In Microsoft Access terminology, any table, form, query, or report is an *object*. (Microsoft Access also has objects called *macros* and *modules*, but only advanced users and programmers work with these.) Thus, a database is a collection of related objects.

4 Microsoft Access offers different ways of looking at an object, and each way is called a *view*. For example, you can look at the results of a query (Datasheet view), or you can look at the instructions that produce the query (Design view). This book will tell you when and how to switch from one view to another.

How to Start a New Database

Recall from the preceding page that a database is a collection of related tables and other objects. You start a new database when you need to enter and manage data that does not fit logically in an existing database. Here you'll learn how to start a new database. Skip ahead to the next page if you need to open and work with an existing database.

- If you do not include an extension in your database name (step 4), Microsoft Access adds the extension .MDB to the name automatically. As you will observe on the next page, this extension makes it somewhat easier to open a database from disk.
- A *network* is a setup where computers are connected to share information such as databases. If you are working on a network and you are creating a database that will be shared by other network users, you should ask the network administrator to help you name the database and choose a storage location for it.
- Each disk or drive on your computer system is assigned a letter. By convention, drive A refers to the disk in your first (and maybe only) floppy-disk drive. If your computer has two floppy-disk drives, drive B is probably the lower or rightmost of the two. Drive C is your hard-disk drive. Any drives higher than C are either network drives or additional areas of your hard disk.

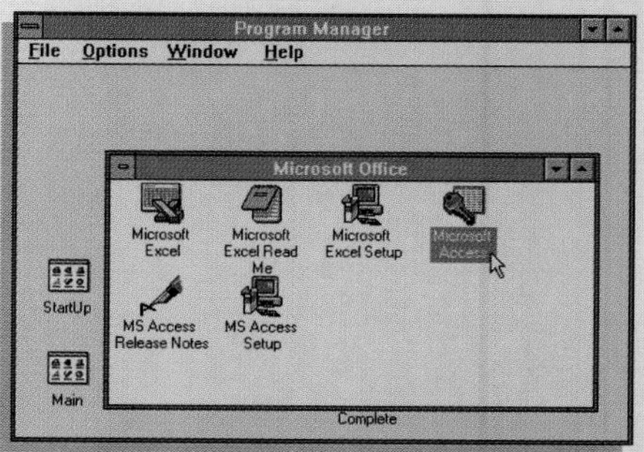

1 Start Microsoft Access if it is not already running.

8 Click on the OK button.

2 Click on File in the menu bar and then click on New Database, the first command in the File menu.

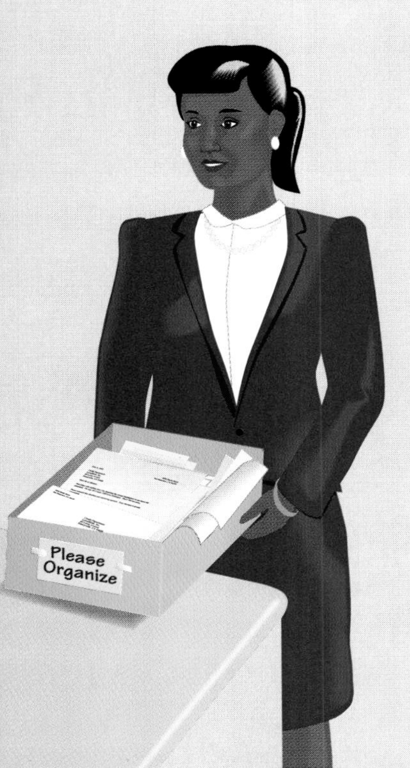

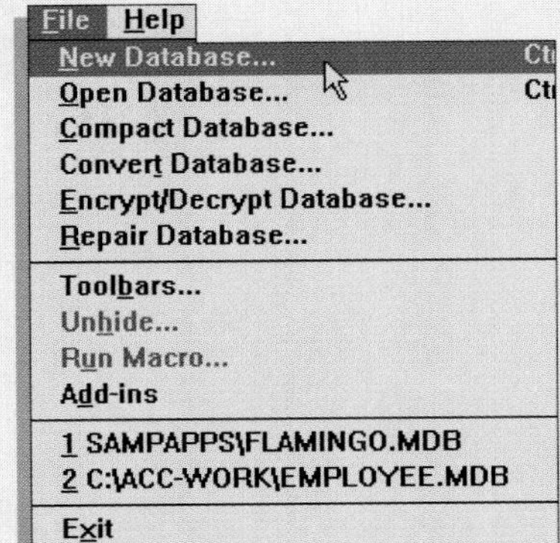

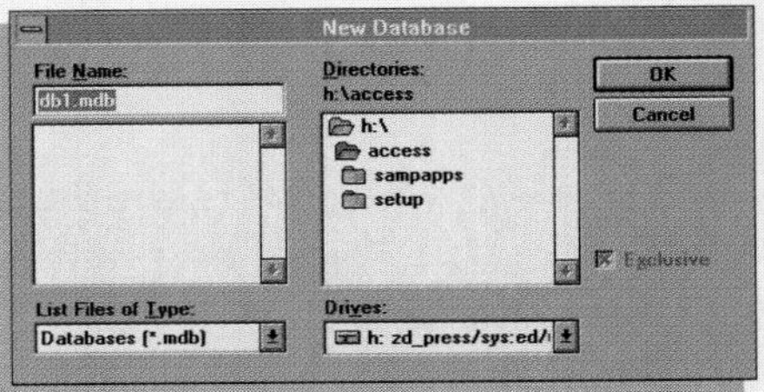

3 The New Database dialog box appears. You need to specify a name and a storage location for the database file you are about to create.

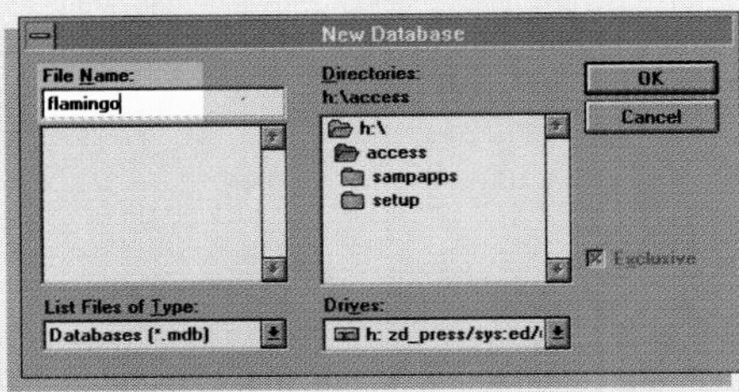

4 Type a file name for the database. (The File Name text box is already active.) A file name can contain up to eight characters, followed optionally by a period and an *extension* of up to three characters. The characters ?*"/[]:|<>+=;, are not permitted in file names. Letter case (upper or lower) does not matter.

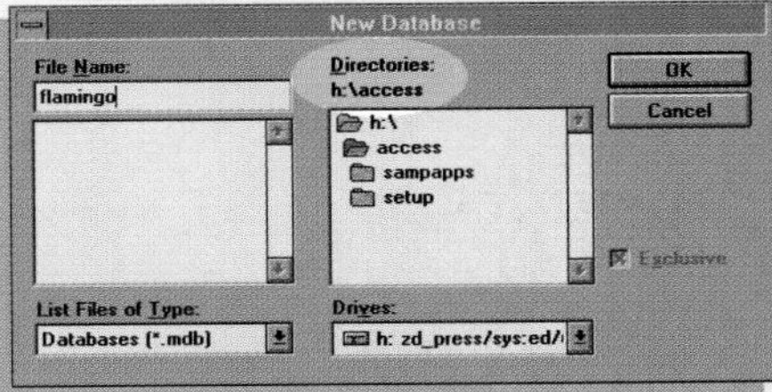

5 Observe the Directories entry in the dialog box. A directory is a division of a disk. Usually a directory contains related data and programs. The directories entry tells you the *drive* (disk) and directory where the database will be stored if you do not specify otherwise. If this location is okay, skip the next two steps.

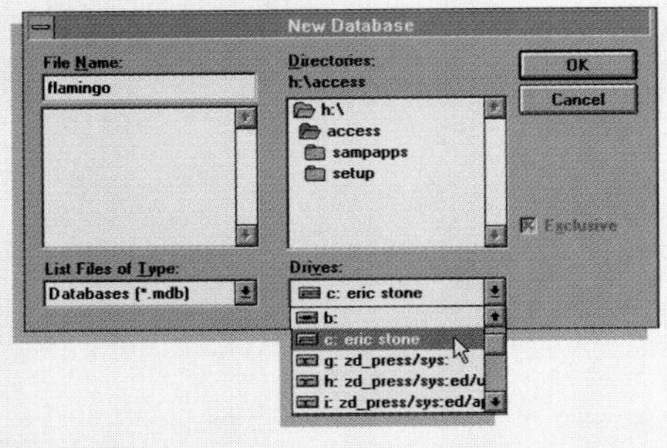

6 To store the database on a different drive, click on the drop-down arrow to the right of the Drives entry, locate the drive you need, and click on it.

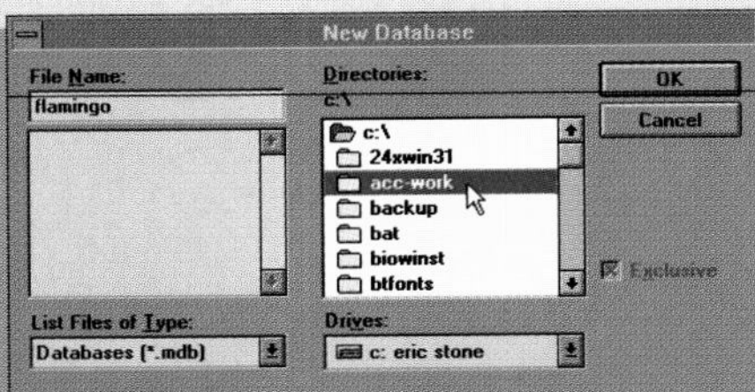

7 To store the database in a different directory, locate the directory name in the Directories list—use the scroll bar if necessary—and double-click on it. Double-clicking on a directory name will also display any directories stored inside that directory. A directory within a directory is called a *subdirectory*.

How to Open a Database from Disk

Opening a database from disk places all objects in the database—tables, queries, and so on—at your fingertips. You can open a database either when no other database is open, or when another database is open but no object is in view.

- Microsoft Access offers a convenient way to open one of the last four databases you worked on. Click on File in the menu bar and notice the database names near the bottom of the menu. If one of these is the database you want to open, simply click on it. If, like many people, you work with the same few databases most of the time, you will usually find the database you need on the File menu and can bypass the Open Database dialog box.
- Only one database can be open at a time. If you open a database when another one is already open, the first one closes. When a database is open and an object is in view, the Open Database command does not even appear on the File menu. You will begin viewing and working with objects in Chapter 4.

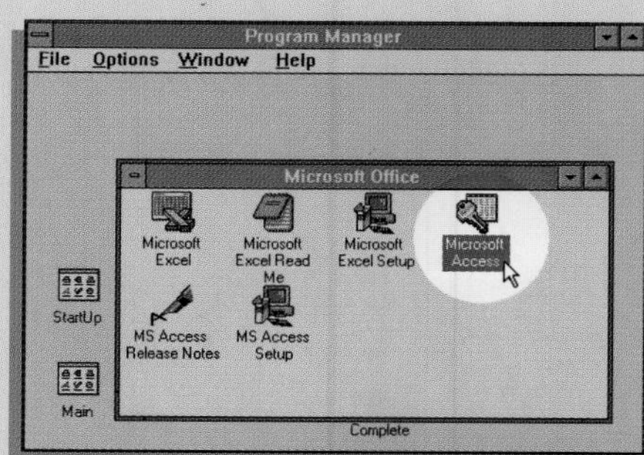

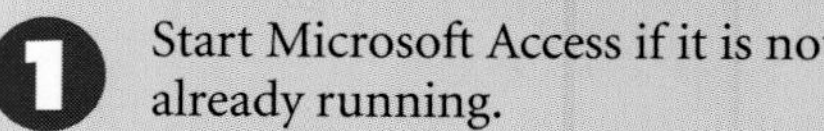

1 Start Microsoft Access if it is not already running.

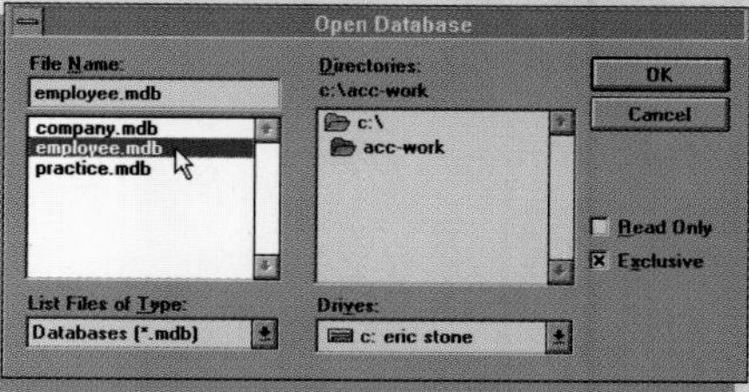

7 In the File Name list, locate the database you want to open—use the scroll bar if necessary—and double-click on it.

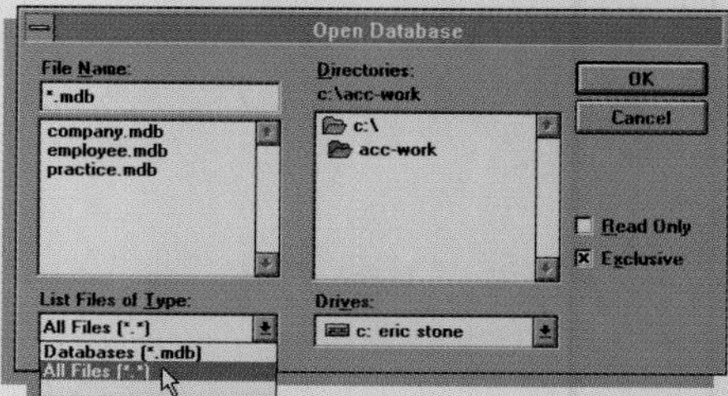

6 Observe the File Name text box in the Open Database dialog box. The notation **.mdb* means that the list below it contains all files that are stored in the current directory (as shown in the Directories entry) and that end with the extension .MDB. Microsoft Access thus makes it somewhat easier to open a database ending with this extension. If the database you need ends with a different extension, click on the drop-down arrow next to the List Files of Type entry, and then click on All Files (*.*). Now the File Name list shows you all documents (and other files) stored in the specified location.

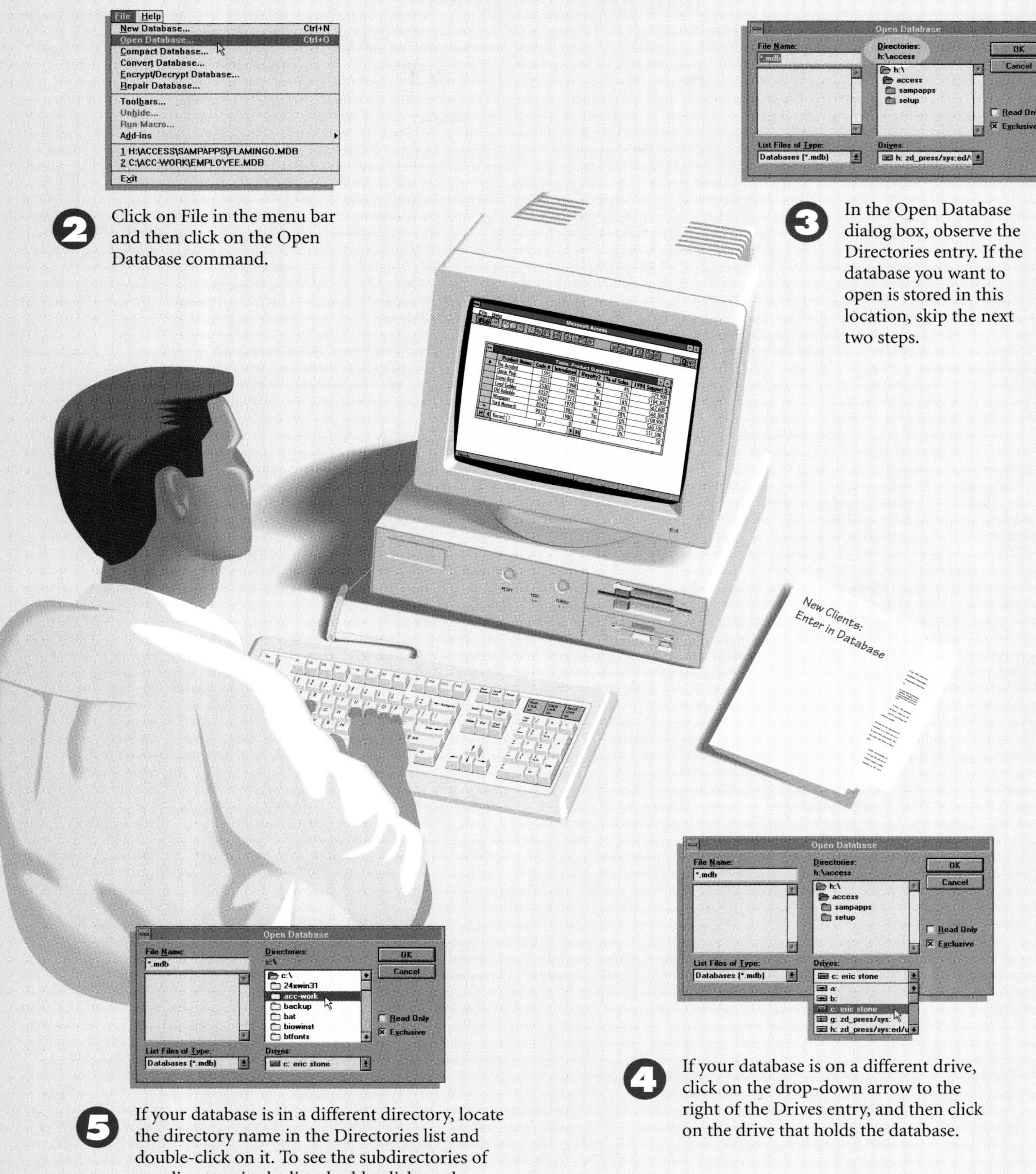

2 Click on File in the menu bar and then click on the Open Database command.

3 In the Open Database dialog box, observe the Directories entry. If the database you want to open is stored in this location, skip the next two steps.

4 If your database is on a different drive, click on the drop-down arrow to the right of the Drives entry, and then click on the drive that holds the database.

5 If your database is in a different directory, locate the directory name in the Directories list and double-click on it. To see the subdirectories of any directory in the list, double-click on the directory name.

CHAPTER 4

Designing Tables

Tables are the backbone of a database. Forms, queries, and reports rely on a database's underlying tables to do their work. All data in your database, even if entered through a form (see Chapter 11), is stored in at least one table.

Given the importance of tables, you should put some energy into planning them. Most broadly, you need to decide how to divide your data into tables. Take, for example, a database containing information about all of your company's customers. Do you have largely the same types of information about every customer? In that case, one customer table is probably all you need. But if you maintain quite different information about commercial and residential customers, or about domestic and international customers, you may want to set up a separate table for each customer category.

In addition, you must decide what information to include in each record of the table and in what sequence. Though you can redesign a table—Chapter 5 shows you how—good planning from the start can save you a lot of effort down the road.

This chapter explains how to set up a table. If you are not responsible for building databases but only for maintaining or interpreting them, you can skip this chapter.

How to Start a New Table

You start a new table when you have to enter and maintain data that does not fit logically in any existing table. This page merely introduces you to the basic database structure and shows how to tell Microsoft Access that you want to build a new table. The larger job of stating what fields the table will contain is covered on the next page.

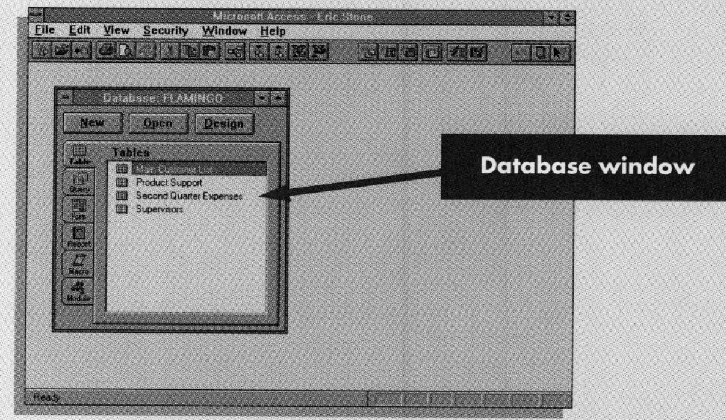

1 This is the *Database window,* a document window that gives you an overview of the database contents. You see the Database window when you start a new database or open an existing database from disk.

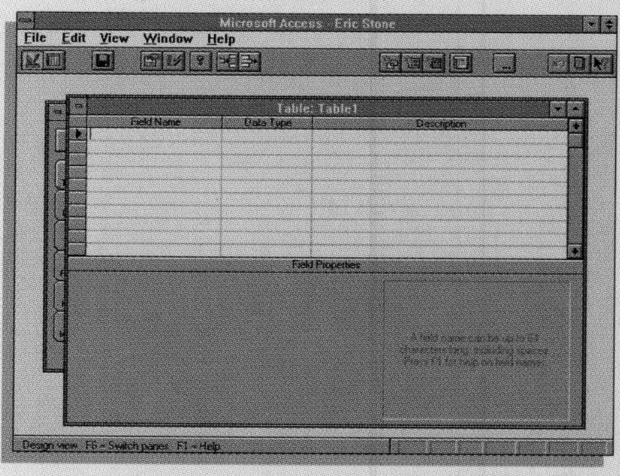

7 You are now viewing a blank table in *Design view.* This is where you will define fields for the table. Turn the page to learn how.

TIP SHEET

- **If your Database window is maximized, it will look a little different from the one shown on this page, but you will work with it exactly as described. Whether you work with maximized or restored windows is a matter of personal preference.**
- **You may have heard of *Wizards,* a Microsoft feature that asks you questions and guides you through complex procedures. In step 6 you declined to use a Wizard to help create a table. Some Wizards ask questions that less experienced users of Microsoft Access are not equipped to answer. In this book, you will take advantage of Wizards only when they are truly helpful to beginners.**

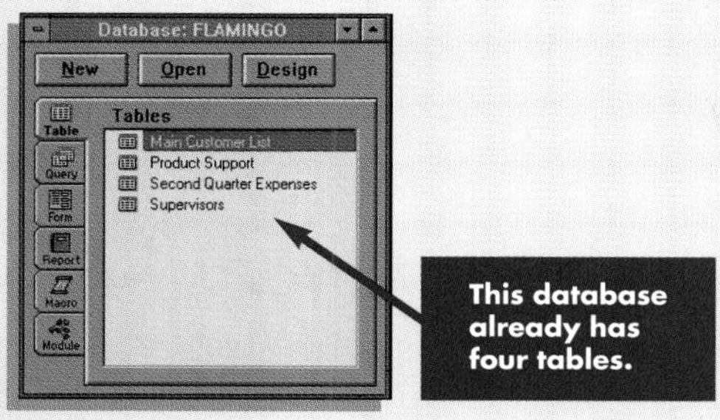

2 Along the left side of the Database window are six *object buttons*, one for each type of Microsoft Access object. One object button is always active, and the list to the right shows you what objects of that type the database contains. Click on any object button to activate it. Of course, a newly created database contains no objects.

3 To start a new table, first open the database or create a new one (see Chapter 3) so that you are viewing the Database window.

4 Click on the Table object button if it is not already active.

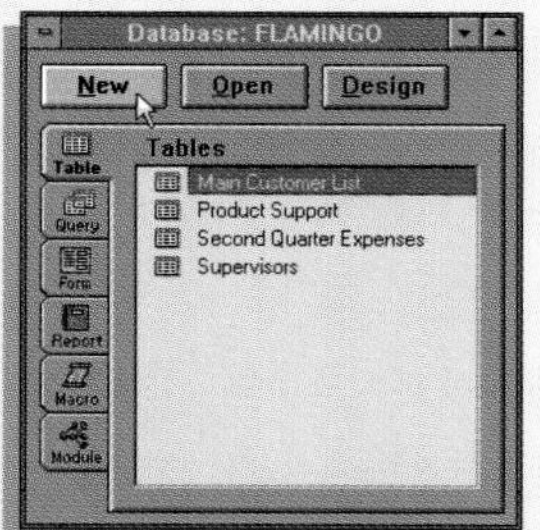

5 Click on the New button near the top of the Database window.

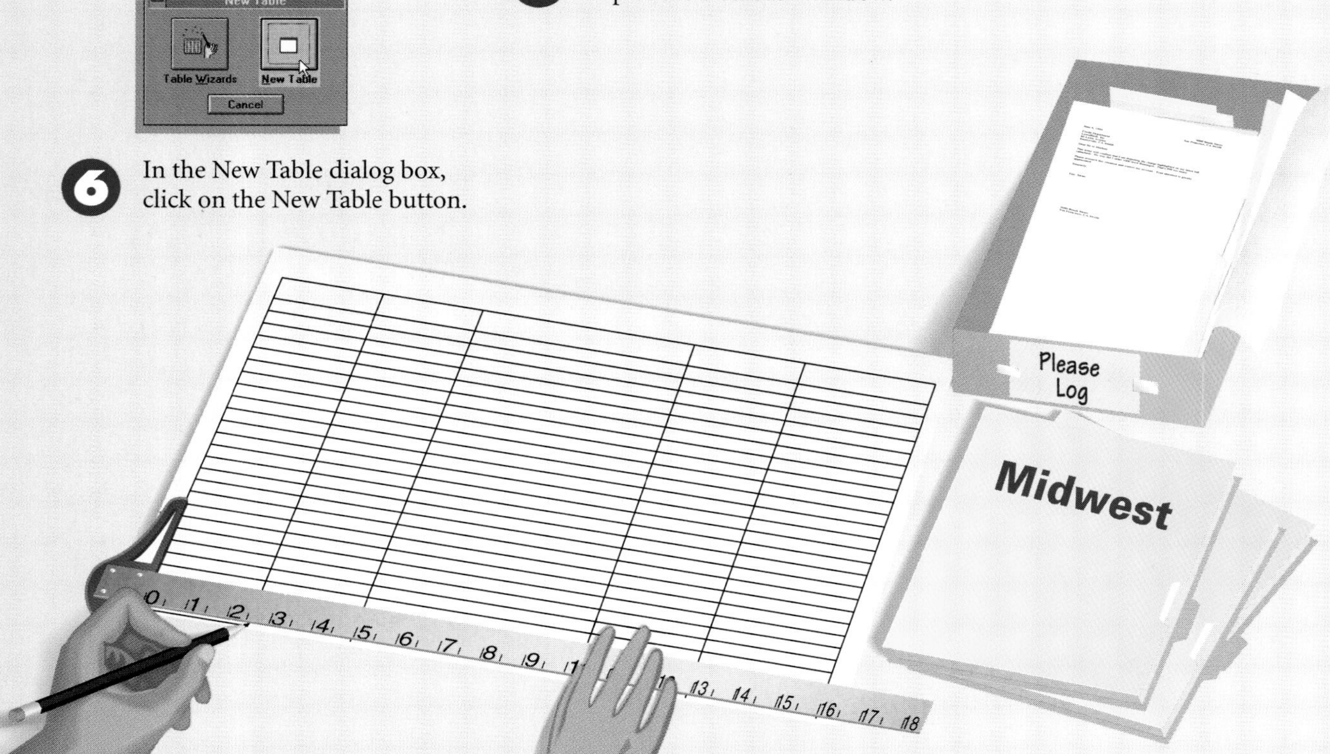

6 In the New Table dialog box, click on the New Table button.

How to Define Fields in a New Table

Defining fields involves not just assigning field names (column headings) but also telling Microsoft Access what type of data will be in the field—text, numbers, dates, and so on. Why is it necessary to state a data type? Well, there are technical reasons, such as the fact that Microsoft Access sets aside different amounts of storage space for different data types. But the most practical reason is that Microsoft Access will prevent you from entering data in a field if it does not match the data type that you specified earlier. For example, if a field containing a customer's credit limit is defined as a Number field and you accidentally enter text (such as a customer's name) in the field, Microsoft Access will alert you to your data-entry error and tell you to insert a number.

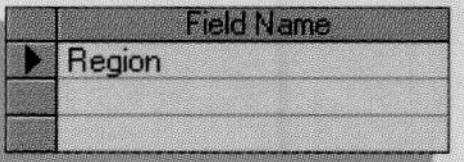

2 Type a name for the field. Microsoft Access field names can be up to 64 characters long and can contain all characters except periods, exclamation points, and brackets.

Insertion point

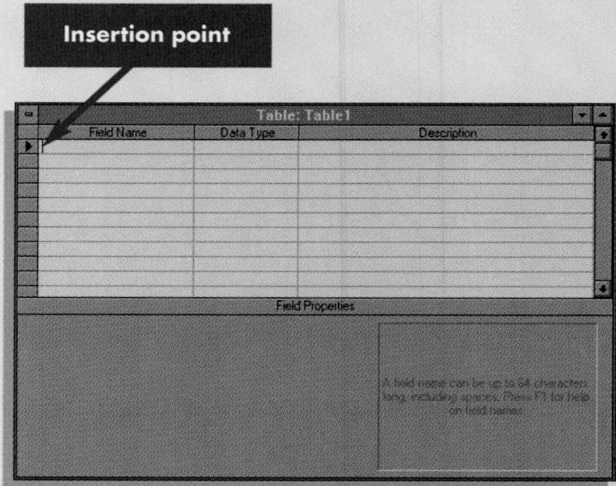

1 Start a new table and display it in Design view as described on the preceding two pages. Click in the top-left blank *cell* (box) of the grid if the flashing *insertion point* is not already there.

TIP SHEET

- **Long field names can make tables awkward to view on the screen and in print. Choose the shortest reasonably descriptive names for your fields.**
- **Why is there a Memo data type when there is already a Text type (step 4)? The underlying reason is technical, but it is enough to understand that if you plan to have text entries longer than 50 characters (the default maximum length for Text fields), you should instead choose the Memo data type, which allows up to 32,000 characters!**

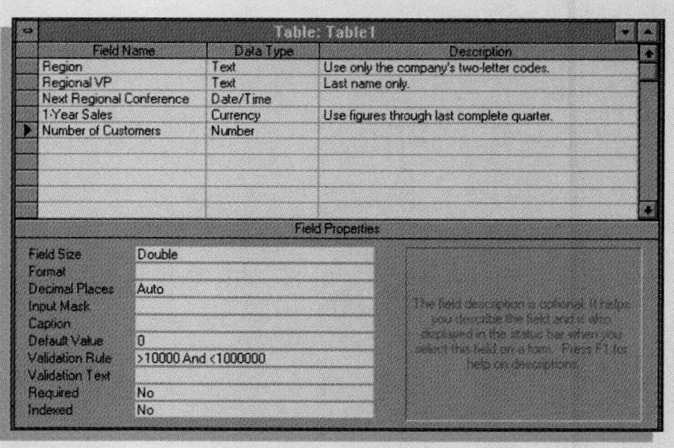

8 To define more fields, click on the next blank cell of the Field Name column and repeat steps 2 through 8. The next page explains what to do when you're done defining fields.

3 Press the Tab key to move to the Data Type column.

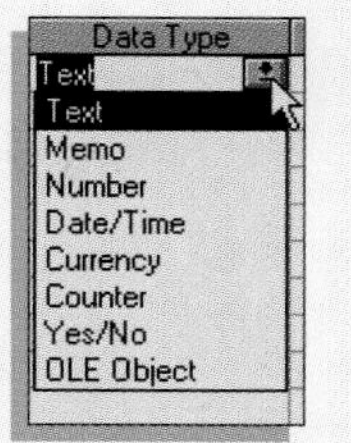

4 Observe that Microsoft Access suggests Text as the data type. To specify a different data type, click on the drop-down arrow that appears and then click on the desired data type. Most data types are self-explanatory. For example, select Currency if the field will contain monetary figures. The Memo data type is for very long text entries. Use the Counter data type to have Microsoft Access automatically insert sequential numbers, such as invoice numbers. The Yes/No data type is for fields with only these two possible values, such as a field that states whether a customer has an active account. Disregard the OLE Object data type.

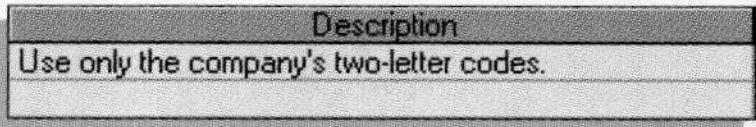

5 Press Tab to move to the Description column and, optionally, type up to 255 characters of information related to the field. You might, for example, state how to fill in the field in an unusual situation. The description will appear as you enter data in the field and may also help others understand the table.

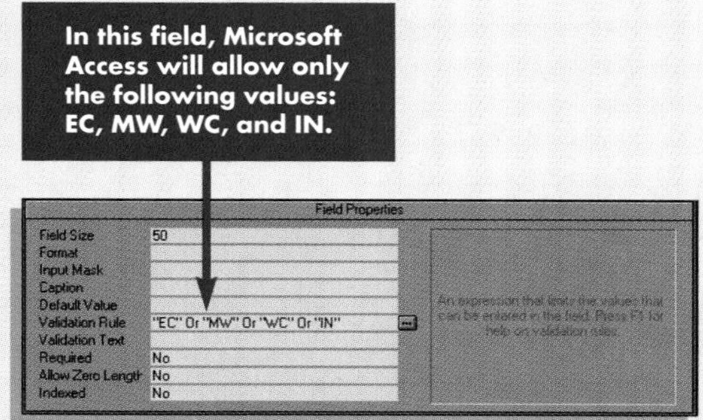

6 Observe the Field Properties area in the bottom half of the window. The entries vary according to the data type, but two major ones are common to most of them. To limit entry in a field to specific values, click in the Validation Rule text box and type the possible values, surrounding them with quotation marks and separating them with the word *Or*. Alternatively, you can specify a range of possible values. For example, enter **<100** to limit entries to numbers under 100. Enter **>100 And <1000** to limit entries to numbers from 101 to 999.

7 By default, Microsoft Access sets up each field to be optional; in other words, you can leave it blank for any record. To prevent a field from ever being left blank, click in the Required text box, click on the drop-down arrow, and click on Yes.

How to Name, Save, and Close a Table

In Microsoft Access, as in any computer program, work you do won't be available for future revision unless you save it on disk. Saving just once is not enough. Every time you change a Microsoft Access object, you need to resave it. If a power outage or other mishap shuts down your computer, you will be able to retrieve your database only as it appeared the last time you saved it. The first time you save a table in Microsoft Access, you also assign a name to it.

TIP SHEET

- **Microsoft Access encourages you to specify a *primary key* for each table. A primary key is a field that uniquely identifies each record and thus can never be duplicated in that field. A common example of such a key is a Social Security number in a personnel table. While in Design view, you can set or change the primary key by clicking anywhere in the field, clicking on Edit in the menu bar, and then clicking on the Set Primary Key command. If you try to close the table without setting a primary key, Microsoft Access asks you if you want one added. If you click on Yes, Microsoft Access adds a field named ID to the table, gives it the Counter data type, and assigns in this field a sequential number for each record.**
- **Table names in Microsoft Access are not file names the way you might expect if you are familiar with other software. That's why the usual 11-character limit for file names does not apply to table names—or to other Microsoft Access object names.**

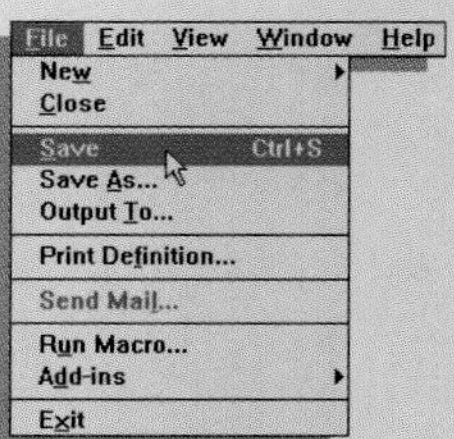

1. Shortly after you begin defining fields for a table, click on File in the menu bar and then click on the Save command.

2. In the Save As dialog box, type a name for the table, replacing the placeholder that Microsoft Access provides. A table name can be up to 64 characters long and can contain all characters except periods, exclamation points, and brackets.

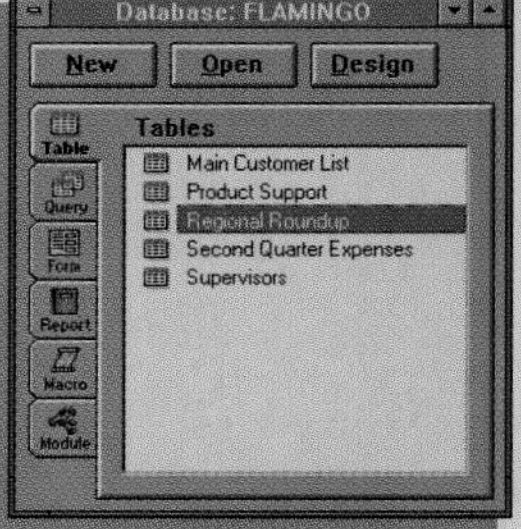

7. You are now back at the Database window. Observe that your newly defined table is now listed as a table object—even though the table does not yet contain any data.

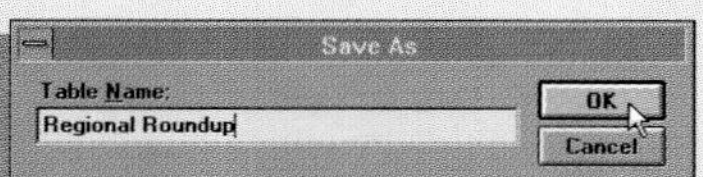

3 Click on the OK button.

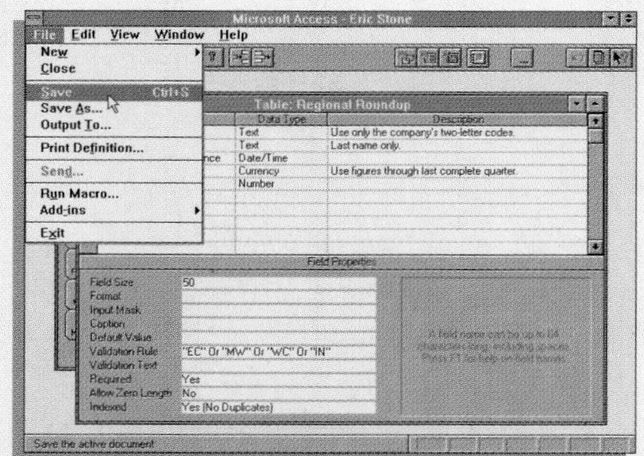

4 Microsoft Access saves the table on disk, closes the dialog box, and displays the newly assigned table name in the title bar. Continue working on the table design as needed. Occasionally click on File in the menu bar and then on the Save command to resave the table with all its changes.

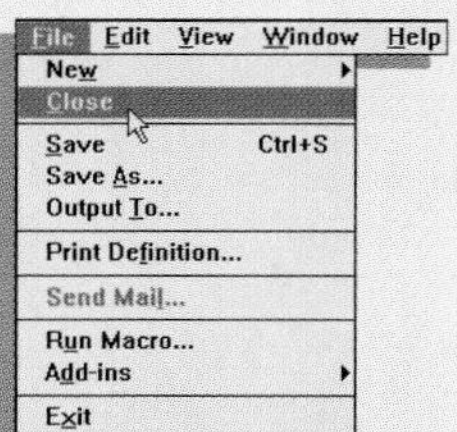

5 When you are ready to stop working on the table design, click on File in the menu bar and then click on the Close command.

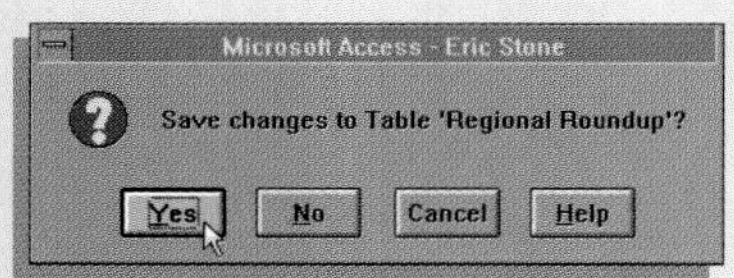

6 If you have changed the table since last saving it, Microsoft Access warns you of this fact. Click on the Yes button to save your changes.

How to Exit Microsoft Access

When you're done using Microsoft Access, it's wise to shut down the program. Technically, it is not necessary to exit a program before using another one or even before exiting Windows to return to the DOS prompt. However, exiting programs you're not using helps your computer run more efficiently. You will also find it easier to use your computer under Windows if the only programs open are the ones you are using or plan to use in the near future.

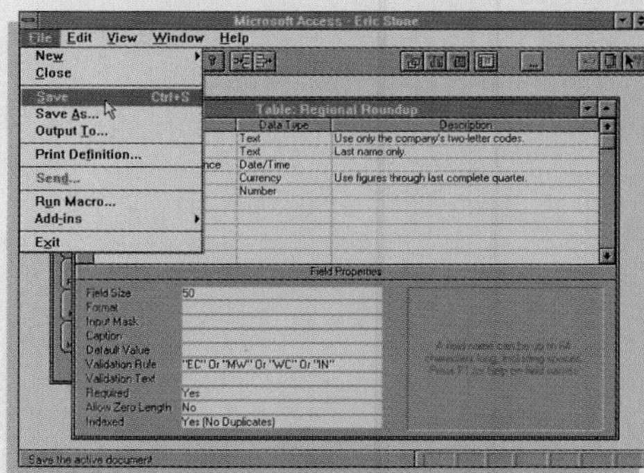

1. Save and close any open objects and return to the Database window (see preceding page). Though Microsoft Access will remind you to save your work if you forget, taking the initiative to save is a good habit to form.

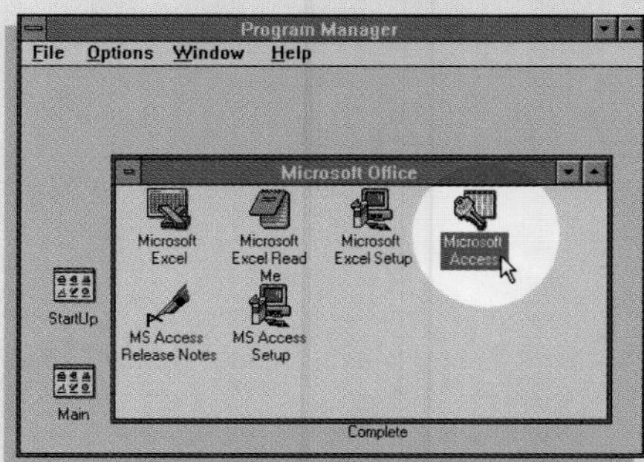

6. Once back in Program Manager, you can restart Microsoft Access anytime by opening the program group containing it and double-clicking on its icon.

TIP SHEET

- **You need not exit Microsoft Access just to use another Windows program briefly. Press Alt+Esc one or more times to switch among Microsoft Access and your other open Windows programs. For example, you can press Alt+Esc to switch to Program Manager, open another program, use it, close it (optional), and press Alt+Esc until you are back in Microsoft Access.**
- **If you exit Windows without closing Microsoft Access and you have left an object unsaved, you will be given a chance to save it (see step 4).**

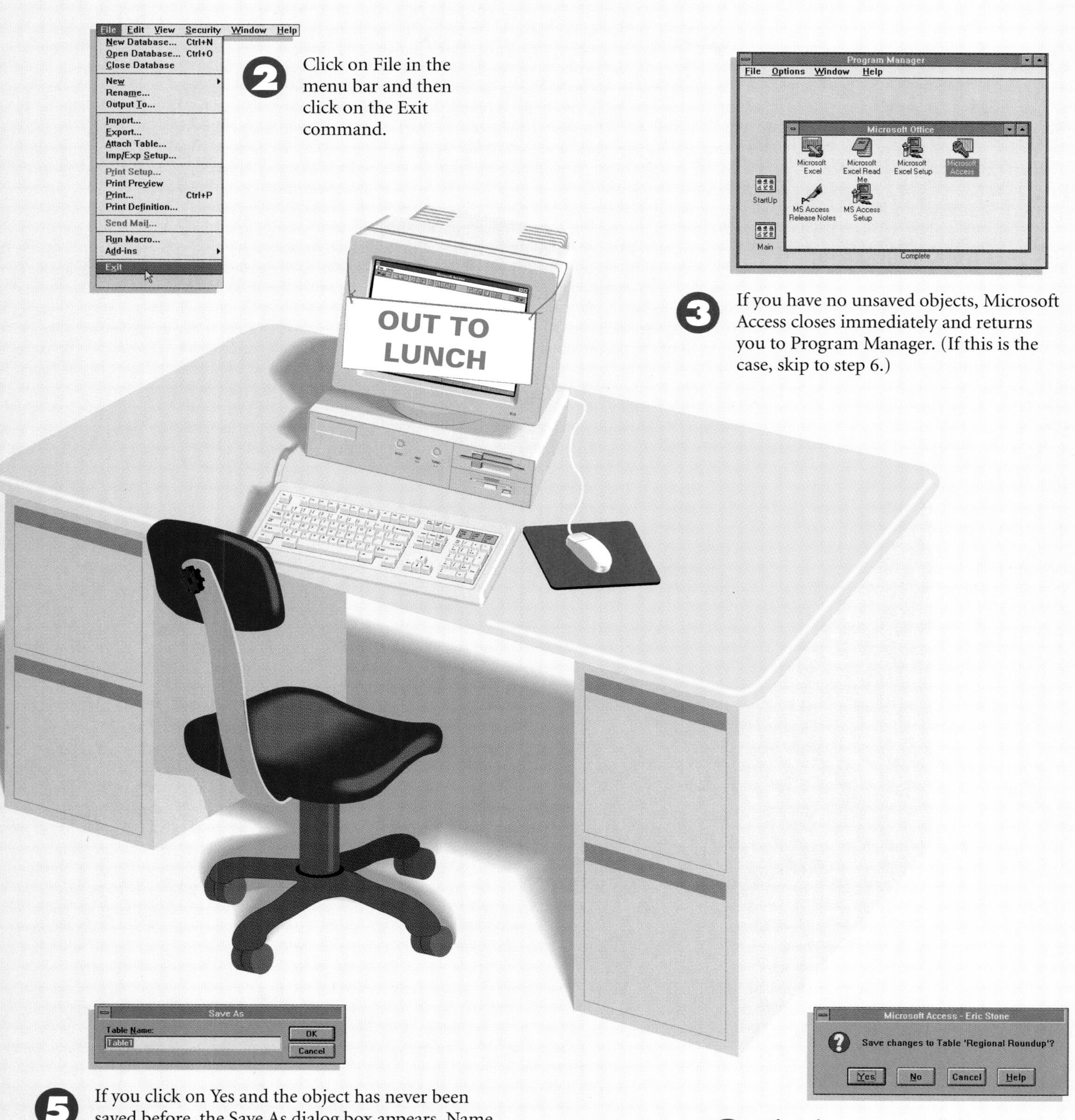

2 Click on File in the menu bar and then click on the Exit command.

3 If you have no unsaved objects, Microsoft Access closes immediately and returns you to Program Manager. (If this is the case, skip to step 6.)

4 If you have an unsaved object, Microsoft Access asks you whether to save it. Click on Yes to save it or on No to abandon it.

5 If you click on Yes and the object has never been saved before, the Save As dialog box appears. Name and save the object. (See "How to Name, Save, and Close a Table" earlier in this chapter. The instructions there apply not just to tables but to all objects.)

CHAPTER 5

Building and Improving Tables

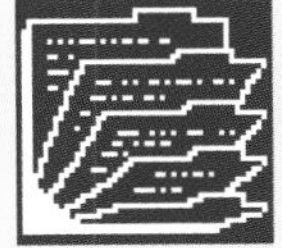

Data entry is the most routine yet perhaps the most important action you will perform on your databases. After all, data entered incorrectly can lead to false query results and reports containing misleading data. Routine though it may be, data entry is worth your attention. This chapter will help.

Fortunately, Microsoft Access provides safeguards that prevent many data-entry errors. As you observed in Chapter 4, you must specify a data type for each field. If you enter data that is plainly the wrong type for the field, Microsoft Access will alert you to your error so you can correct it. For example, Microsoft Access will alert you if you enter text or a plain number in a field of the Date/Time data type.

In addition, if you entered a validation rule for a field (see "How to Define Fields in a New Table" in Chapter 4), Microsoft Access will prevent the entry in this field of any data that violates the rule.

This chapter will help you enter and edit data in a table, redesign a table, and print a table.

How to Open and View a Table

When you open a table for viewing or data entry, Microsoft Access displays the table in *Datasheet view*. This is just a fancy way of saying that you are looking at the table as a table, rather than seeing the underlying table design as you did in Chapter 4. In Datasheet view, you see the whole table in standard row-and-column format, with the field names as the column headings.

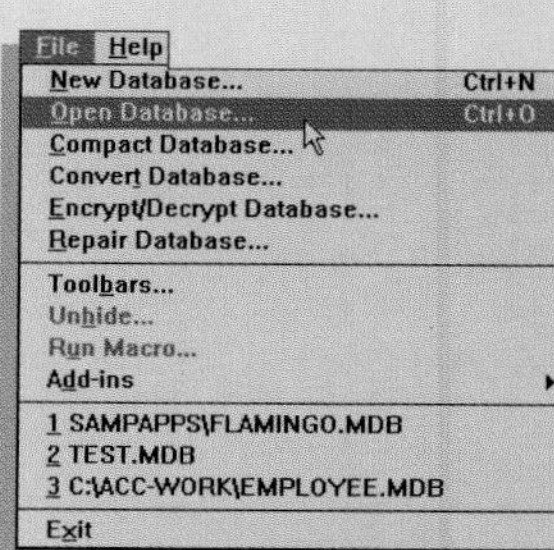

1 Open the database from disk and display the Database window (Chapter 3).

TIP SHEET

- **Instead of clicking on the table name and then clicking on the Open button (steps 3 and 4), you can simply double-click on a table name to open the table in Datasheet view.**
- **When viewing a table containing many fields, you may wish to maximize the window by clicking on its maximize button. Doing so will place as much of the table as possible on the screen at one time. If parts of the table are still out of view, use the scroll bars to scroll to the section you want to see.**
- **Recall that you can also enter and view records in forms, which are helpful when you want to think about one record at a time. See Chapters 10 and 11.**

Notice the shape of the mouse pointer for this operation.

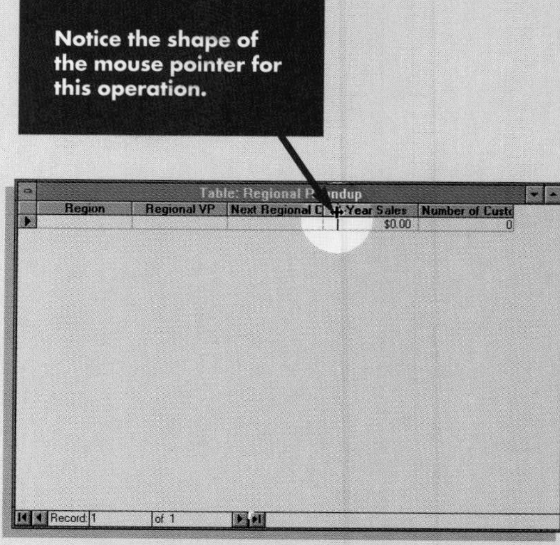

6 The default column width may not be enough to display the field names completely. To widen (or narrow) a column, point to the right column border in the column heading and drag the mouse as far as needed.

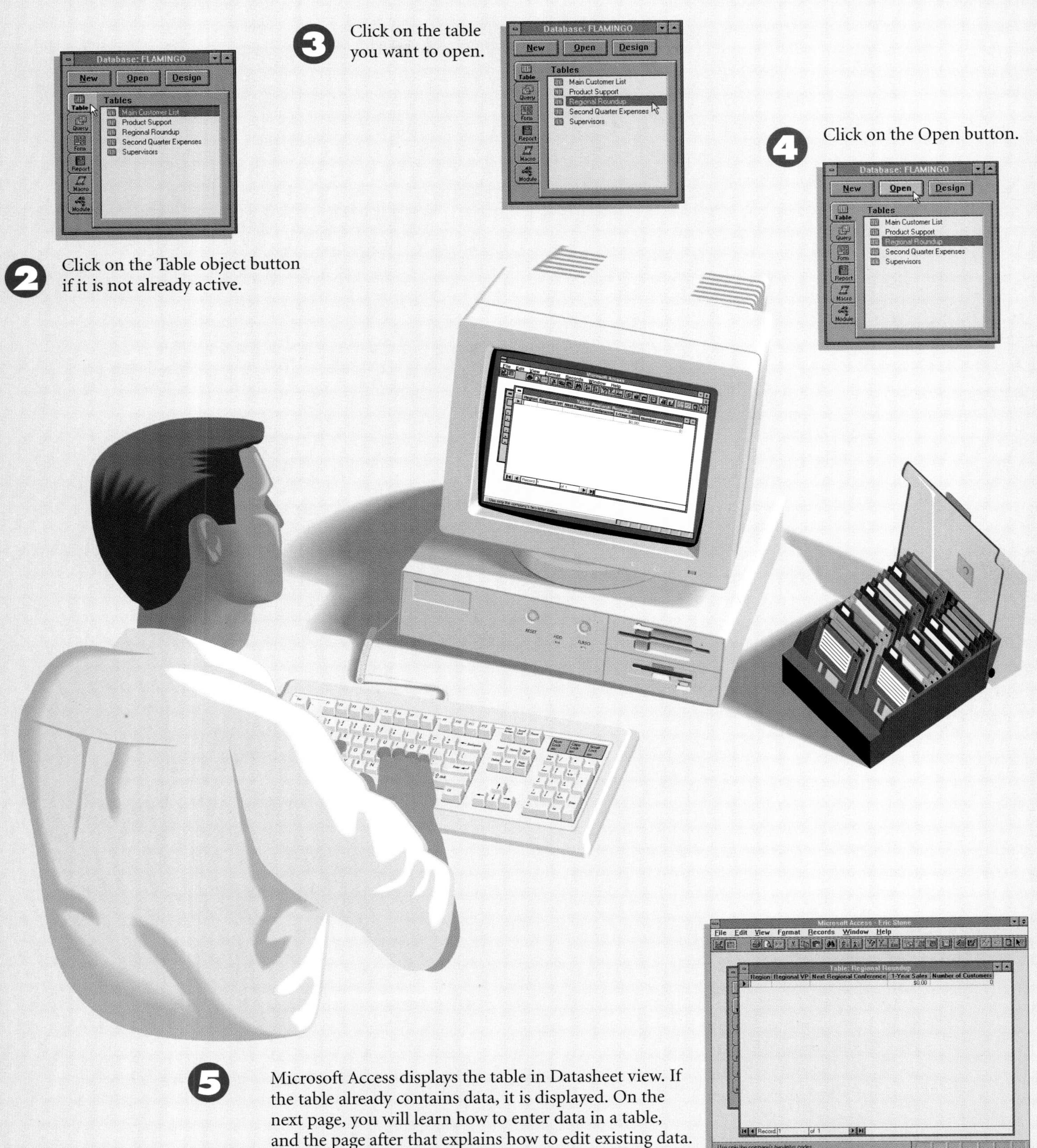

2 Click on the Table object button if it is not already active.

3 Click on the table you want to open.

4 Click on the Open button.

5 Microsoft Access displays the table in Datasheet view. If the table already contains data, it is displayed. On the next page, you will learn how to enter data in a table, and the page after that explains how to edit existing data.

How to Enter Data in a Table

You can enter data whenever a table is open in Datasheet view. As you'll observe, Microsoft Access alerts you to certain obvious data-entry errors, but not to all possible errors. Pay attention as you enter data in a table, lest errors come back to haunt you in faulty query results and inaccurate reports.

TIP SHEET

- **Don't worry about entering records in any particular sequence. Whenever you open a table, Microsoft Access sorts the records according to the primary key, if any (see Chapter 4). You can always sort records differently later (see Chapter 6).**
- **In Datasheet view, Microsoft Access always leaves a blank record at the bottom of the table. Except when the table is empty, this blank record is noted with an asterisk (*) in the left margin. The blank record will not show up in your table printouts or affect any other Microsoft Access operations.**
- **As you enter data, the status bar shows you the description (if any) you entered for the active field when designing the table. This may help you remember any validation rules or other guidelines you should follow when entering data in this field. See "How to Change the Design of a Table" later in this chapter to learn how to add or change a field description if you didn't enter a useful one the first time around.**

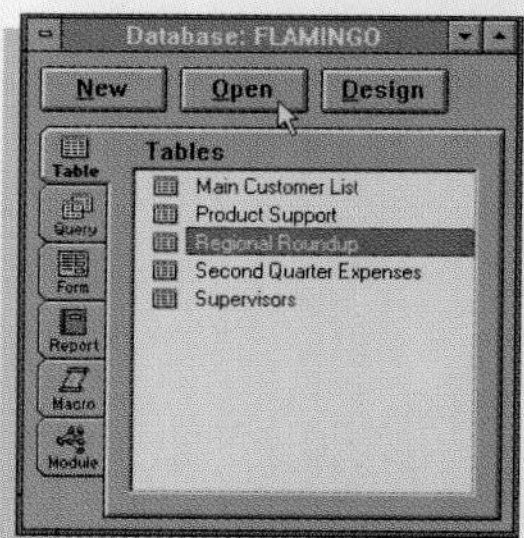

1 Open the table in Datasheet view (see preceding topic).

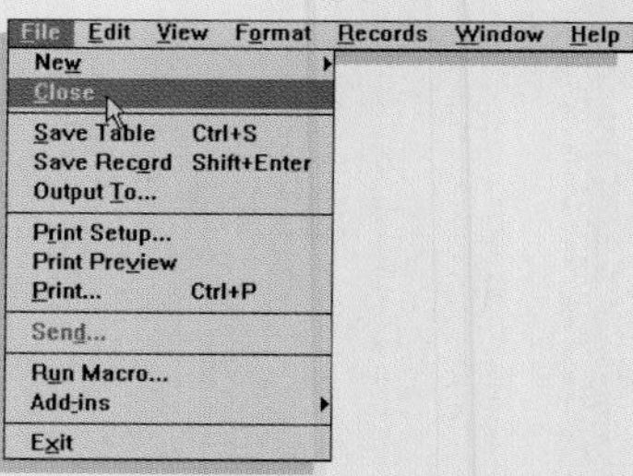

8 When done entering data, you can close the table by clicking on File in the menu bar and then clicking on the Close command. You need not take any extra steps to save your data; Microsoft Access saves any unsaved data when it closes the table.

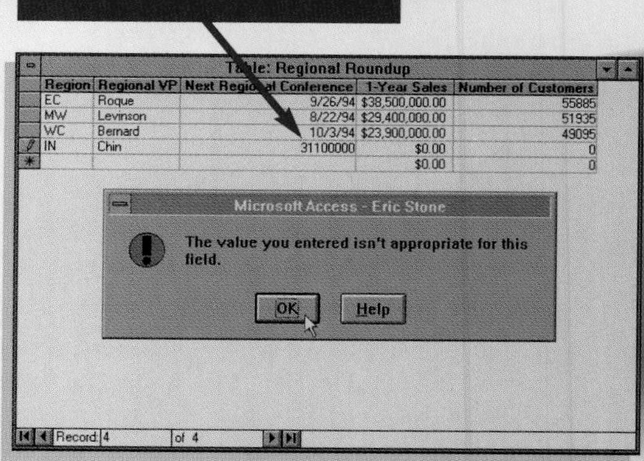

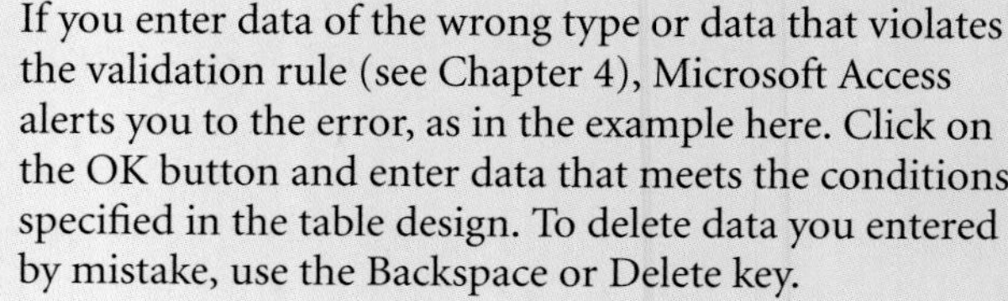

7 If you enter data of the wrong type or data that violates the validation rule (see Chapter 4), Microsoft Access alerts you to the error, as in the example here. Click on the OK button and enter data that meets the conditions specified in the table design. To delete data you entered by mistake, use the Backspace or Delete key.

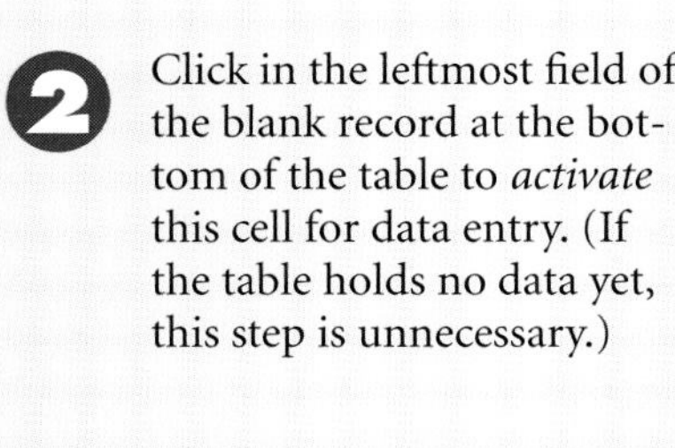

2 Click in the leftmost field of the blank record at the bottom of the table to *activate* this cell for data entry. (If the table holds no data yet, this step is unnecessary.)

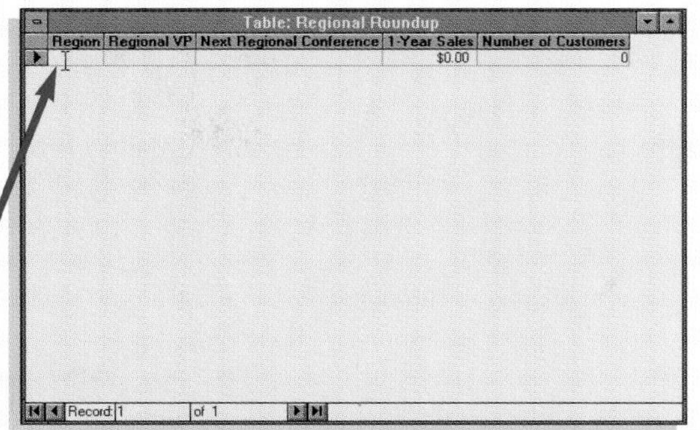

Mouse pointer

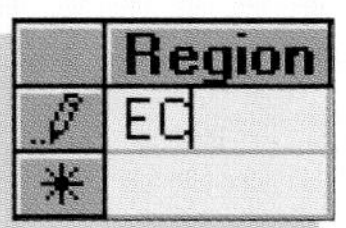

3 Type the data for this field. Notice the pencil in the left margin of the record. This indicates that the record you are entering has not yet been saved.

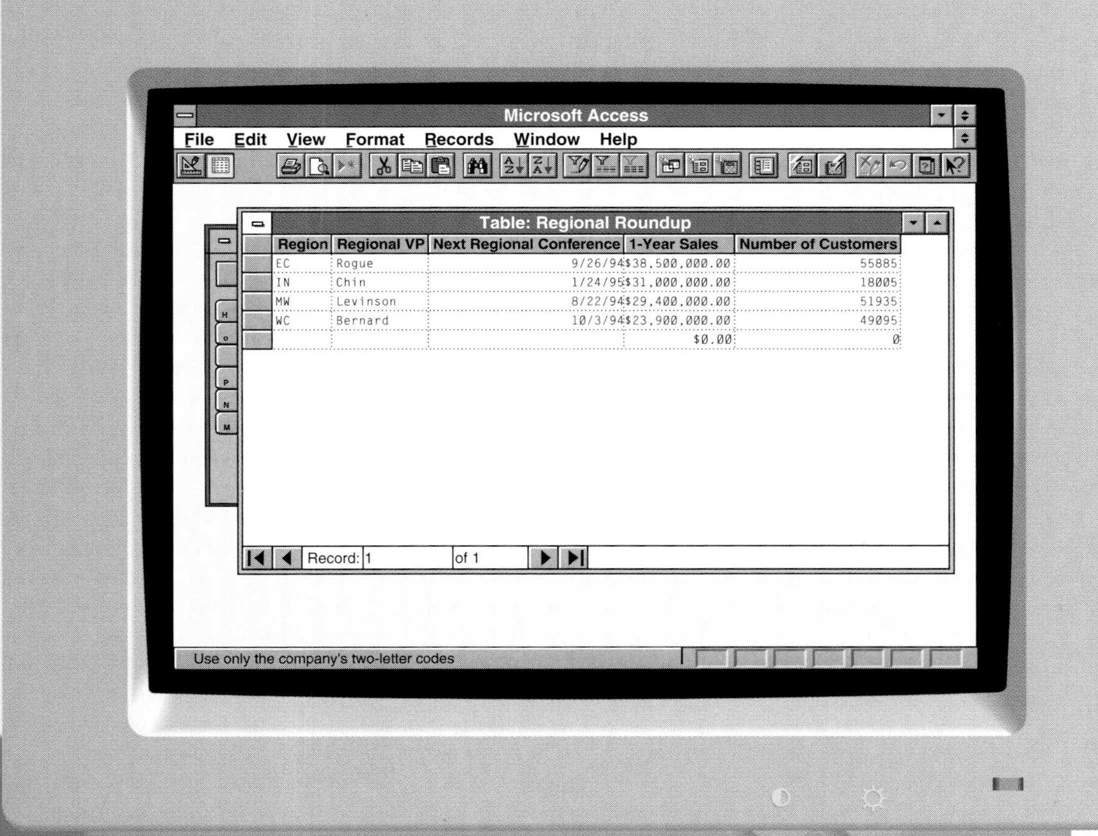

Region	Regional VP	Next Regional Conference	1-Year Sales	Number of Customers
EC	Rogue	9/26/94	$38,500,000.00	55885
IN	Chin	1/24/95	$31,000,000.00	18005
MW	Levinson	8/22/94	$29,400,000.00	51935
WC	Bernard	10/3/94	$23,900,000.00	49095
			$0.00	0

4 Press the Tab key to activate the next field.

5 Repeat steps 3 and 4 until you have entered a complete record.

Table: Regional Roundup

Region	Regional VP	Next Regional Conference	1-Year Sales	Number of Customers
EC	Rogue	9/26/94	$38,500,000.00	55885
MW	Levinson	8/22/94	$29,400,000.00	51935
WC	Bernard	10/3/94	$23,900,000.00	49095
			$0.00	0

Record: 4 of 4

6 Press Tab to move down to the next row and enter more records. As soon as you leave the record you have just entered, that record is saved automatically.

How to Change the Contents of a Table

Making changes to table contents is practically inevitable, even if you enter the data perfectly the first time. That's because editing a table does not necessarily mean correcting errors. Addresses and phone numbers change, customers drop off your mailing list, sales territories are reassigned—the list of possible changes is endless. This page explains how to change and delete records. To simply add new records to a table, see the preceding page.

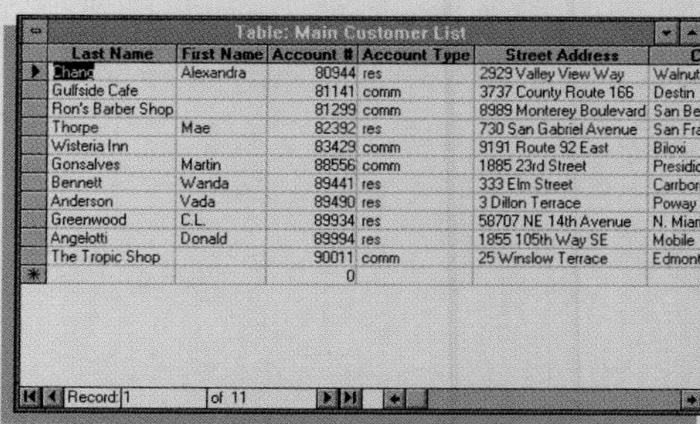

Table: Main Customer List

Last Name	First Name	Account #	Account Type	Street Address	Ci
Chang	Alexandra	80944	res	2929 Valley View Way	Walnut
Gulfside Cafe		81141	comm	3737 County Route 166	Destin
Ron's Barber Shop		81299	comm	8989 Monterey Boulevard	San Be
Thorpe	Mae	82392	res	730 San Gabriel Avenue	San Fra
Wisteria Inn		83429	comm	9191 Route 92 East	Biloxi
Gonsalves	Martin	88556	comm	1885 23rd Street	Presidio
Bennett	Wanda	89441	res	333 Elm Street	Carrborc
Anderson	Vada	89490	res	3 Dillon Terrace	Poway
Greenwood	C.L.	89934	res	58707 NE 14th Avenue	N. Miam
Angelotti	Donald	89994	res	1855 105th Way SE	Mobile
The Tropic Shop		90011	comm	25 Winslow Terrace	Edmont
		0			

Record: 1 of 11

1 Display the table in Datasheet view. (See "How to Open and View a Table" earlier in this chapter.)

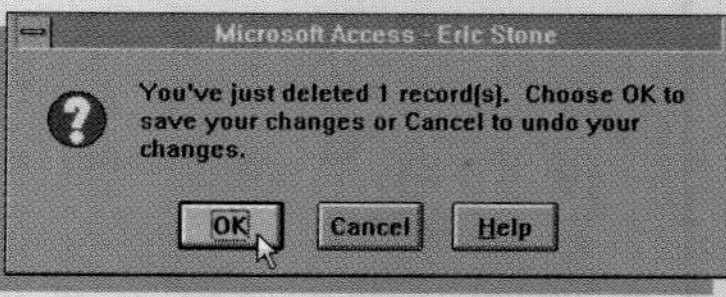

7 When Microsoft Access asks you to confirm the deletion, click on the OK button.

6 Then delete the record by pressing the Delete key.

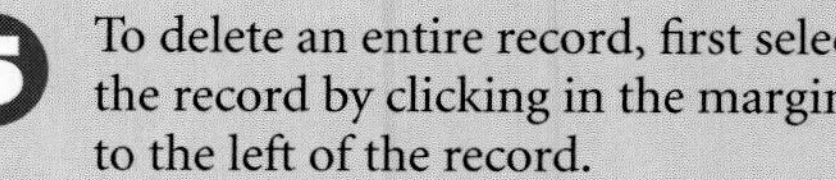

Table: Main Customer List

Last Name	First Name	Account #	Account Type	Street Address	Ci
Chang	Alexandra	80944	res	2929 Valley View Way	Walnut
Gulfside Cafe		81141	comm	3737 County Route 166	Destin
Ron's Barber Shop		81299	comm	8989 Monterey Boulevard	San Be
Thorpe	Mae	82392	res	730 San Gabriel Avenue	San Fra
Wisteria Inn		83429	comm	9191 Route 92 East	Biloxi
Gonsalves	Martin	88556	comm	1885 23rd Street	Presidio
Bennett	Wanda	89441	res	333 Elm Street	Carrborc
Anderson	Vada	89490	res	3 Dillon Terrace	Poway
Greenwood	C.L.	89934	res	58707 NE 14th Avenue	N. Miam
Angelotti	Donald	89994	res	1855 105th Way SE	Mobile
The Tropic Shop		90011	comm	25 Winslow Terrace	Edmont
		0			

5 To delete an entire record, first select the record by clicking in the margin to the left of the record.

TIP SHEET

- **To completely replace the data in a cell, drag across the data to select (highlight) it, and then type the new data.**
- **If you are working with a large table and are having trouble finding the data you need to edit, see Chapter 6 for help.**
- **If you make a mistake while editing data and notice it immediately, press Ctrl+Z to issue the Undo command and reverse the error. More about this lifesaving command in Chapter 7.**

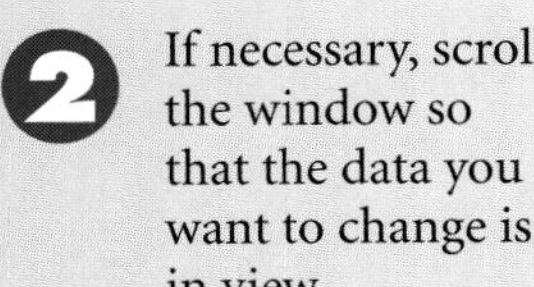

2 If necessary, scroll the window so that the data you want to change is in view.

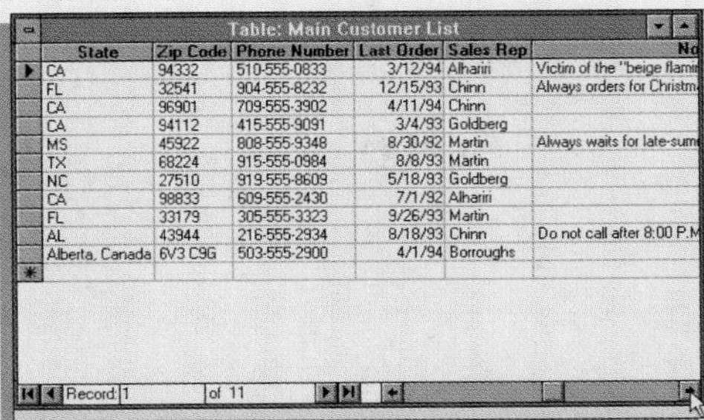

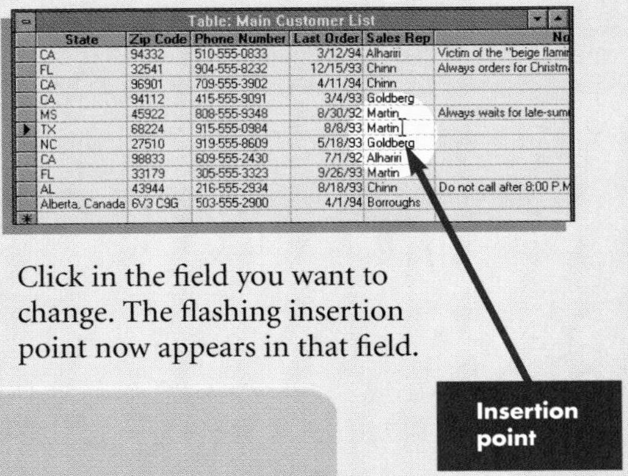

Table: Main Customer List

State	Zip Code	Phone Number	Last Order	Sales Rep	No
CA	94332	510-555-0833	3/12/94	Alhariri	Victim of the "beige flami
FL	32541	904-555-8232	12/15/93	Chinn	Always orders for Christm
CA	96901	709-555-3902	4/11/94	Chinn	
CA	94112	415-555-9091	3/4/93	Goldberg	
MS	45922	808-555-9348	8/30/92	Martin	Always waits for late-sum
TX	68224	915-555-0984	8/8/93	Martin	
NC	27510	919-555-8609	5/18/93	Goldberg	
CA	98833	609-555-2430	7/1/92	Alhariri	
FL	33179	305-555-3323	9/26/93	Martin	
AL	43944	216-555-2934	8/18/93	Chinn	Do not call after 8:00 P.M
Alberta, Canada	6V3 C9G	503-555-2900	4/1/94	Borroughs	

Record: 1 of 11

3 Click in the field you want to change. The flashing insertion point now appears in that field.

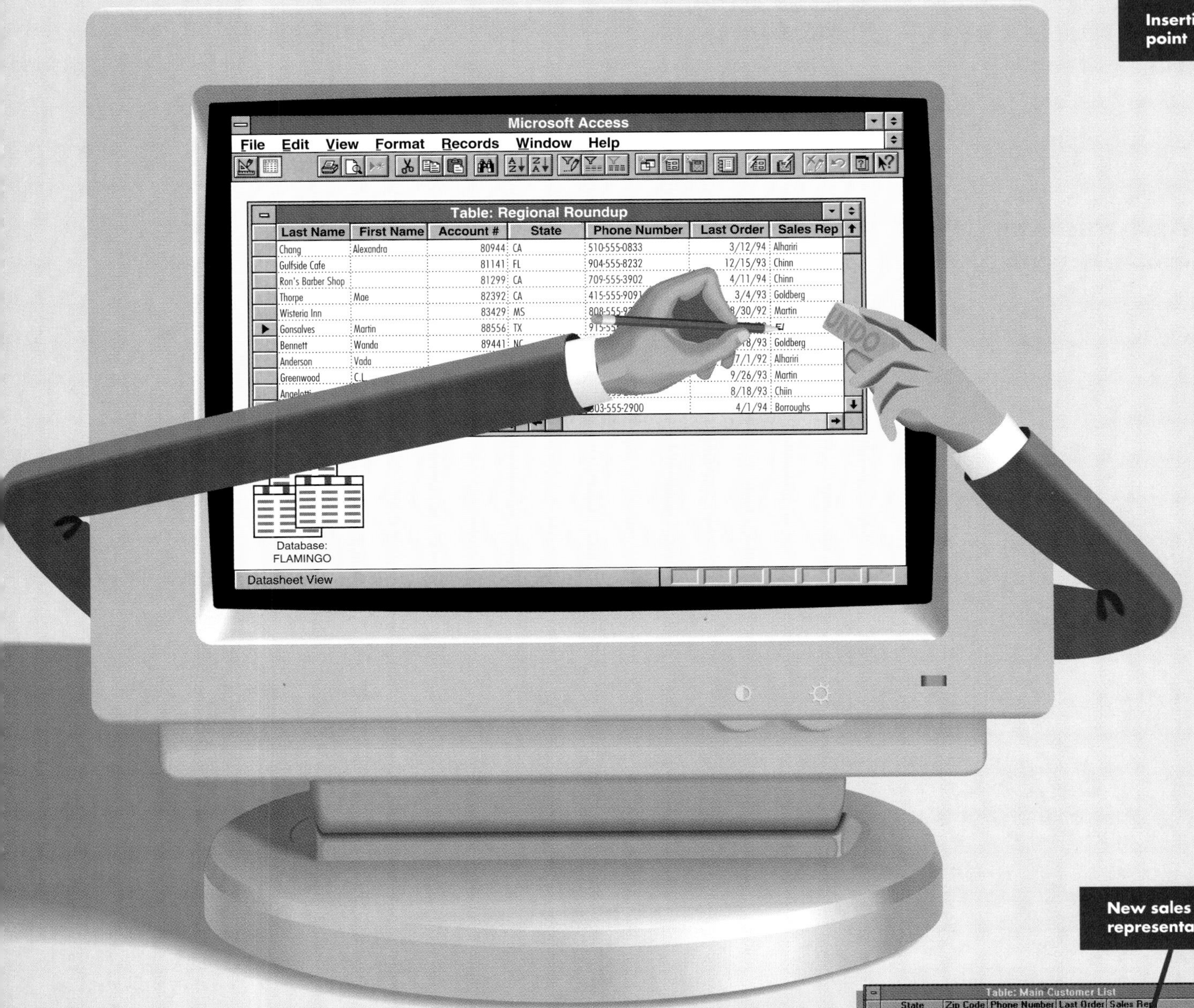

Insertion point

4 Type and delete characters as needed. Use the Left and Right Arrow keys to move the insertion point. Press the Backspace key to delete the character to the left of the insertion point. Press the Delete key to delete the character to the right of the insertion point.

New sales representative

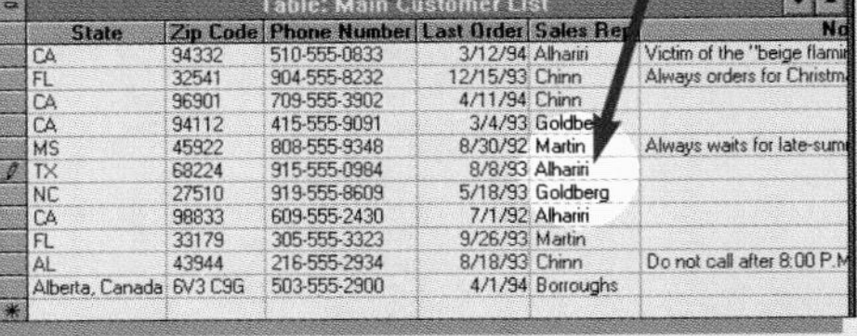

Table: Main Customer List

State	Zip Code	Phone Number	Last Order	Sales Rep	No
CA	94332	510-555-0833	3/12/94	Alhariri	Victim of the "beige flami
FL	32541	904-555-8232	12/15/93	Chinn	Always orders for Christm
CA	96901	709-555-3902	4/11/94	Chinn	
CA	94112	415-555-9091	3/4/93	Goldbe	
MS	45922	808-555-9348	8/30/92	Martin	Always waits for late-sum
TX	68224	915-555-0984	8/8/93	Alhariri	
NC	27510	919-555-8609	5/18/93	Goldberg	
CA	98833	609-555-2430	7/1/92	Alhariri	
FL	33179	305-555-3323	9/26/93	Martin	
AL	43944	216-555-2934	8/18/93	Chinn	Do not call after 8:00 P.M
Alberta, Canada	6V3 C9G	503-555-2900	4/1/94	Borroughs	

How to Change the Design of a Table

Let's say you designed a customer table with one field for the customer's city and state. Later you'll realize that this setup is preventing you from sorting records by state or pulling out records from certain states in a query. In this case, you need to redesign your table to include a separate field for the customer's state. Similarly, you may wish to change the way a field looks or works by changing the field name, data type, or field description. This page shows you how to make these and other design changes.

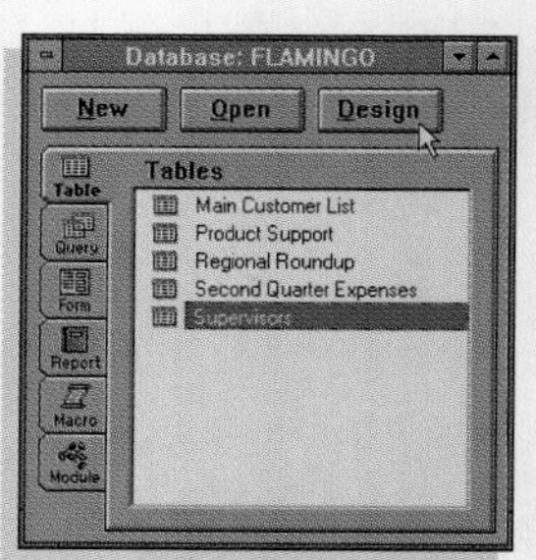

1 From the Database window, open the table in Design view. To do so, click on the Table object button, click on the table you want to redesign, and then click on the Design button.

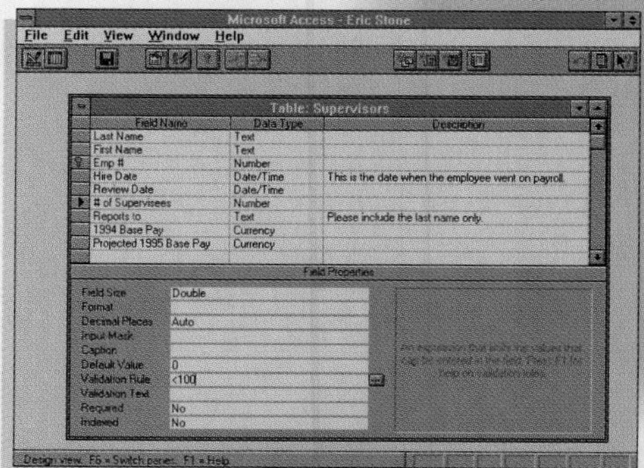

7 To change the required status of a field, or to add or change a validation rule, click anywhere in the field definition and then change the appropriate setting in the Field Properties area (see Chapter 4).

8 Click on File in the menu bar and then click on the Save command to save your changes to the table design. Unlike changes to table contents, changes to table design are not saved automatically.

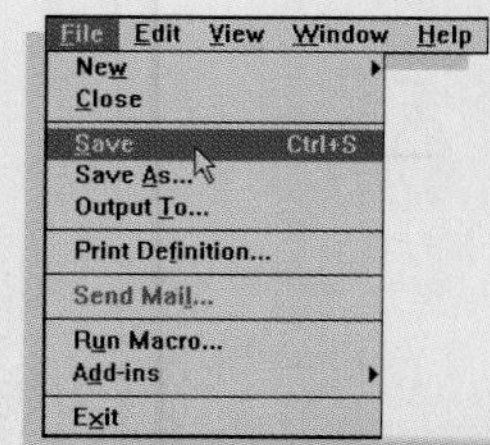

9 When done redesigning the table, you can either click on File and then on Close to return to the Database window, or click on View and then on Datasheet to view the table contents.

TIP SHEET

- **When looking at a table in Datasheet view, you can go directly to Design view and make changes. Simply click on View in the menu bar and then click on the Table Design command.**
- **Design changes may make some data in your table invalid. For example, if you add or change a validation rule, some existing data in the field may violate the new rule. In this case, Microsoft Access alerts you to the problem and asks you what to do. If existing data violates a new validation rule, you can abandon the rule or allow the offending data to remain in the table. (You might then wish to edit it so it meets the rule.) If you changed the data type for a field and some existing data is of the wrong type, Microsoft Access will ask you whether to delete that data or cancel the type change.**

2 To add a field, click anywhere in the field *below* the point where you want to add the new field. Then click on Edit in the menu bar and click on the Insert Row command. In the newly added blank row, define a field as described in Chapter 4.

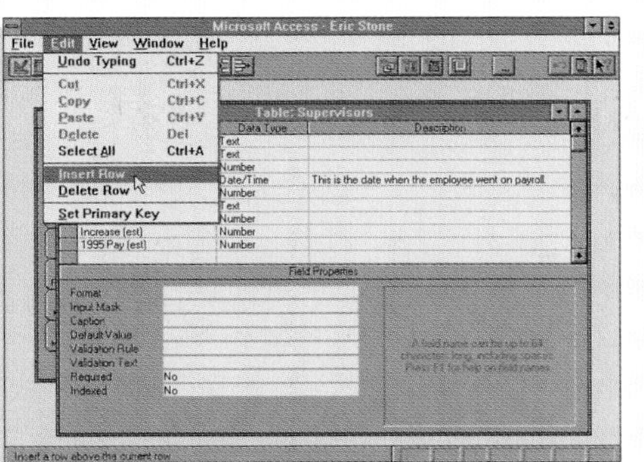

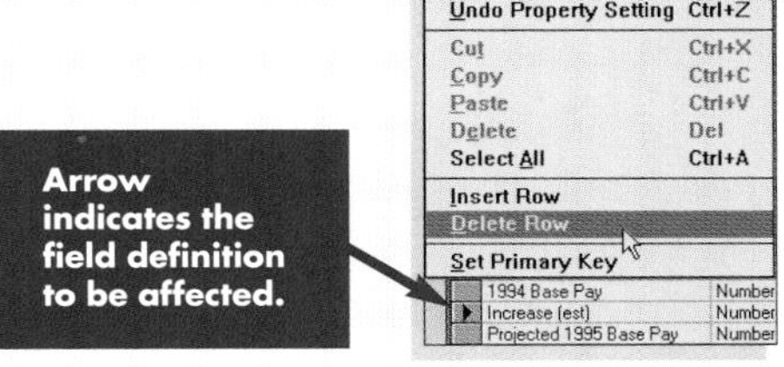

3 To delete a field, click anywhere in the field definition, click on Edit in the menu bar, and then click on the Delete Row command.

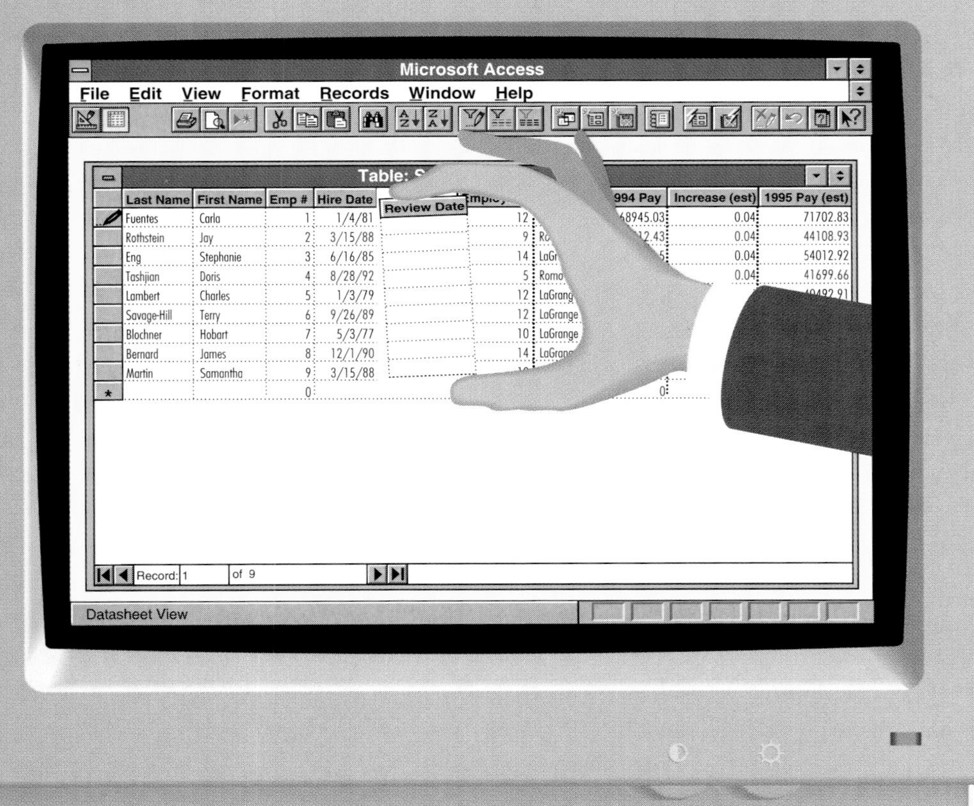

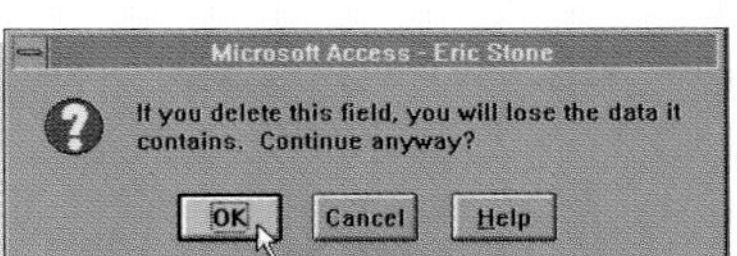

4 When you delete a field, Microsoft Access reminds you that you will delete any data the field contains. Click on the OK button to confirm the deletion.

5 To change the name or description of a field, click in the appropriate field to place the insertion point there, and then edit the text. Use the arrow keys to move the insertion point, and use Backspace and Delete to delete characters.

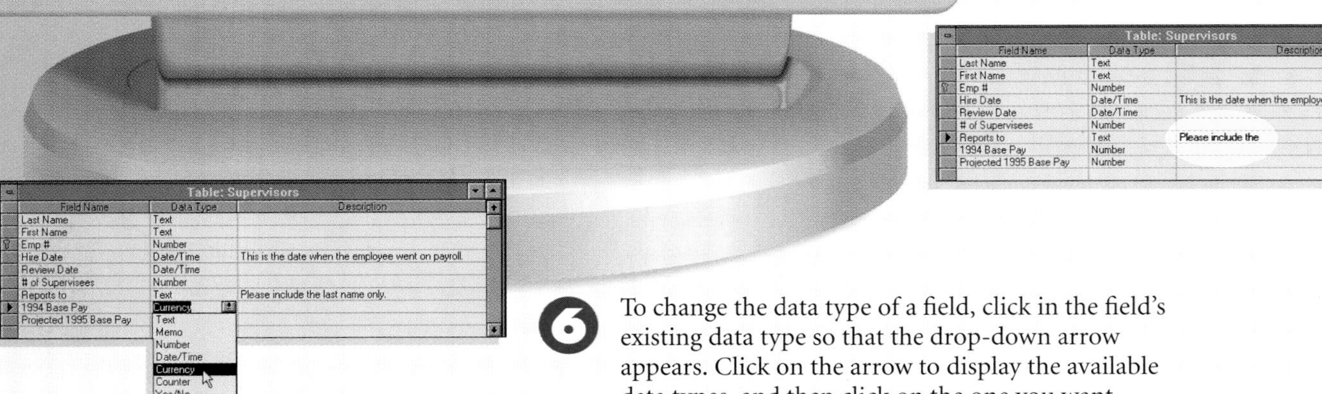

6 To change the data type of a field, click in the field's existing data type so that the drop-down arrow appears. Click on the arrow to display the available data types, and then click on the one you want.

How to Print a Table

Printing a table is not the best way to present your data. Rows and columns of data are no fun to wade through and interpret. This is especially true of tables too long and/or wide to fit on one page. Nonetheless, a quick printout of a table may come in handy—especially when you have to work away from your computer.

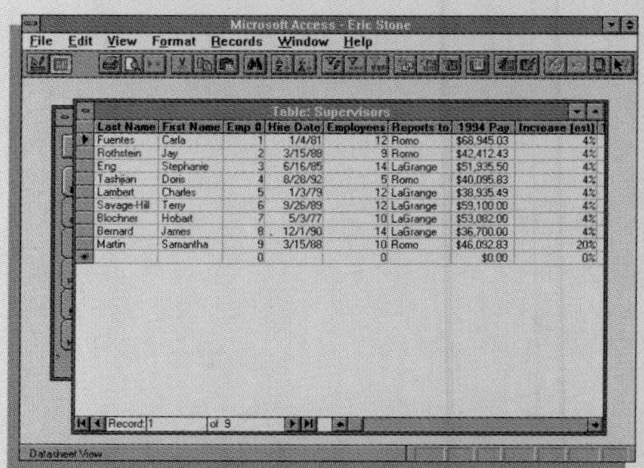

1 Display the table in Datasheet view. (For help, see "How to Open and View a Table" earlier in this chapter.)

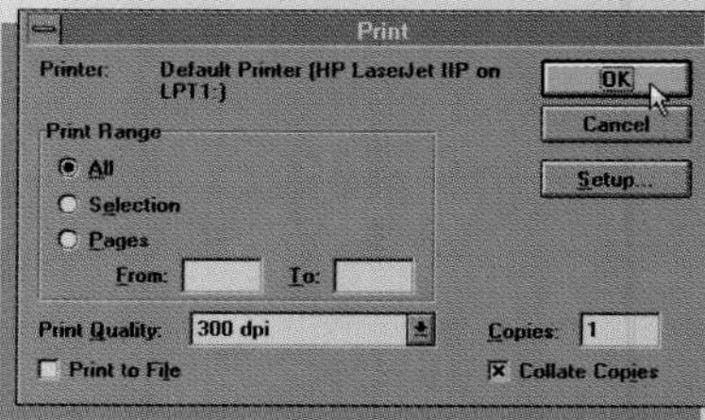

8 Make sure your printer is on and is stocked with paper. Then, click on the OK button to print your table.

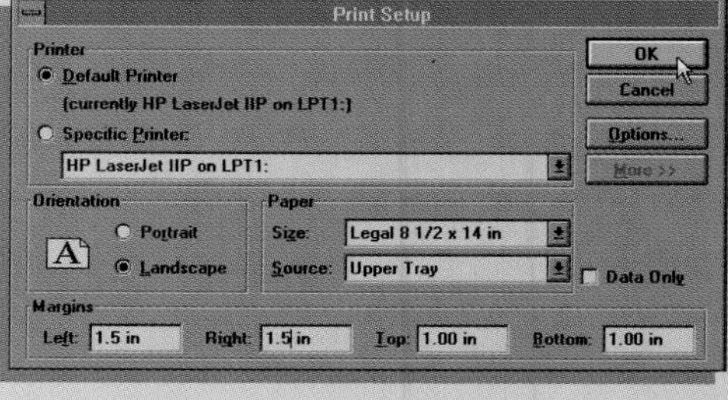

7 Click on the OK button to return to the Print dialog box.

- **Sometimes, switching to landscape orientation (step 4) is all it takes to fit a wide table on one page.**
- **Reports, covered in Chapters 12 and 13, are the way to produce sharp-looking printouts that are easy to understand.**

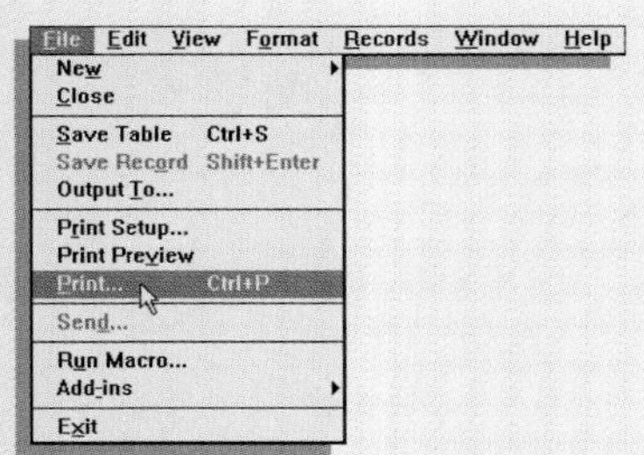

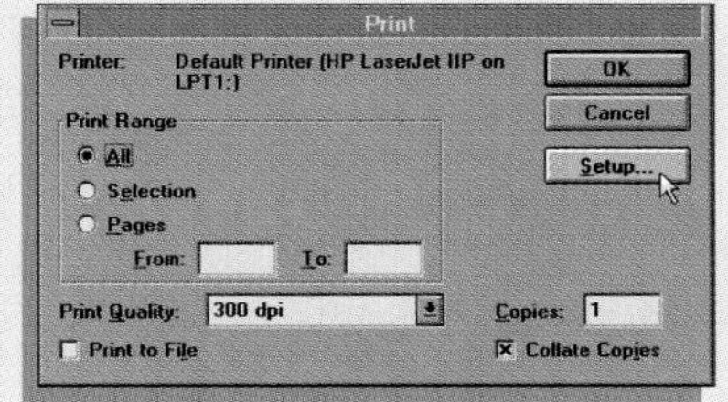

2 Click on File in the menu bar and then click on the Print command.

3 The Print dialog box appears. By default, Microsoft Access prints in portrait orientation (upright rather than sideways) on 8.5-by-11-inch paper with 1-inch margins on all four sides. If these settings are fine, skip to step 8. Otherwise, click on the Setup button.

4 The Print Setup dialog box appears. To print in landscape (sideways) orientation rather than portrait, click on the Landscape radio button.

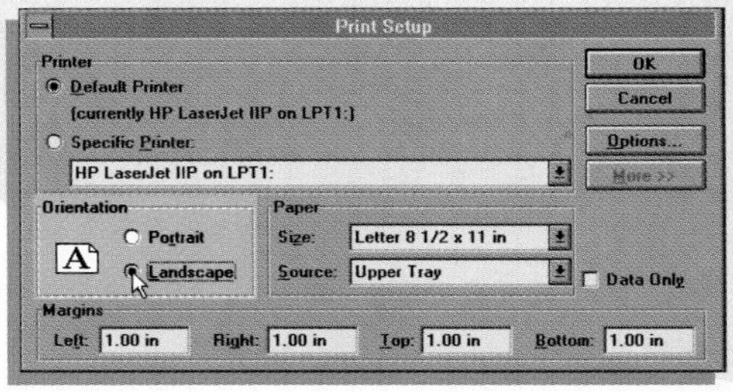

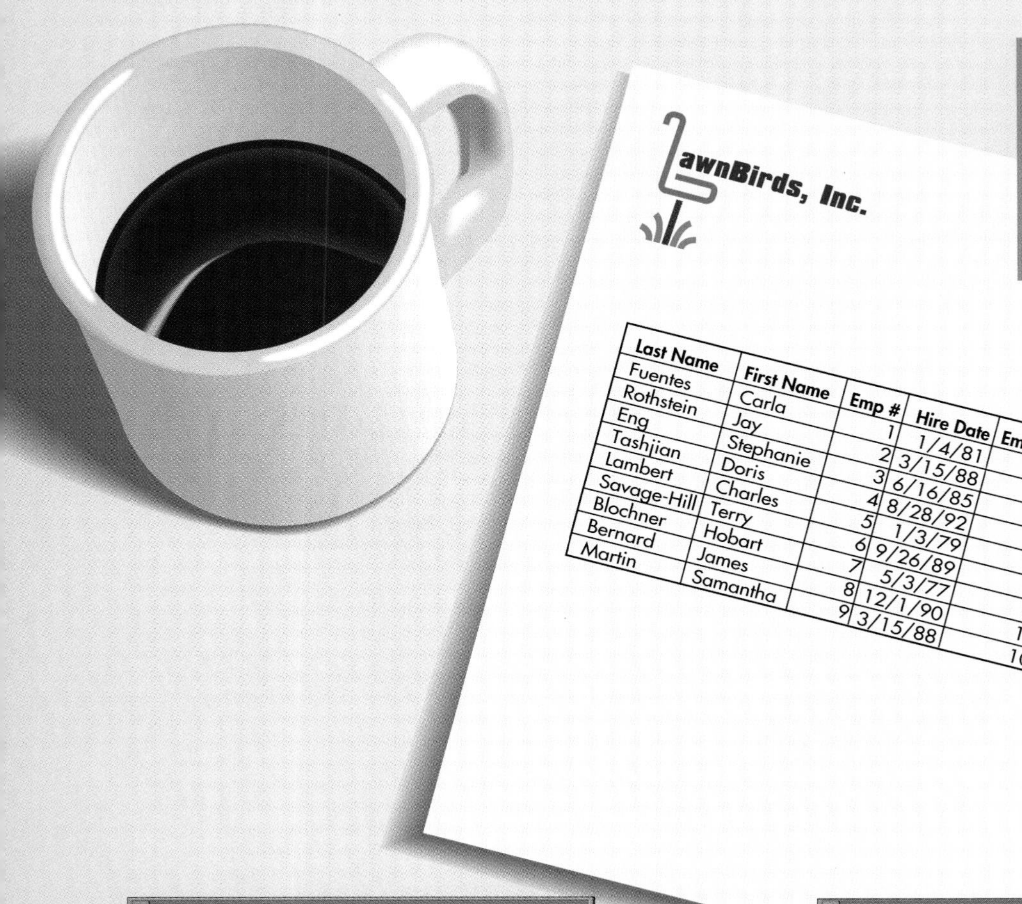

LawnBirds, Inc.

Supervisors

11/5/94

Last Name	First Name	Emp #	Hire Date	Employees	Reports to	1994 Pay	Increase (est)	1995 Pay (est)
Fuentes	Carla	1	1/4/81	12	Romo	$68,945.03	4%	$71,702.83
Rothstein	Jay	2	3/15/88	9	Romo	$42,412.43	4%	$44,108.93
Eng	Stephanie	3	6/16/85	14	LaGrange	$51,935.50	4%	$54,012.92
Tashjian	Doris	4	8/28/92	5	Romo	$40,095.83	4%	$41,699.66
Lambert	Charles	5	1/3/79	12	LaGrange	$38,935.49	4%	$40,492.91
Savage-Hill	Terry	6	9/26/89	12	LaGrange	$59,100.00	4%	$61,464.00
Blochner	Hobart	7	5/3/77	10	LaGrange	$53,082.00	4%	$55,205.78
Bernard	James	8	12/1/90	14	LaGrange	$36,700.00	4%	$38,168.00
Martin	Samantha	9	3/15/88	10	Romo	$46,092.83	20%	$55,311.40

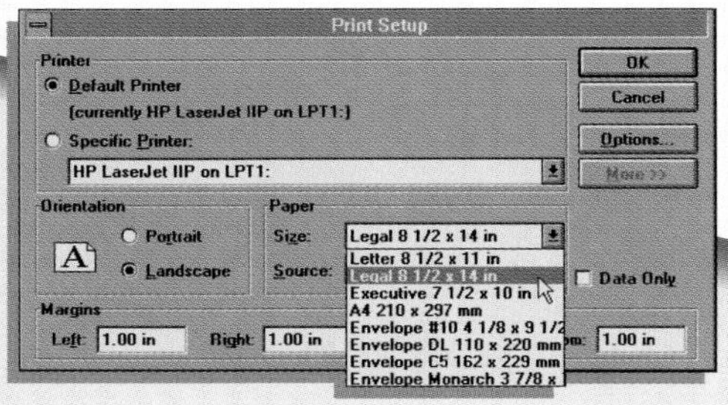

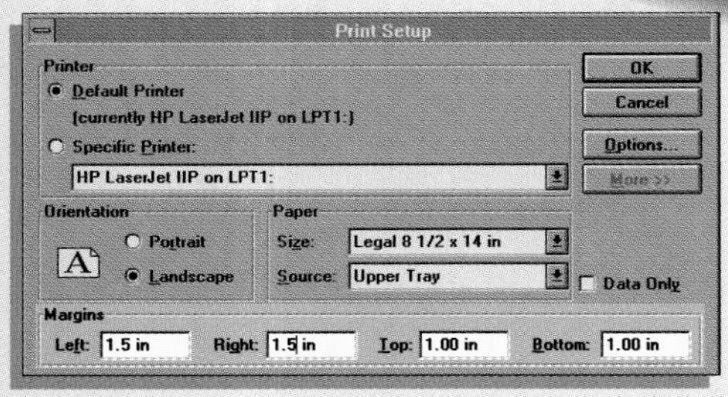

6 To change the left, right, top, or bottom margin, click in the appropriate text box, delete the existing setting, and type a new margin setting in inches.

5 To specify a different paper size, click on the Size drop-down arrow and select the size you plan to use. Also, if necessary, click on the Source drop-down arrow and specify where the paper being used is stored. The available options vary by printer.

CHAPTER 6

Working with Large Tables

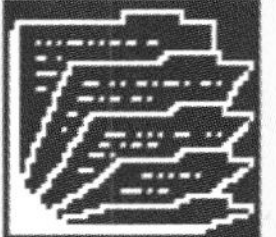

For simplicity's sake, the tables shown as examples in this book are small. But the ones you work with in real life are likely to be much bigger. Tables containing many thousands of records are common in the business world. Imagine, for example, the customer list of a major mail-order retailer.

The fact that this book shows small tables is of no real consequence. In Microsoft Access, the size of a table has no bearing on the things you can do with it—and how you do them. Everything you read about in this book applies to tables of any size.

But large tables do pose certain challenges, particularly when it comes to finding and arranging data. When a table is so large that you can't view all of your records at one time, you need ways to find the data you want to work with. This chapter covers the Microsoft Access features that make large tables more manageable.

How to Find Data

If you can think of any unique or nearly unique content of a record in a table, you can use the Find feature in Microsoft Access to jump immediately to the record. Let's say you need to change a customer's credit limit. To find the record, just tell Microsoft Access the customer's name or account number and have the program search for it.

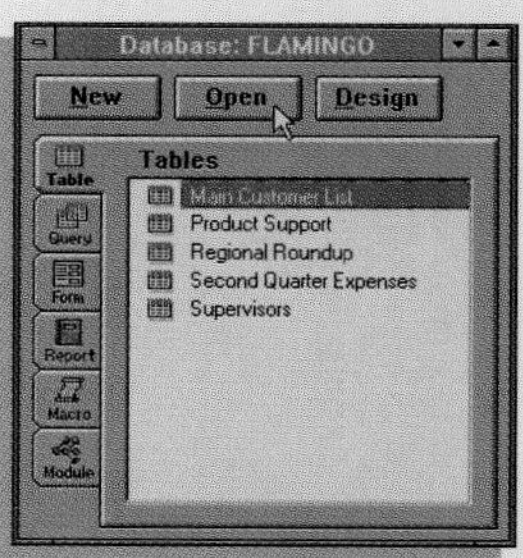

1 Open the table in Datasheet view.

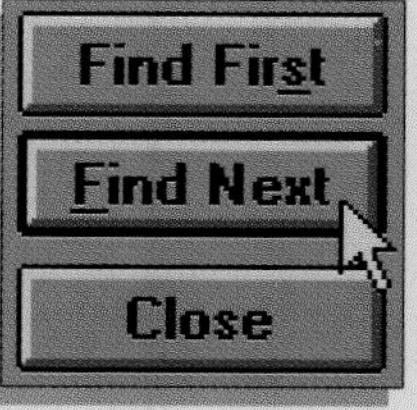

7 Click on the Find Next button. Microsoft Access jumps to the first instance of the search text, but the dialog box stays open.

8 If this is the record you want to work with, click on Close to close the Find dialog box. Otherwise, click on the Find Next button again to jump to the next instance of the search text, and continue clicking on Find Next until you reach the correct record.

TIP SHEET

- **After Microsoft Access finds the search text, you can move the Find dialog box to an out-of-the-way part of the screen so that you can view the table. To move a dialog box, simply drag its title bar.**
- **If Microsoft Access reaches the bottom of the table (or the top if you are searching upward) without finding the search text, it asks you whether to continue searching at the other end. Click on Yes to continue the search or No to quit.**
- **What if the Find feature fails to locate your search text? Three problems can typically trip up a search. First, you may have mistyped the search text in the Find dialog box. Check it carefully and edit it if necessary. Second, you may have placed the insertion point in the wrong field (step 2). And finally, the search text may simply be absent from the table.**

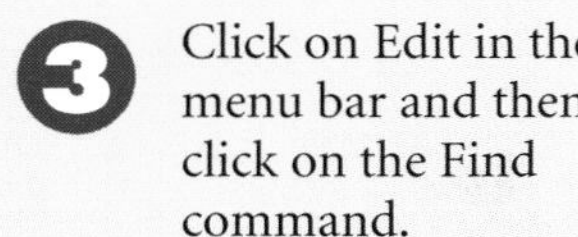

Table: Main Customer List

Last Name	First Name	Account #	Account Type	Street Address	City
Chang	Alexandra	809440	res	2929 Valley View Way	Walnut Creek
Gulfside Cafe		811411	comm	3737 County Route 166	Destin
Ron's Barber Shop		812991	comm	8989 Monterey Boulevard	San Bernardino
Thorpe	Mae	823920	res	730 San Gabriel Avenue	San Francisco
Wisteria Inn		834291	comm	9191 Route 92 East	Biloxi
Gonsalves	Martin	885560	comm	1885 23rd Street	Presidio
Bennett	Wanda	894411	res	333 Elm Street	Carrboro
Anderson	Vada	894901	res	3 Dillon Terrace	Poway
Greenwood	C.L.	899341	res	58707 NE 14th Avenue	N. Miami Beach
Angelotti	Donald	899941	res	1855 105th Way SE	Mobile
The Tropic Shop		900112	comm	25 Winslow Terrace	Edmonton
		0			

2 Click anywhere in the field you want to search. For example, if you want to search for a record based on its account number, click in the field containing account numbers.

3 Click on Edit in the menu bar and then click on the Find command.

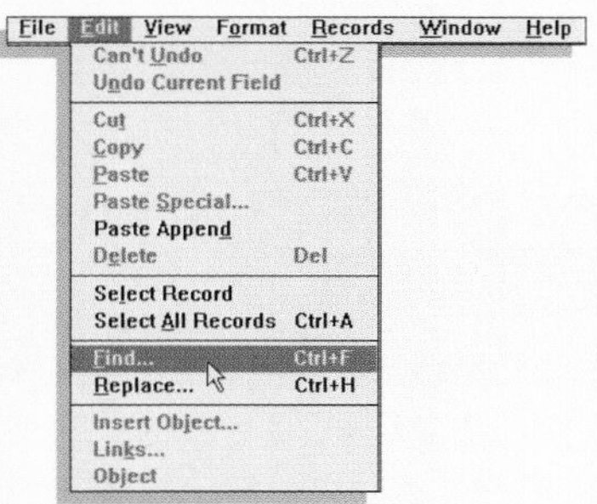

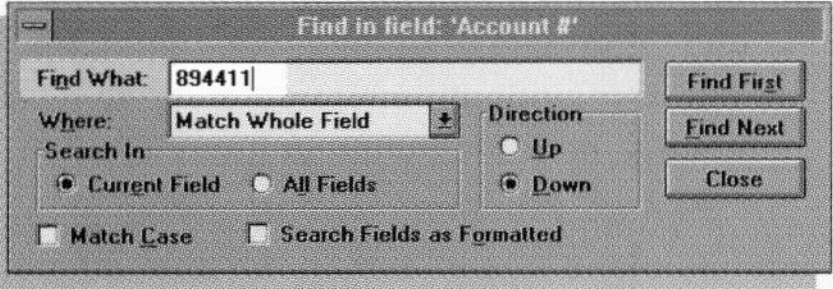

4 In the Find What text box, type the text you want to search for.

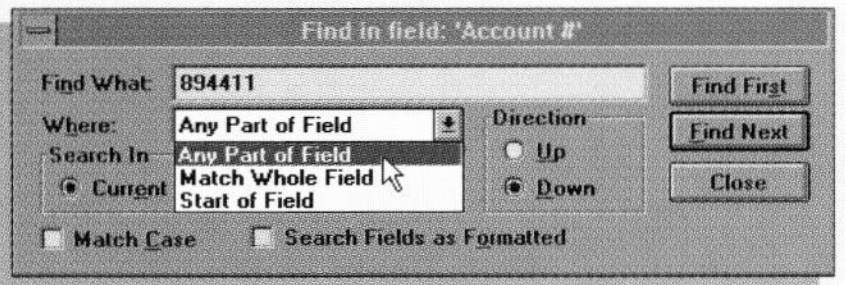

5 By default, Microsoft Access assumes that this text makes up the entire field contents. If this text makes up only part of the field contents, click on the Where drop-down arrow and then click on Any Part of Field. That way, if you type **Smith**, the Find Command will locate not only people named Smith but also Smithson, Naismith, and so on. Alternatively, click on Start of Field to locate the text only if it appears at the beginning of the field.

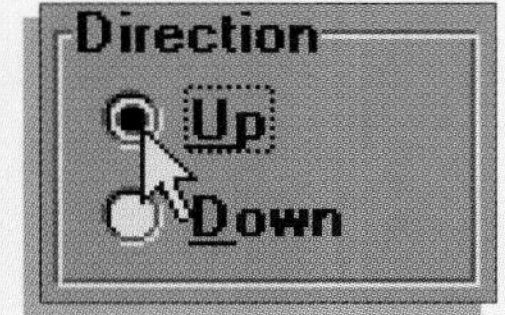

6 By default, Microsoft Access searches downward from the cell containing the insertion point. If you want to search upward instead, click on the Up radio button.

How to Sort a Table

Microsoft Access automatically sorts your tables on the primary key, if any (see Chapter 4). If there is no primary key defined, it displays records in the order in which they were entered. But sometimes it's useful to view tables another way—a personnel table sorted by salary, a client list sorted by state, and so on. The Quick Sort command can instantly sort records in ascending or descending order based on the contents of any field.

1. Open the table in Datasheet view.

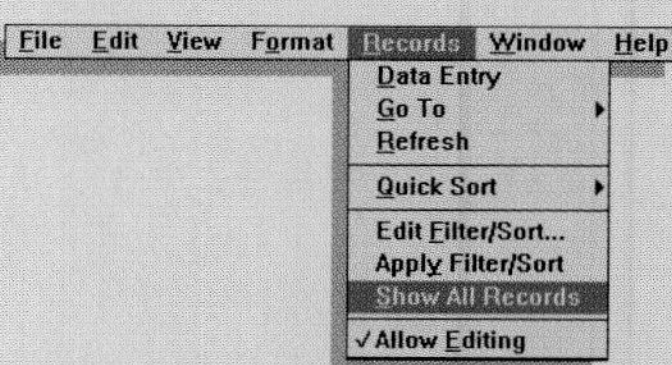

6. Next time you open the table in Datasheet view, the old sort order (primary key or data-entry order) will be restored, but if you want to restore it immediately after sorting, click on Records in the menu bar and then click on the Show All Records command.

TIP SHEET

- **As noted in step 6, the results of the Quick Sort command are temporary. Microsoft Access reverts to the old sort order when you reopen the table. If you want a more permanent way to look at records in a certain order, you can sort them through a query and then run the query whenever necessary. See Chapters 8 and 9.**
- **After sorting a table, observe the notation *FLTR* in the status bar. This stands for *filter*, and technically it means that you have taken advantage of a Microsoft Access feature that "filters" data to show only records that meet a certain condition. Of course, you have not really filtered the data through the Quick Sort command; you have merely rearranged it temporarily. However, the *FLTR* notation is a reminder that you are viewing a temporarily sorted table.**

Table: Main Customer List

First Name	Account #	Account Type	Street Address	City	State	Zi
Alexandra	809440	res	2929 Valley View Way	Walnut Creek	CA	943
	811411	comm	3737 County Route 166	Destin	FL	325
	812991	comm	8989 Monterey Boulevard	San Bernardino	CA	969
Mae	823920	res	730 San Gabriel Avenue	San Francisco	CA	941
	834291	comm	9191 Route 92 East	Biloxi	MS	459
Martin	885560	comm	1885 23rd Street	Presidio	TX	682
Wanda	894411	res	333 Elm Street	Carrboro	NC	275
Vada	894901	res	3 Dillon Terrace	Poway	CA	988
C.L.	899341	res	58707 NE 14th Avenue	N. Miami Beach	FL	331
Donald	899941	res	1855 105th Way SE	Mobile	AL	439
	900112	comm	25 Winslow Terrace	Edmonton	Alberta, Canada	6V
	0					

2 Click anywhere in the field containing the data by which you want the table sorted. For instance, if you want the table sorted alphabetically by state, click in the State field.

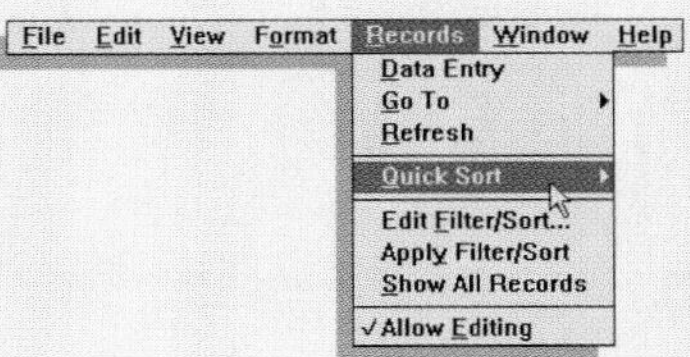

3 Click on Records in the menu bar and then click on the Quick Sort command.

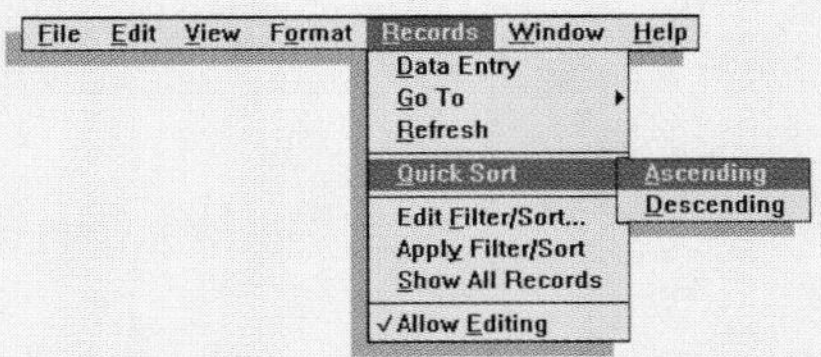

4 Click on Ascending or Descending to specify the sort order. Ascending order is standard numerical or alphabetical order; descending order is the reverse.

Records are sorted alphabetically by state.

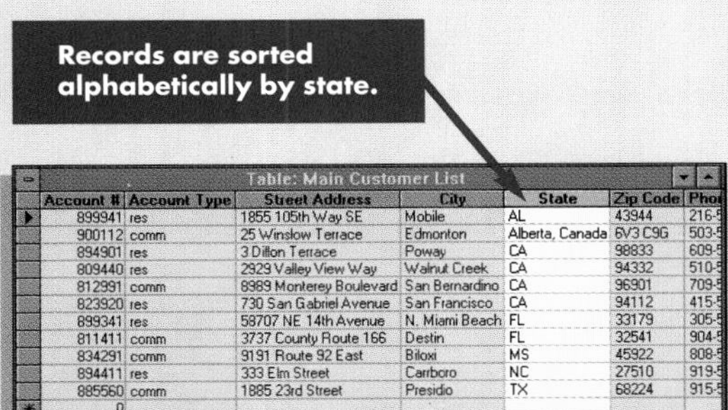

Table: Main Customer List

Account #	Account Type	Street Address	City	State	Zip Code	Pho
899941	res	1855 105th Way SE	Mobile	AL	43944	216-5
900112	comm	25 Winslow Terrace	Edmonton	Alberta, Canada	6V3 C9G	503-5
894901	res	3 Dillon Terrace	Poway	CA	98833	609-5
809440	res	2929 Valley View Way	Walnut Creek	CA	94332	510-5
812991	comm	8989 Monterey Boulevard	San Bernardino	CA	96901	709-5
823920	res	730 San Gabriel Avenue	San Francisco	CA	94112	415-5
899341	res	58707 NE 14th Avenue	N. Miami Beach	FL	33179	305-5
811411	comm	3737 County Route 166	Destin	FL	32541	904-5
834291	comm	9191 Route 92 East	Biloxi	MS	45922	808-5
894411	res	333 Elm Street	Carrboro	NC	27510	919-5
885560	comm	1885 23rd Street	Presidio	TX	68224	915-5
0						

5 Microsoft Access instantly sorts the records. Observe the results and work with the table as needed.

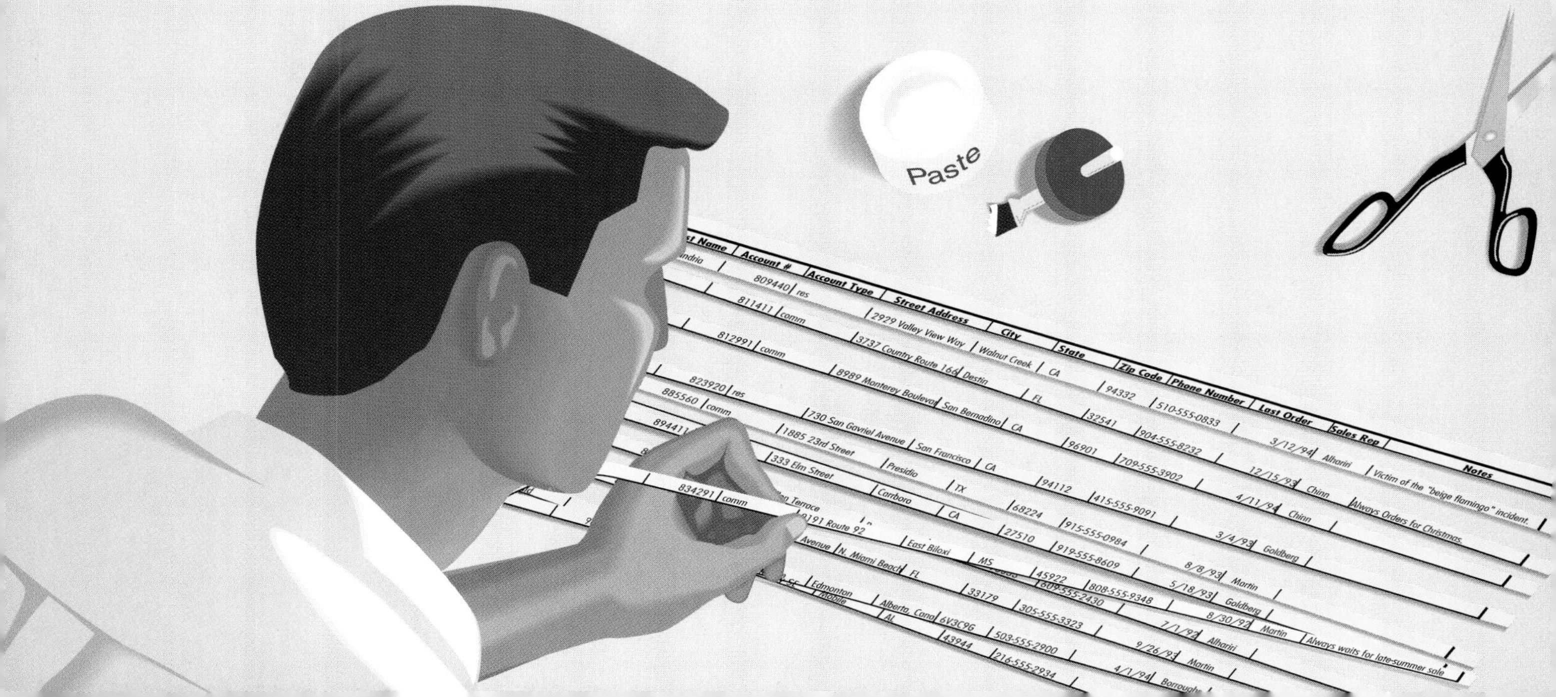

CHAPTER 7

Rescue

Sure, you can turn to this book when you have a database management problem or need information on a Microsoft Access text. But often you can get past your troubles without even turning away from your computer screen.

Microsoft Access comes with a valuable command named Undo. It reverses the action you have performed most recently, such as editing data, changing a table design feature—in fact, most actions you'll learn about in this book. Though it cannot reverse every action, Undo is a good bet to get you out of hot water.

Microsoft Access also comes with *on-line help* that you can display on your screen and peruse much as you'd flip through a reference book. The on-line help system is *context-sensitive,* which means that it usually brings you directly to information on the action in progress. For example, if you issue the Help command when a dialog box is displayed, you get information about that dialog box.

How to Undo an Action

If it hasn't happened to you yet, it will. You'll insert Larry's data in Curly's record, delete a field when you meant to edit it, or experience some other common mishap—and be dismayed or even horrified by the results. Not to worry. If you notice a mistake fast enough, you can probably reverse it instantly by issuing the Undo command. This command can reverse most actions you take on objects in Microsoft Access. Beware, however, that Microsoft Access cannot undo certain actions, such as deleting an entire record.

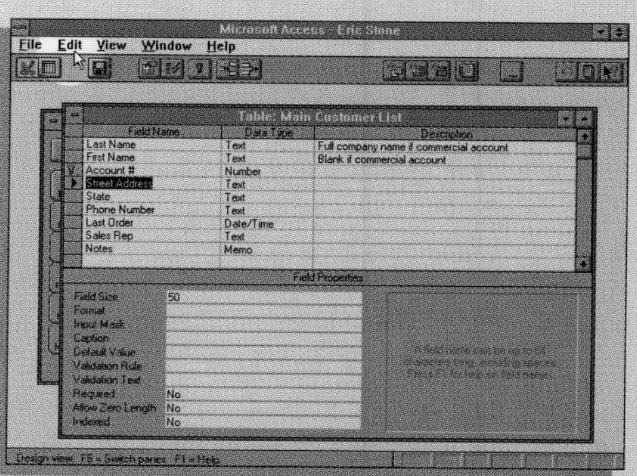

1 Click on Edit in the menu bar as soon as you realize that you want to undo your last action. Once you perform another action, the previous action may become irreversible.

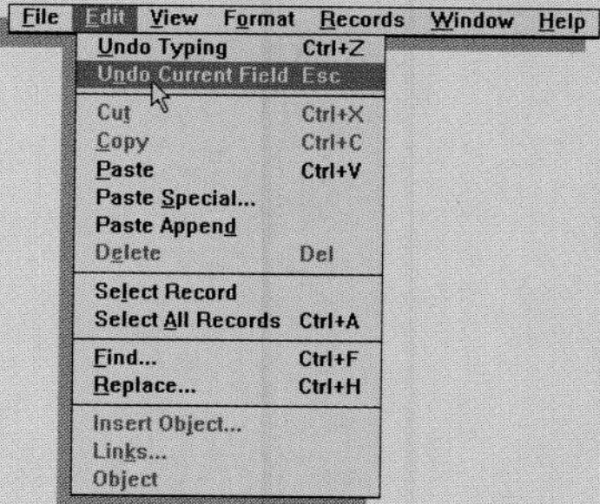

4 If the Undo command (or either Undo command) reflects the action you want to reverse, click on it. Otherwise, click outside the menu to close it.

TIP SHEET

- **As noted in Chapter 5, Microsoft Access saves an edited record as soon as you move the insertion point to another record. Typically, saving is an irreversible action. However, Microsoft Access lets you undo a saved record, restoring the record to what it was before you started editing it. After moving the insertion point to a new record, simply click on Edit in the menu bar and then click on Undo Saved Record. You must do this before taking any editing action on another record.**
- **It is somewhat surprising that Microsoft Access cannot reverse the deletion of an entire record. However, before allowing you to delete a record, the program does require you to confirm your intentions (see Chapter 5). Other types of deletions, such as deleting a field from a table design, are reversible.**

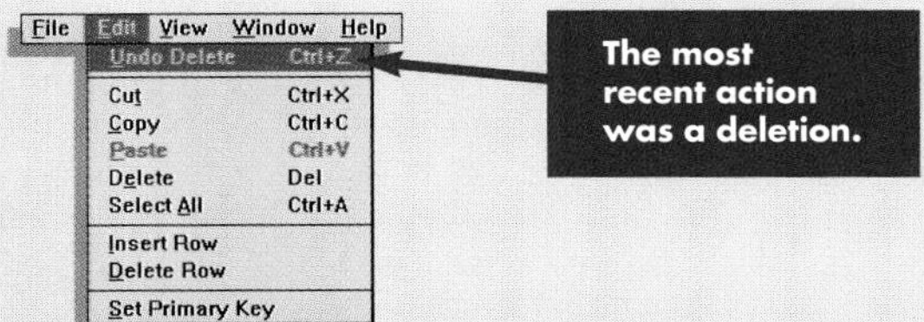

2 Observe the first command on the Edit menu. It reads *Undo* followed by the last action you took. If your last action is irreversible, the menu reads *Can't Undo*.

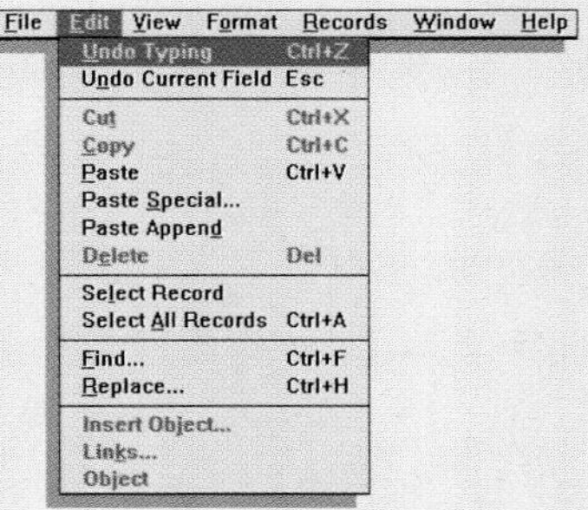

3 In some circumstances, there are two Undo commands. For example, if you are editing a cell in a table, you have a choice of Undo Typing, which reverses the last editing action you took within the field, and Undo Current Field, which restores the cell contents to what they were before you started editing.

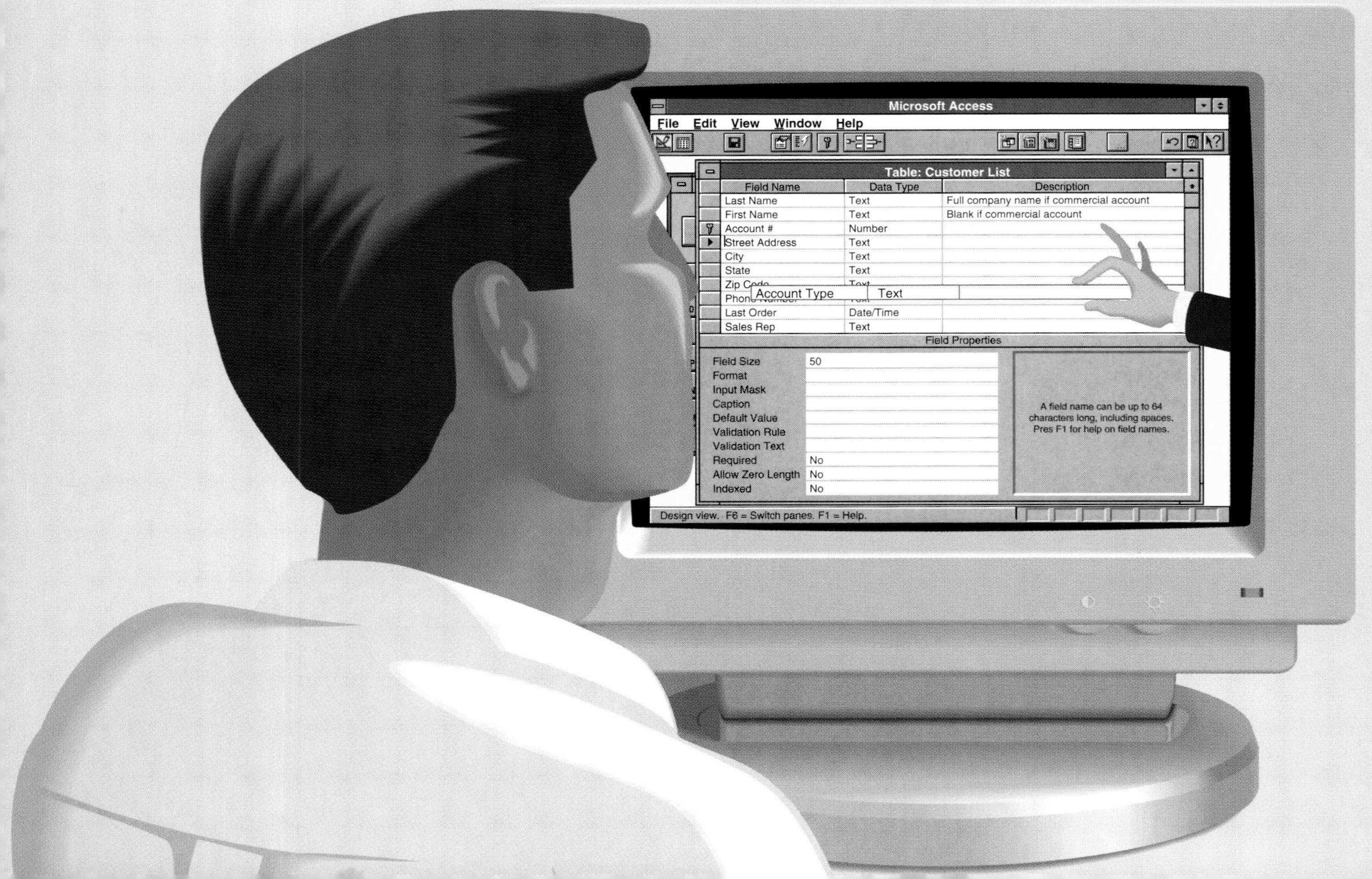

How to Get Help from Microsoft Access

If you have questions as you work with Microsoft Access, you can turn to this book for help. But you may well be able to find the information you need without even taking your hands off the keyboard and mouse. The Help command usually gives information related to the action in progress—and if it doesn't, you can search through the help system for the information you need. The Help command works in virtually all contexts, even when a menu is pulled down or a dialog box is displayed.

1 Press F1 to issue the Help command. Microsoft Access brings you directly to the information it assumes you need. For example, if a dialog box was open, you see information about that dialog box. If a menu was pulled down, you see information about the highlighted command. If you were editing a table, you see information about tables.

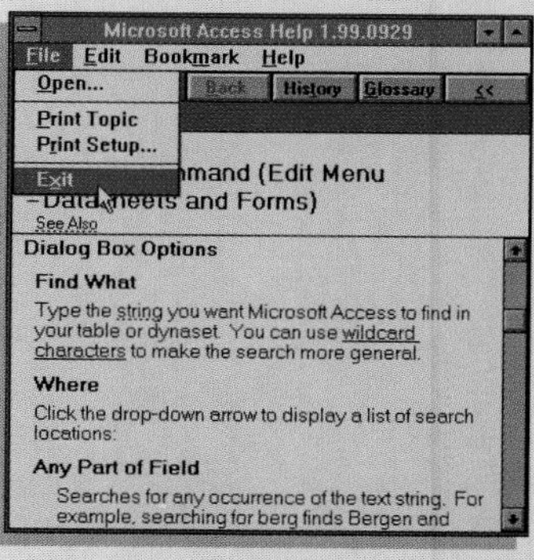

6 Observe that the Help window has its own menu bar, separate from that of Microsoft Access. When done using the help system, click on File in the Help window menu bar and then click on the Exit command.

TIP SHEET

- **The Help window is an application window. You can maximize, minimize, restore, resize, and move it. One advantage to this is that you can arrange the Help window so that it does not cover the screen portion you need help with, such as a dialog box. See Chapter 2 for more information on window manipulation.**
- **You may have observed that the Microsoft Access menu bar offers a Help menu and that some dialog boxes have Help buttons. Indeed, the Help menu and Help buttons are other ways to enter the help system. This page stresses the F1 key because it is available no matter what you are doing in Microsoft Access.**

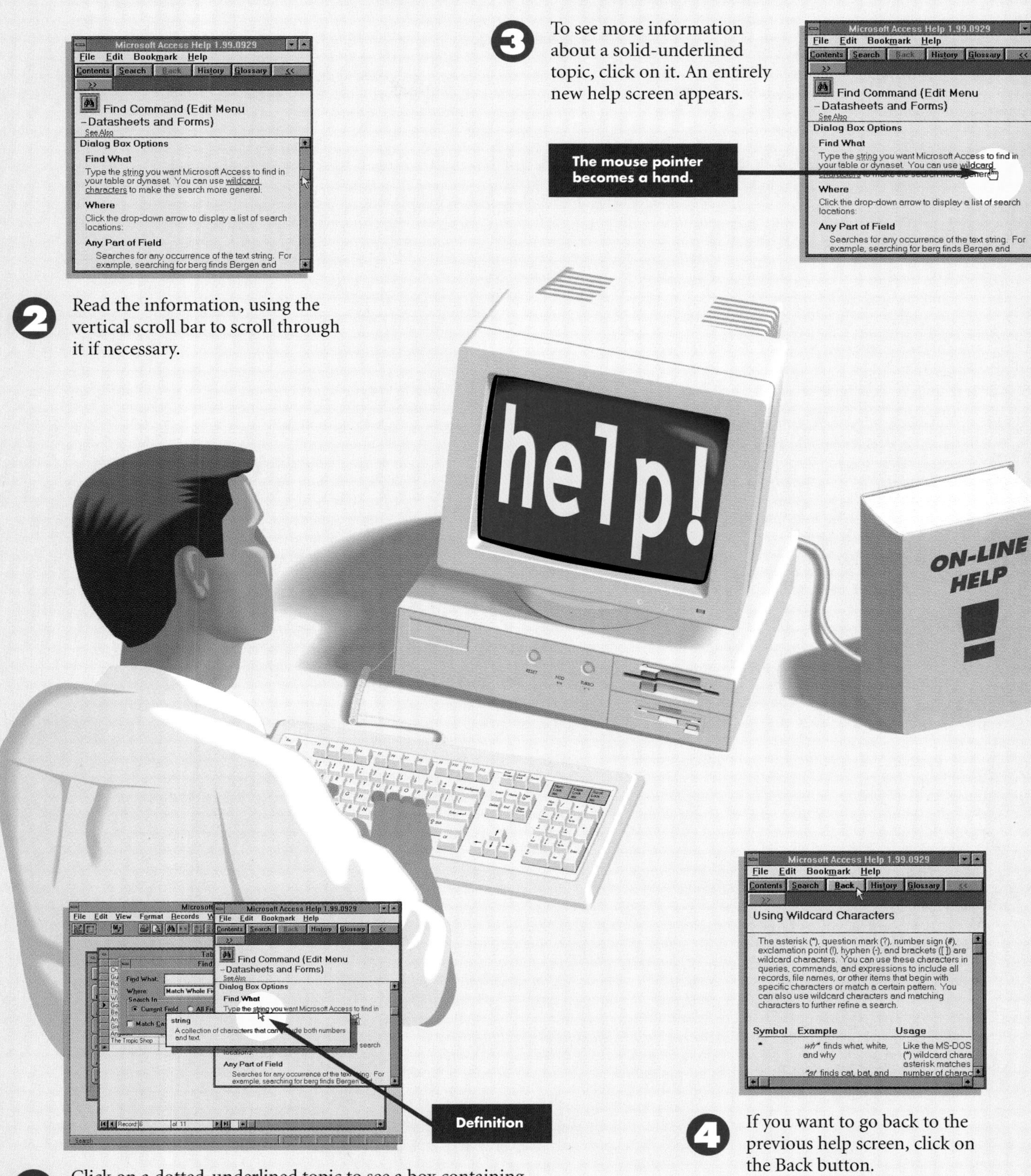

2 Read the information, using the vertical scroll bar to scroll through it if necessary.

3 To see more information about a solid-underlined topic, click on it. An entirely new help screen appears.

4 If you want to go back to the previous help screen, click on the Back button.

5 Click on a dotted-underlined topic to see a box containing either the definition of a term or a list of more specific topics. Click outside the box to close it, or click on an underlined topic within the box to read about it.

TRY IT!

Here is an opportunity to try out the many skills you have acquired in the first seven chapters of this book. Follow each step carefully at your computer to design and build the table pictured here. Though smaller than typical tables in Microsoft Access, this example illustrates all the major skills you need to create tables of any size. Chapter numbers are included with most steps to help you find more information on the skills required.

Start Microsoft Access if it is not already running. *Chapter 3*

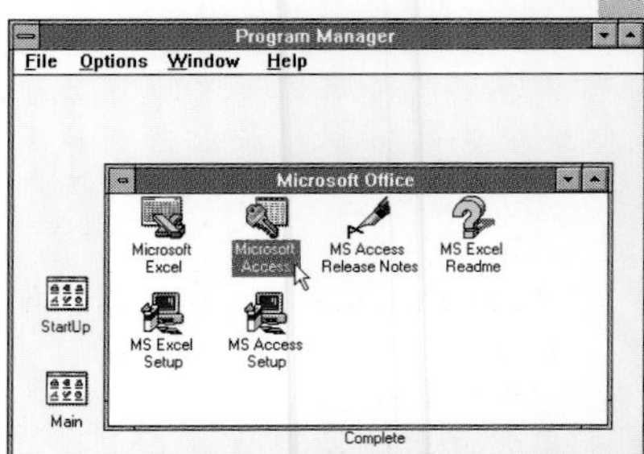

You should see either the blank Microsoft Access application window or the Database window. *Only if* you are viewing a table (or other object), close it by clicking on File in the menu bar and then clicking on the Close command. *Chapters 3 to 5*

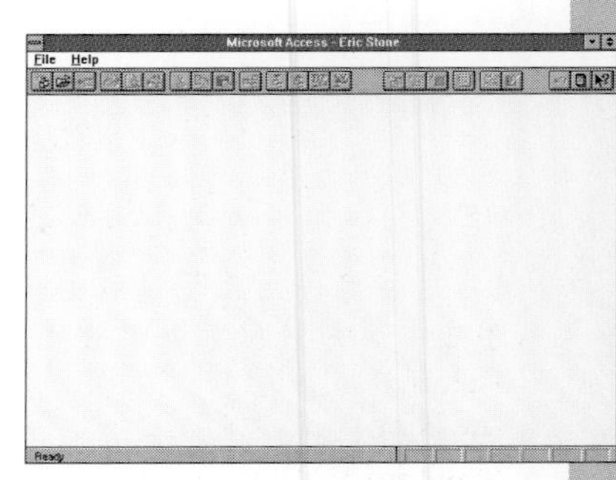

Microsoft Access

Table: Product Support

Product Name	Code #	Introduced	Royalty	Sales	1994 Support $
Old Reliable	1595	9/26/85	No	$608,905.22	$29,900.00
Yard Monarch	2355	8/2/68	No	$3,980,055.94	$104,300.00
Econo-Bird	3530	1/24/90	Yes	$1,488,033.07	$62,600.00
Coral Gables	4352	4/11/72	No	$1,008,934.05	$68,300.00
The Acrobat	5034	9/19/78	No	$4,290,347.37	$108,900.00
Wingspan	8242	9/20/85	Yes	$949,837.10	$60,100.00
Classic Pink	9053	1/3/80	No	$880,932.25	$51,500.00

Ready

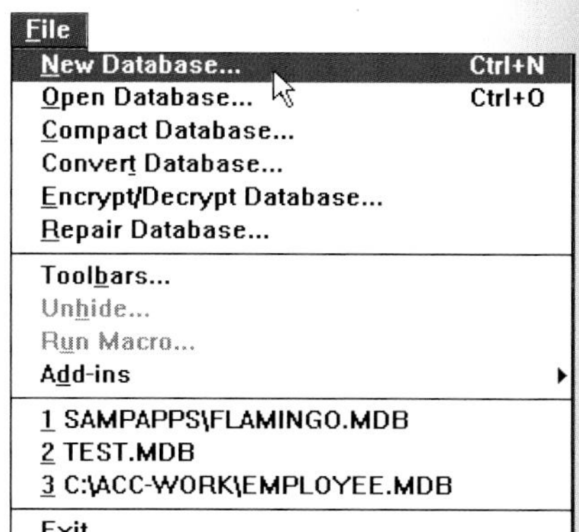

Click on File in the menu bar and then click on the New Database command. *Chapter 4*

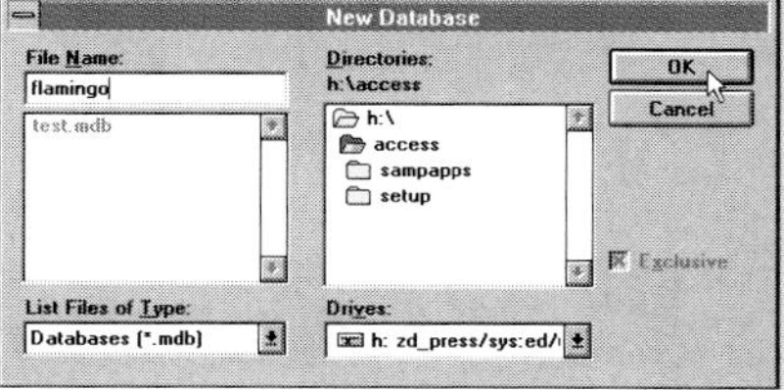

Type **flamingo** in the New Database dialog box and click on the OK button. The new database will be named FLAMINGO.MDB and will be stored in your default location. *Chapter 3*

In the Database window, click on the New button to start a new table. *Chapter 4*

Click on New Table. *Chapter 4*

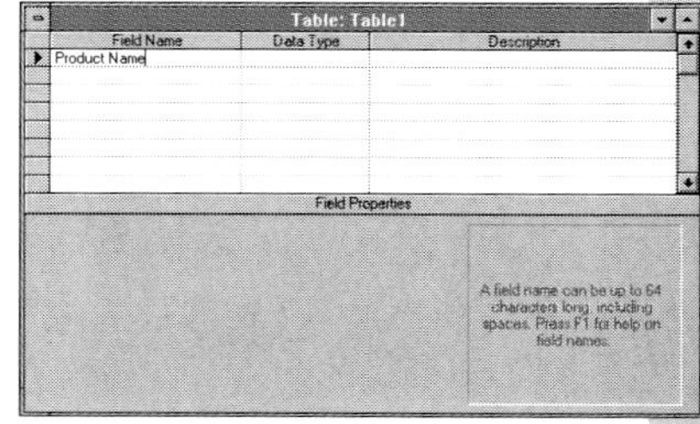

The new table opens in Design view. Type the first field name, **Product Name**, and press the Tab key. *Chapter 4*

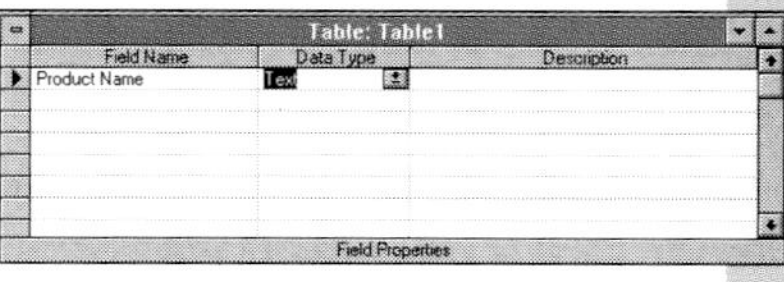

Microsoft Access suggests the data type you want (Text), so just press Tab again to move to the Description column. *Chapter 4*

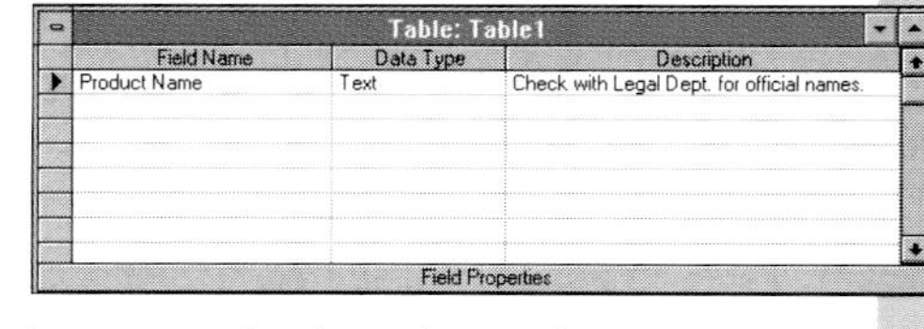

For the field description, type **Check with Legal Dept. for official names.** Then press Tab to move to the next field definition. *Chapter 4*

Continue to next page ▸

TRY IT!

Continue below

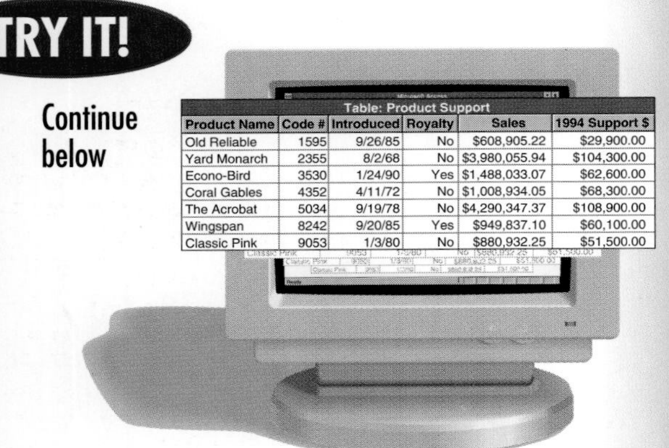

Table: Product Support

Product Name	Code #	Introduced	Royalty	Sales	1994 Support $
Old Reliable	1595	9/26/85	No	$608,905.22	$29,900.00
Yard Monarch	2355	8/2/68	No	$3,980,055.94	$104,300.00
Econo-Bird	3530	1/24/90	Yes	$1,488,033.07	$62,600.00
Coral Gables	4352	4/11/72	No	$1,008,934.05	$68,300.00
The Acrobat	5034	9/19/78	No	$4,290,347.37	$108,900.00
Wingspan	8242	9/20/85	Yes	$949,837.10	$60,100.00
Classic Pink	9053	1/3/80	No	$880,932.25	$51,500.00

10

Table: Table1

Field Name	Data Type	Description
Product Name	Text	Check with Legal Dept. for official names.
Code #		

For the next field name, type **Code #** and press Tab. *Chapter 4*

11

For the data type, click on the drop-down arrow and then click on Number. *Chapter 4*

12

In the Field Properties area, click on the Validation Rule text box and type **>999 And <10000** to restrict entries in this field to four-digit numbers (that is, numbers greater than 999 and less than 10,000). *Chapter 4*

13

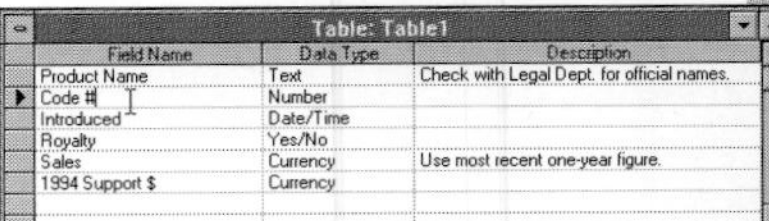

Table: Table1

Field Name	Data Type	Description
Product Name	Text	Check with Legal Dept. for official names.
Code #	Number	
Introduced	Date/Time	
Royalty	Yes/No	
Sales	Currency	Use most recent one-year figure.
1994 Support $	Currency	

Define the remaining fields as shown here, pressing Tab to move from one entry to the next. *Chapter 4*

14

Table: Table1

Field Name	Data Type	Description
Product Name	Text	Check with Legal Dept. for official names.
Code #	Number	
Introduced	Date/Time	
Royalty	Yes/No	
Sales	Currency	Use most recent one-year figure.
1994 Support $	Currency	

Click anywhere in the definition of the Code # field.

15

Click on Edit in the menu bar and then click on the Set Primary Key command. *Chapter 4*

16

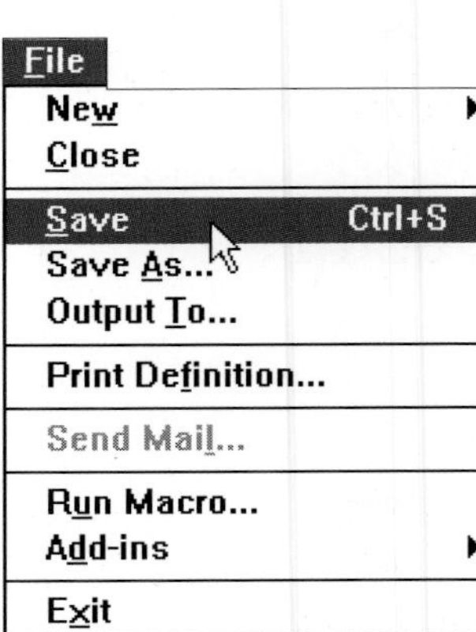

Click on File in the menu bar and then click on the Save command. *Chapter 4*

17

In the Save As dialog box, type **Product Support** and click on the OK button to save the table design. *Chapter 4*

Click on View in the menu bar and then click on the Datasheet command. *Chapter 5*

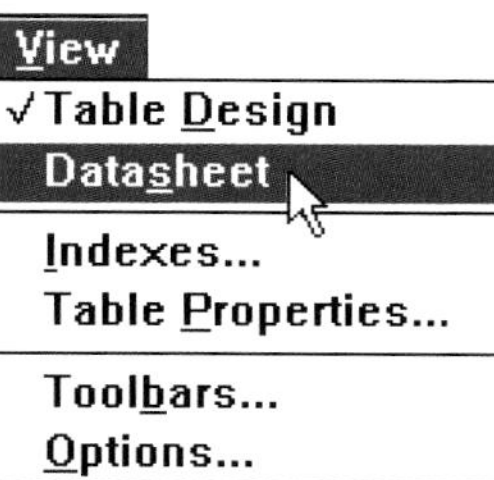

Product Name	Code #	Introduced	Royalty	Sales	1994 Support $
Old Reliable	1595	9/26/85	No	$608,905.22	$29,900.00
Yard Monarch	2355	8/2/68	No	$3,980,055.94	$104,300.00
Econo-Bird	3530	1/24/90	Yes	$1,488,033.07	$62,600.00
Coral Gables	4352	4/11/72	No	$1,008,934.05	$68,300.00
The Acrobat	5034	9/19/78	No	$4,290,347.37	$108,900.00
Wingspan	8242	9/20/85	Yes	$949,837.10	$60,100.00
Classic Pink	9053	1/3/80	No	$880,932.25	$51,500.00

You are now viewing the table in Datasheet view. Enter the data in the table, pressing Tab to move from one cell to the next. (The preceding page shows the table in larger type.) You may wish to widen or narrow columns so that they display their complete contents without wasting space. To do so, drag the right border of the column heading. *Chapter 5*

Click on any cell in the Product Name field.

Product Name
Old Reliable
Yard Monarch
Econo-Bird
Coral Gables
The Acrobat
Wingspan
Classic Pink

21

Click on Records, click on Quick Sort, and then click on Ascending. Microsoft Access sorts the records alphabetically by product name. *Chapter 6*

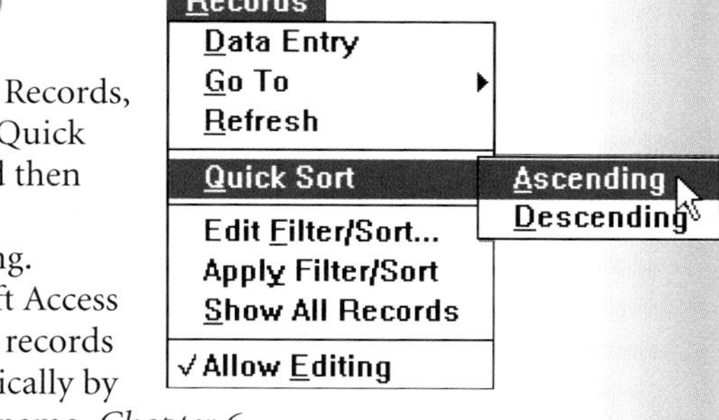

22

Click on File in the menu bar and then click on the Close command to close the table. (If you changed the width of any column in step 19, Microsoft Access will ask you whether to save the layout change. Click on Yes.) *Chapter 4*

File
New
Close
Save Table Ctrl+S
Save Record Shift+Enter
Output To...
Print Setup...
Print Preview
Print... Ctrl+P
Send...
Run Macro...
Add-ins
Exit

23

In the Database window, double-click on the Product Support table object to re-display your new table in Datasheet view. *Chapter 5*

Product Name	Code #	Introduced	Royalty	Sales	1994 Support $
Old Reliable	1595	9/26/85	No	$608,905.22	$29,900.00
Yard Monarch	2355	8/2/68	No	$3,980,055.94	$104,300.00
Econo-Bird	3530	1/24/90	Yes	$1,488,033.07	$62,600.00
Coral Gables	4352	4/11/72	No	$1,008,934.05	$68,300.00
The Acrobat	5034	9/19/78	No	$4,290,347.37	$108,900.00
Wingspan	8242	9/20/85	Yes	$949,837.10	$60,100.00
Classic Pink	9053	1/3/80	No	$880,932.25	$51,500.00

Observe that Microsoft Access now sorts the table by the primary key, the Code # field. The results of the Quick Sort in step 21 are lost. *Chapter 6*

Click on File in the menu bar and then click on the Close command. *Chapter 4*

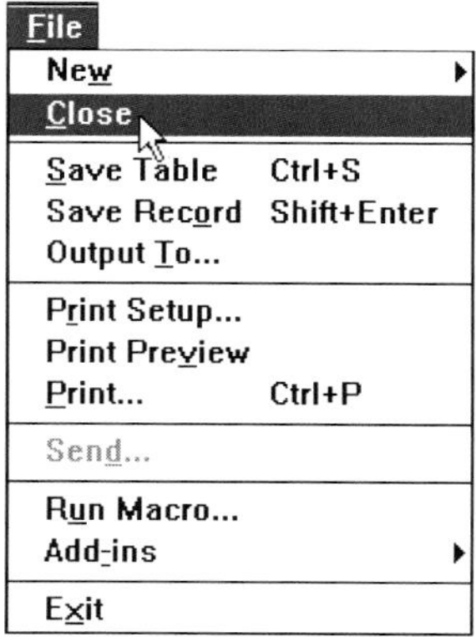

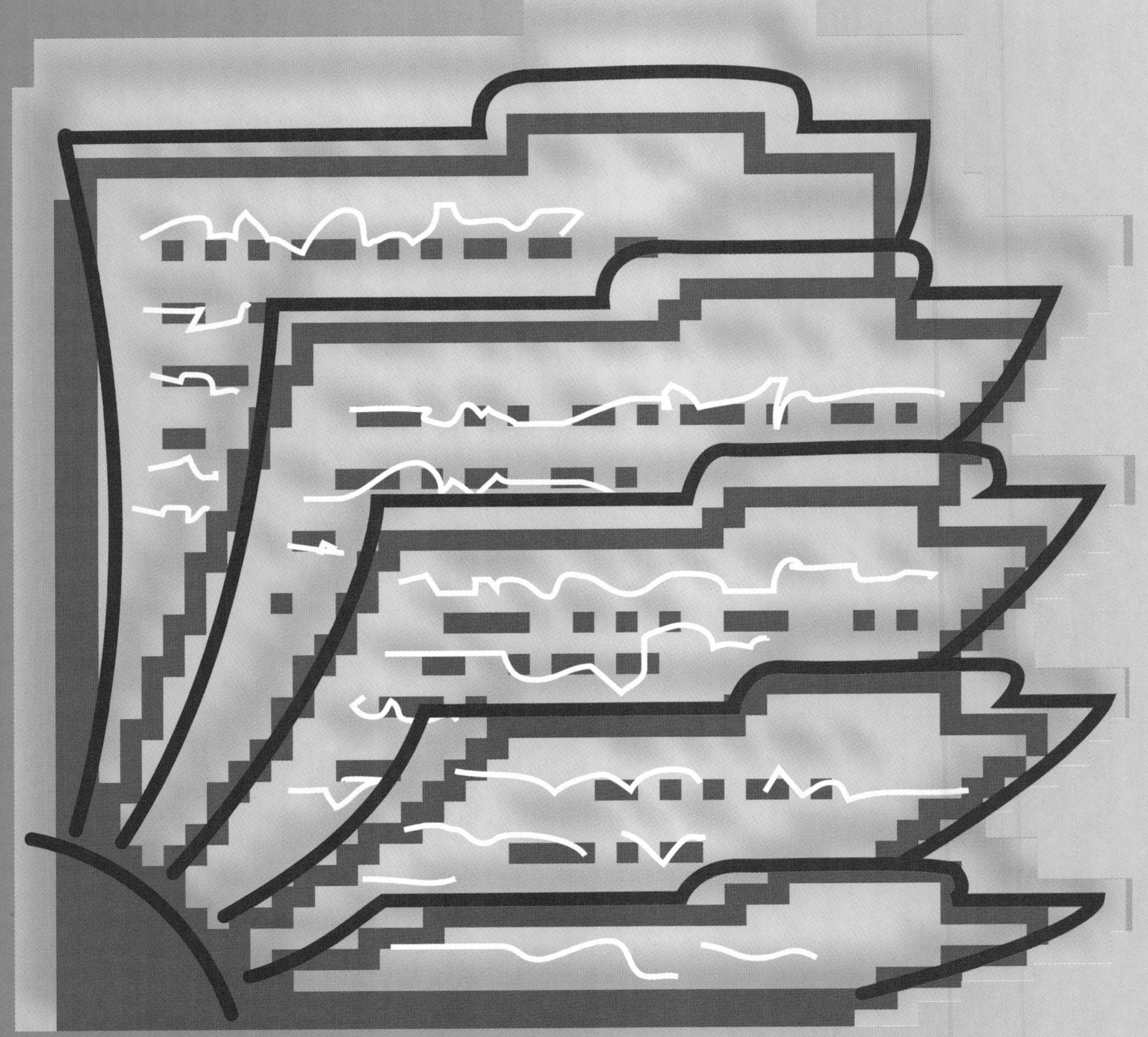

CHAPTER 8

Pulling Information from a Table

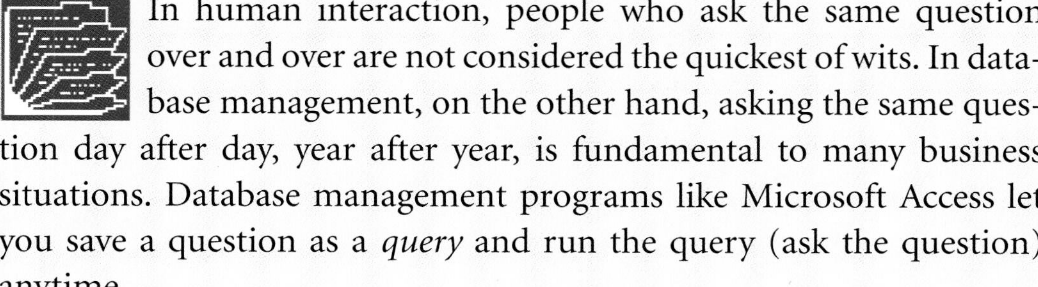

In human interaction, people who ask the same question over and over are not considered the quickest of wits. In database management, on the other hand, asking the same question day after day, year after year, is fundamental to many business situations. Database management programs like Microsoft Access let you save a question as a *query* and run the query (ask the question) anytime.

Why keep asking the same question? Imagine a table containing inventory information. Your inventory changes daily as new product comes in and existing product sells. Now imagine that at the end of each workday your supervisor needs to know what products are in short supply—say, fewer than 100 in stock. In Microsoft Access you can build a query that, in effect, asks the table, "What products are in short supply and how many of each are in stock?" At the end of each day, you run the query and see that day's answer.

Tables are a nice way to arrange data, but pulling information from tables through carefully planned queries is the way you really get some performance out of your database management software. This chapter explains how to build and run a query.

How to Start a New Query

Building a query takes quite a few steps. Therefore, each of the first four pages in this chapter covers a small part of the process. This page just helps you inform Microsoft Access that you're ready to build a query. In upcoming pages you will learn how to specify exactly what the query will do.

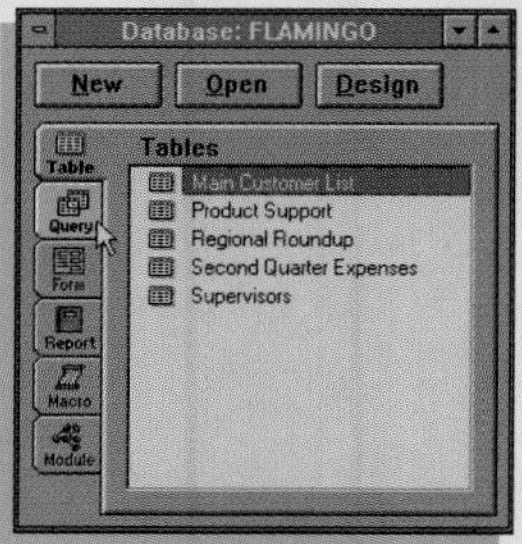

2 In the Database window, click on the Query object button.

1 Open the database containing the table from which you want to pull information (see Chapter 3).

TIP SHEET

- **You can base a query on another query rather than on a table. For example, if one query pulls out the name, account number, and address of all customers who spent more than $500 with your company last year, another query could whittle down the list further by pulling out those customers who spent more than $500 *and* are from California. This technique can save considerable time. To base a query on another query, in step 6 click on the Queries radio button in the Add Table dialog box, click on the query on which to base the new query, and then proceed with the remaining steps as described. Before trying this, it's best to get some experience building and running ordinary queries.**

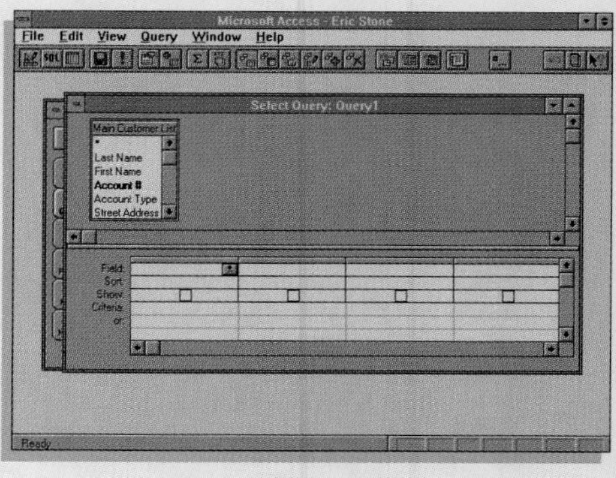

8 Now you see only the blank grid. The next two pages explain how to work with it.

3 Now you are viewing a list of queries (if any) that are already defined for this database. But you don't want to work with an existing query; you want to start a new one. Click on the New button.

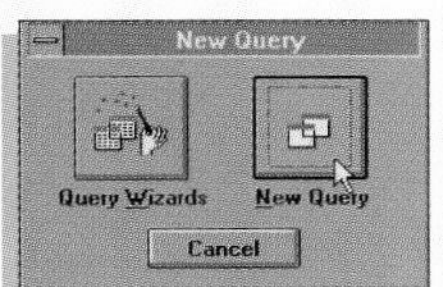

4 Click on New Query.

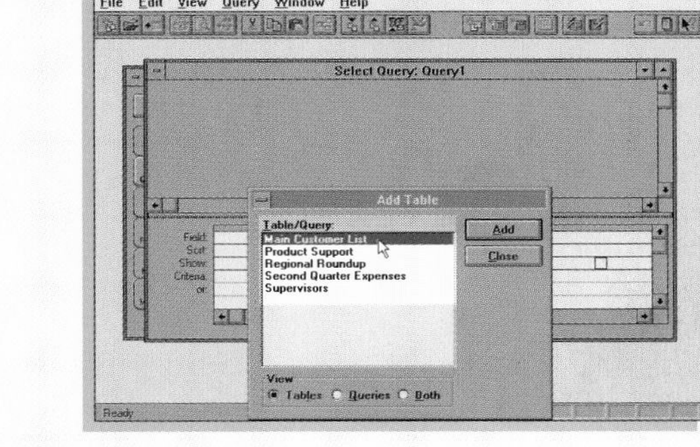

5 Microsoft Access displays a blank grid in which you will build the query. Overlapping it is the Add Table dialog box. Click on the table from which you want to pull information.

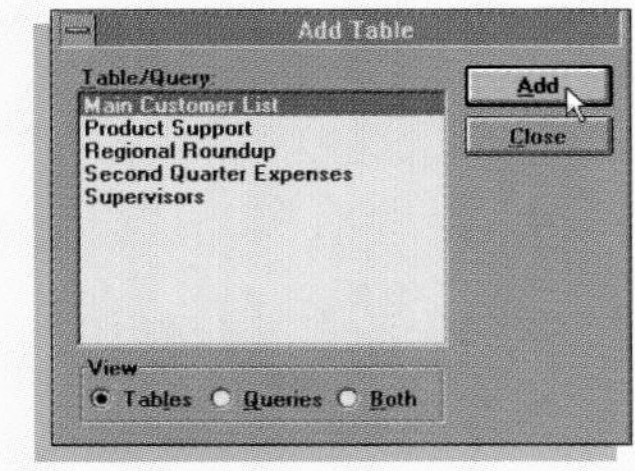

6 Click on the Add button.

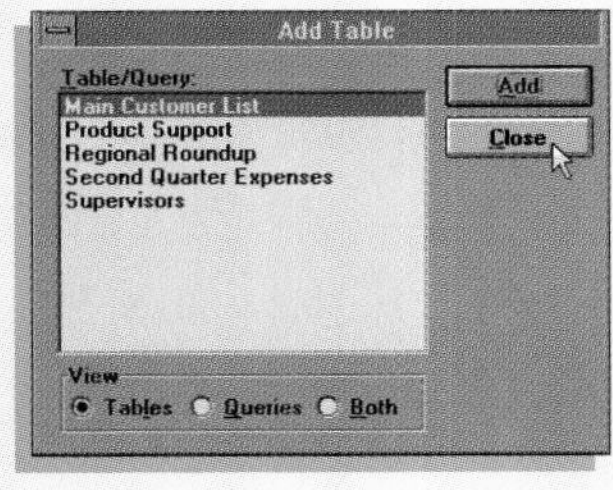

7 Click on the Close button.

How to Specify What Fields a Query Will Display

Queries do not merely pull out records that meet certain criteria. They also make data easier to view by showing only those fields that are of interest. For example, you may keep dozens of items of information (fields) on each of your customers, but to prepare a special promotion you may need only the name, account number, and date of last purchase for California customers who have made recent purchases. This page explains how to tell Microsoft Access what fields to display when you run a query.

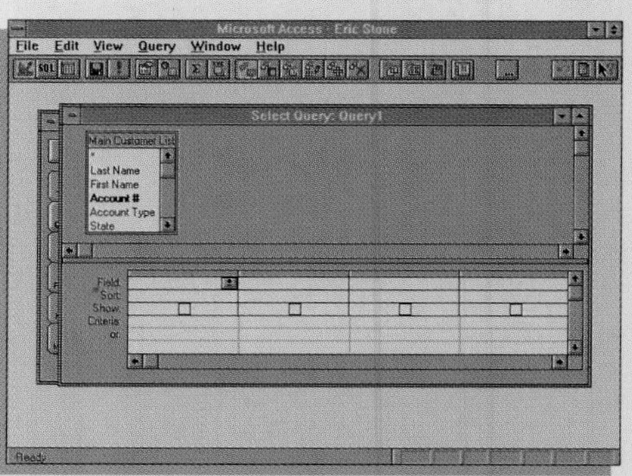

1 Start a new query as described on the preceding page.

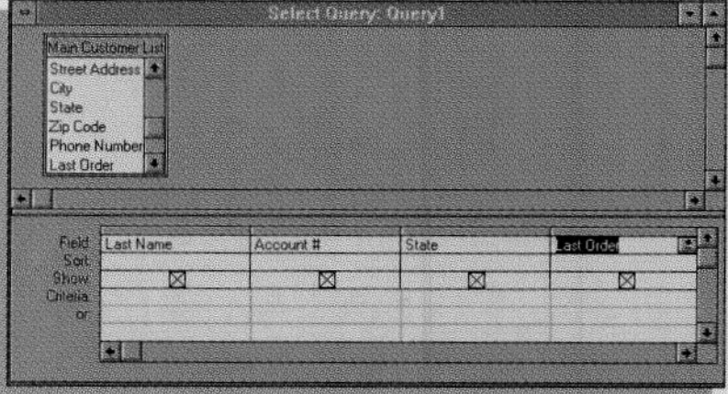

5 Drag additional field names to additional cells in the top row of the grid. The sequence in which you place field names in the grid is the sequence in which they will appear when you run the query. You can include as many fields as you want—even all of them.

TIP SHEET

- **Whenever you drag a field name to the grid, the Show check box below the field name is marked. Clear the Show text box to use that field in determining the query results without showing the field. For example, if you are pulling from a customer table all customers who live in California, you will need to include the State field in order to extract the necessary records, but there's no need to see this field when you run the query.**
- **You may observe in the list of field names that one name is boldfaced. This simply identifies the primary key (see Chapter 4).**
- **Don't worry if you make mistakes selecting the fields to include in a query. In the next chapter you will learn how to add and remove fields, and how to change their sequence.**

2 Observe that above the grid there is a list of all the fields in the table on which you are basing the query. The scroll arrows can help you see the whole list.

3 Point to the first field you want to include in the query, and hold down the left mouse button.

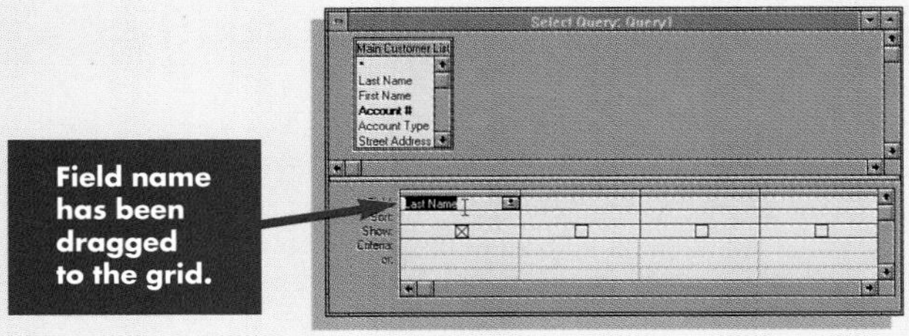

Field name has been dragged to the grid.

4 Drag the mouse to the upper-left cell in the grid, and release the mouse button. Microsoft Access places the field name in the grid.

How to Specify What Records a Query Will Display

The condition a record must meet to be included in the query results is called a *criterion.* (The more familiar plural is *criteria.*) In spoken language, you might express a criterion in a statement such as, "The employee must work in a California office," or "The customer must have placed an order in the past six months." However, in Microsoft Access you express criteria according to a stricter format. This page explains how.

1 Set up a new query and specify what fields it is to include, as described on the preceding pages.

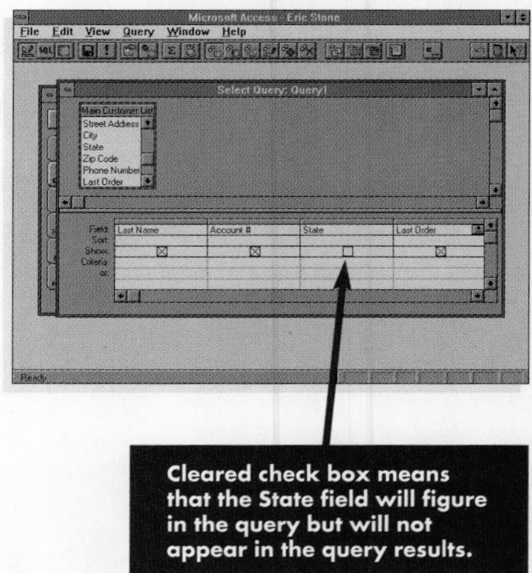

TIP SHEET

- **If you forget the quotation marks when typing a criterion for a text field, Microsoft Access will add them for you when you move the insertion point out of the cell. However, typing the quotation marks yourself removes the possibility that Microsoft Access will misinterpret your expression and place the quotation marks in the wrong places.**
- **You can disregard case (upper or lower) when entering a criterion. For example, typing "ny" OR "nj" as your criterion will pull records from New York and New Jersey even if you used uppercase abbreviations (NY and NJ) in the table.**
- **Queries do not change the underlying table. For example, you can sort on any field within a query, and the records will still be sorted on the primary key when you next open the table in Datasheet view.**

Field:	Last Name	Account #	State	Last Order
Sort:				
Show:	☒	☒	☐	☒
Criteria:			"CA"	>=#1/1/94#
or:				

5 Optionally, enter a criterion for one or more additional fields. A record must meet each criterion to be displayed in the query results. For example, you might wish to determine which of your California customers (criterion 1) have ordered this year (criterion 2).

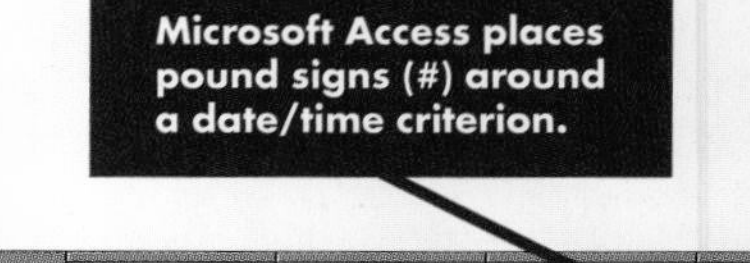

6 You can also sort the query results in ascending or descending order, based on any field. The field on which you sort is known as the *key.* In the Sort row of the grid, click beneath the key you want to use. A drop-down arrow appears in the cell. Click on the drop-down arrow and then click on either Ascending or Descending.

Field:	Last Name	Account #	State	Last Order
Sort:				
Show:	☒	☒	☐	☒
Criteria:				
or:				

2 Along the top row of the grid, locate the field whose content will serve as the criterion. Beneath that field name, click in the Criteria cell.

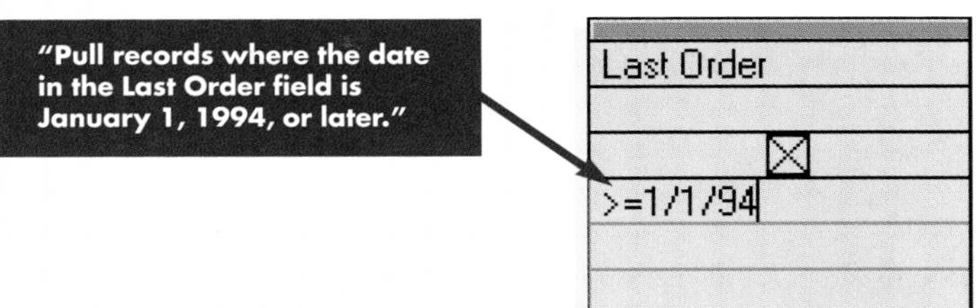

3 Type a criterion using standard mathematical operators. Separate multiple criteria, if any, with *And* or *Or*. Place the content of text fields in quotation marks. Examples follow in step 4.

4 Here are a few examples of criteria: If a field contains the date on which accounts were opened, **>=1/1/94** finds accounts opened on or after the first day of 1994. For a field containing a state of residence, **"CA" OR "NV" OR "AZ"** pulls records where the state is California, Nevada, or Arizona. (Observe that Microsoft Access assumes an equal sign at the beginning of the expression if you omit a mathematical operator.) The expression **<>"NY"** finds all customers except those from New York. To extract records of customers who have spent between $500 and $1,000 with your company, enter **>=500 And <=1000**.

How to Name, Save, and Close a Query

As your tables change, you'll want to run queries over and over again to see the new results. Therefore, you need to save each query as a Microsoft Access object. That way, the query will be available whenever the database is open. The first time you save a query, you also assign a name to it. The next page explains how to run a query.

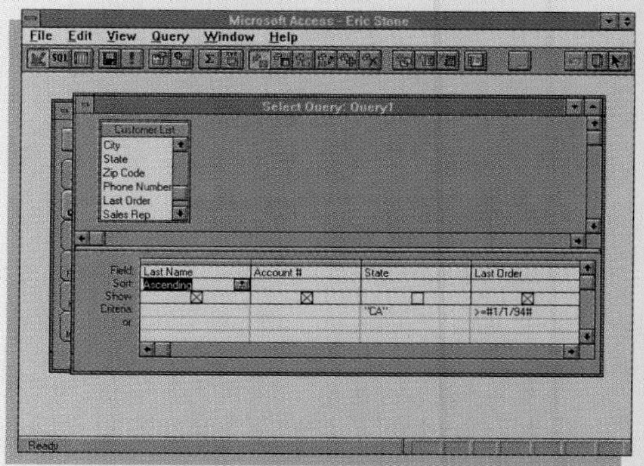

1 Create the query as described on the preceding pages.

2 Click on File in the menu bar and then click on the Save command.

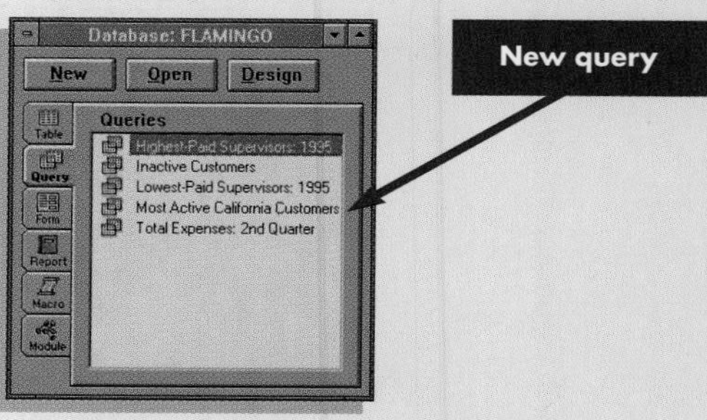

7 Observe in the Database window that your newly defined query is now listed as an object.

TIP SHEET

- **Though it's wise to take the initiative of saving your queries frequently as you change them (step 5), Microsoft Access can rescue you if you're careless. When you issue the Close command in step 6 without having saved the modified query, Microsoft Access warns you of this fact. Click on the Yes button to save your changes and close the query.**

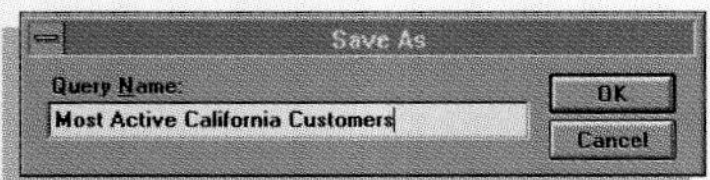

3. In the Save As dialog box, type a name for the query, replacing the placeholder Microsoft Access provides. Like all object names, a query name can be up to 64 characters long and can contain all characters except periods, exclamation points, and brackets.

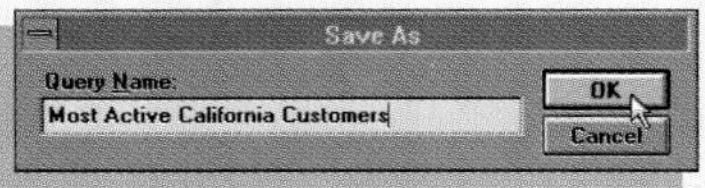

4. Click on the OK button.

5. Microsoft Access saves the table on disk, closes the dialog box, and displays the query name in the title bar. Continue working on the query if necessary. Occasionally click on File in the menu bar and then on the Save command to resave the query with all its changes.

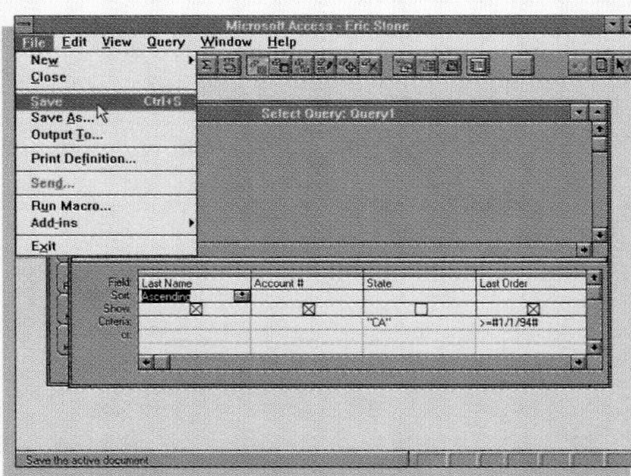

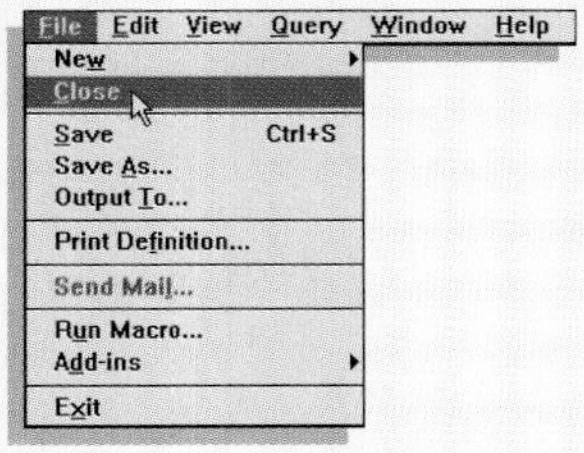

6. When done working on the query, click on File in the menu bar and then click on the Close command.

How to Run a Query

You run a query to see the *dynaset* it produces. A dynaset is a *dyna*mic sub*set* of your table; it contains only those fields and records that meet your query definition at that moment. Next time you run the query, you're bound to get a different dynaset reflecting changes to the underlying table.

1 In the Database window, click on the Query object button to display a list of the queries available in the database.

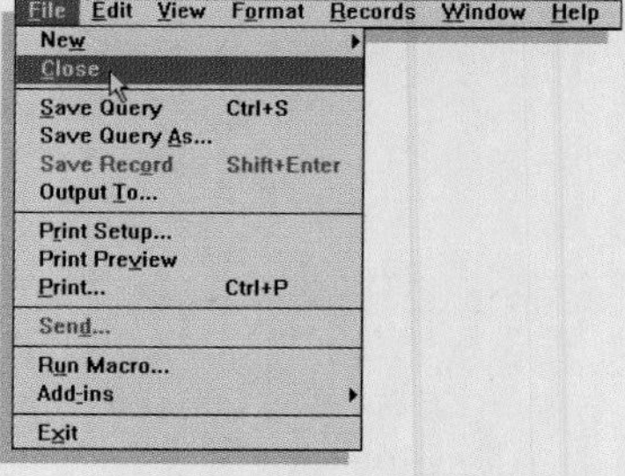

6 When done working with the dynaset, click on File in the menu bar and then click on the Close command. Microsoft Access returns you to the Database window.

TIP SHEET

- **If a query does not produce the results you expected, you will have to change the query definition. See the next chapter for help.**
- **To print the dynaset from Datasheet view, click on File in the menu bar, click on the Print command, and then click on the OK button in the Print dialog box.**
- **Now that you can create two kinds of objects (tables and queries), it's worthwhile to know how to delete an object that you no longer need. In the Database window, click on the object, click on Edit in the menu bar, and then click on the Delete command. When asked to confirm the deletion, click on the OK button. Deleting a query is not especially dangerous, because no underlying data is deleted. On the other hand, you should reflect carefully before deleting a table.**

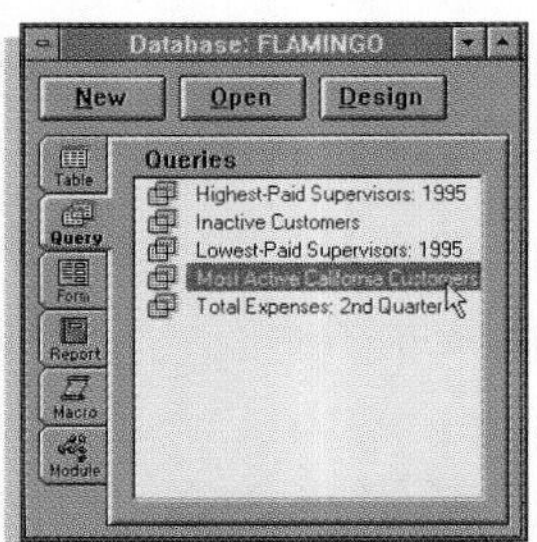

2 Click on the query you want to run.

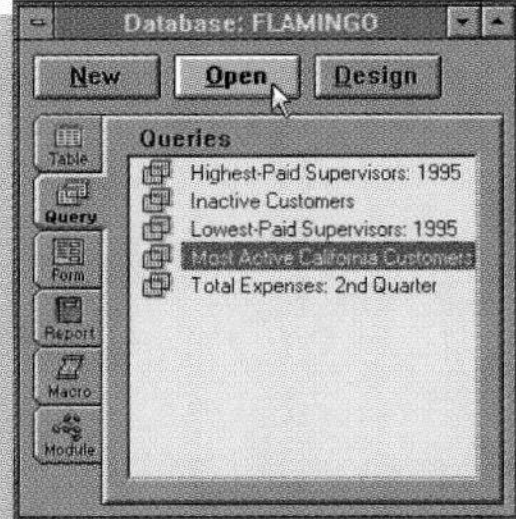

3 Click on the Open button.

Table

Last Name	First Name	Account #	Account Type	Street Address	City	State	Zip Code	Phone Number	Last Order	Sales Rep	Notes
Chang	Alexandra	809440	res	2929 Valley View Way	Walnut Creek	CA	94332	510-555-0833	3/12/94	Alhariri	Victim of the "beige flamingo" incident.
Golfside Cafe		811411	comm	3737 Country Route 166	Destin	FL	32541	904-555-8232	12/15/93	Chinn	Always orders for Christmas.
Ron's Barber Shop		812991	comm	8989 Monterey Boulevar	San Bernadino	CA	96901	709-555-3902	4/11/94	Chinn	
Thorpe	Mae	823920	res	730 San Gabriel Avenue	San Francisco	CA	94112	415-555-9091	3/4/93	Goldberg	
Wisteria Inn		834291	comm	9191 Route 92	EastBiloxi	MS	45922	808-555-9348	3/30/94	Martin	Always waits for late-summer sale.
Gonsalves	Martin	885560	comm	1885 23rd Street	Presidio	TX	68224	915-555-0984	8/8/93	Martin	
Bennett	Wanda	894411	res	333 Elm Street	Carrboro	NC	N27510	919-555-8609	5/18/93	Goldberg	
Anderson	Vada	894901	res	3 Dillon Terrace	Poway	CA	98833	609-555-2430	7/1/92	Alhariri	
Greenwood	C.L.	899341	res	58707 NE 14th Avenue	N. Miami Beac	FL	33179	305-555-3323	9/26/93	Martin	
Angelotti	Donald	899941	res	1855 105th Way SE	Mobile	AL	43944	216-555-2934	8/18/93	Chinn	Do not call after 8:00 P.M.
The Tropic Shop		900112	comm	25 Winslow Terrace	Edmonton	Alberta, Cana	6V3 C9G	503-555-2900	4/1/94	Borroughs	

Last Name	Account #	Last Order
Chang	809440	3/12/94
Ron's Barber Shop	812991	4/11/94
Wisteria Inn	834291	3/30/94

Dynaset of customers who have ordered in 1994

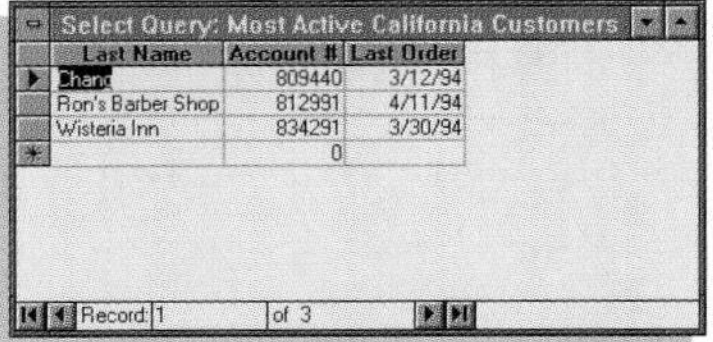

4 Microsoft Access displays the query results—the dynaset—in Datasheet view. Observe that it shows only the fields you included in the query definition and only the records that meet your criteria.

5 You can edit your table from within the dynaset. Just edit text and numbers the same way you do when viewing the complete table in Datasheet view (see Chapter 5). Next time you view the table, you will observe the results of the changes you made in the dynaset.

CHAPTER 9

Improving Queries

A query may be part of your computing life for a long time. But you don't have to live with a query that isn't performing up to par. Microsoft Access enables you to revisit the query design and change any feature of a query—the fields it displays, the criteria, and so on. This chapter explains how.

In this chapter you will also learn how to beef up a query by having it perform a calculation. For example, if a table contains month-by-month expense figures for each department in your company, a query can display departmental quarterly totals. Pretty impressive.

How to Correct and Improve a Query

Why change a query? It's not just to fix mistakes in a query that produces unwanted results. You may also wish to add optional improvements to a query. For example, you can add a second criterion or change the way query results are sorted. To edit a query, you display it in Design view and work with it much as you did when creating the query (see Chapter 8). This page provides the details.

TIP SHEET

- **As you work with a query design, periodically save your changes by clicking on File in the menu bar and then clicking on the Save command. If you issue the Close command (step 9) while the query contains unsaved changes, Microsoft Access will prompt you to save them.**
- **Unfortunately, the Undo command (see Chapter 7) does not reverse changes to query design. If you make a mistake that you cannot easily undo on your own *and* you have not saved the query since making the mistake, close the query (see step 9) and answer *No* when asked whether to save your changes. When you reopen the query (step 1), it appears as it did the last time you saved it.**
- **After editing a query, you can immediately run the query to see the effects of your changes. Simply click on View in the menu bar and then click on the Datasheet command. Likewise, if you are viewing query results and you decide to edit the underlying query, click on View and then click on Query Design to display the query in Design view.**
- **When you change a query significantly, you may wish to rename it so the name better reflects the query's purpose. In the Database window, click on the query name. Click on File in the menu bar, click on Rename, type the new name, and click on OK.**

1. Display the Database window, click on the Query object button, click on the query you want to change, and then click on the Design button.

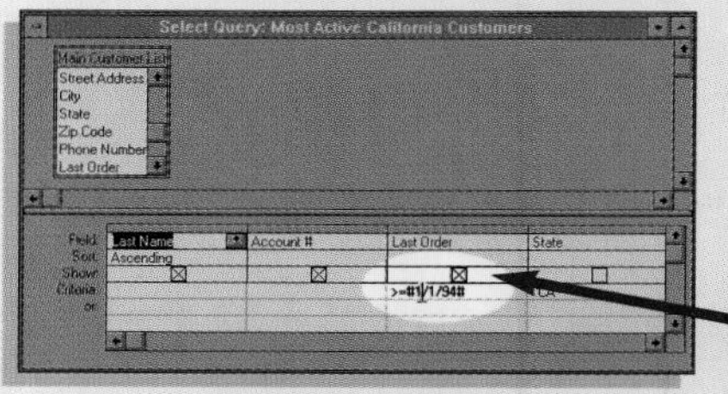

2. You now observe the query in Design view, the same view in which you built the query originally. To edit a criterion, click in it and then change it using Backspace, Delete, and the typing keys. To add a criterion, click in the Criteria cell for the field and type the condition as described in Chapter 8. To remove a criterion, simply click in it and delete it completely.

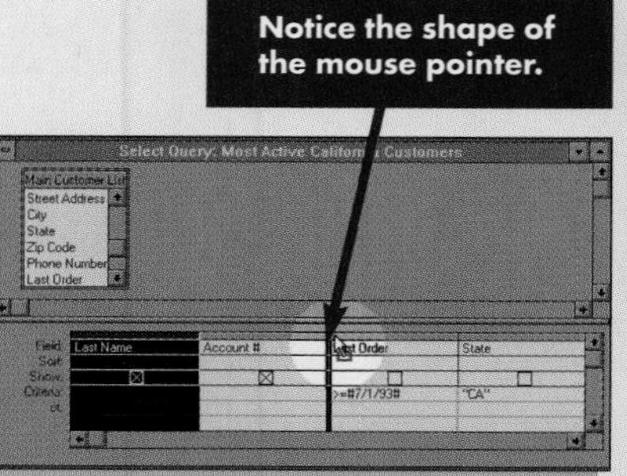

8. Next, position the mouse pointer over the top part of the selected field, hold down the mouse button, and drag to the left or right. When the column border where you want to insert the field darkens, release the mouse button. Click anywhere to remove the selection highlighting.

9. When done working with the query, click on File in the menu bar and then click on the Close command.

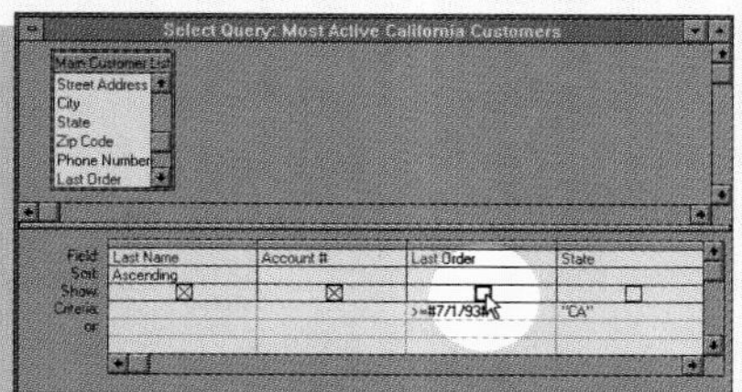

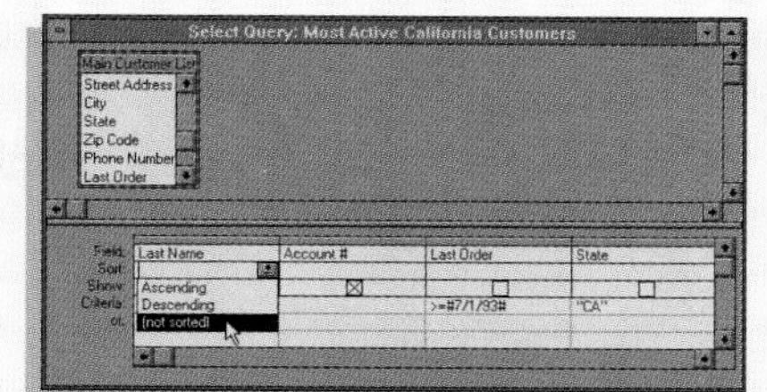

4 To add a sort key, click in the Sort cell for the key field, click on the drop-down arrow, and specify Ascending or Descending sort order. To cancel a sort key, click on its Sort drop-down arrow and then click on *(not sorted)*.

3 To determine whether a field that figures in the query is actually displayed as part of the query results, mark or clear the Show check box for that field.

5 To add a field at any position, click anywhere in the column to the right of that position, click on Edit in the menu bar, and then click on Insert Column. Define the new field as explained in Chapter 8.

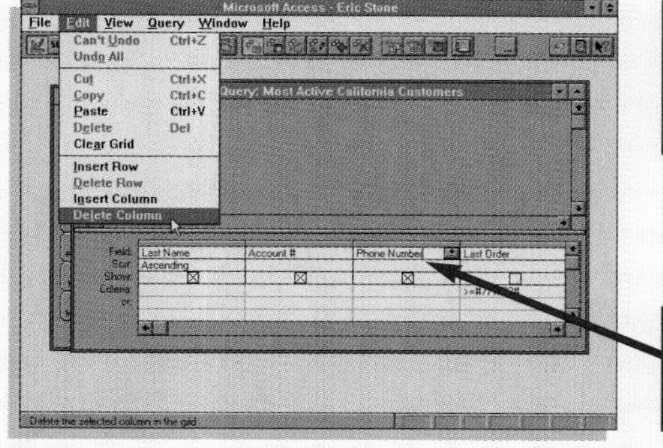

Column will be inserted to the left of the column containing the insertion point.

Column containing the insertion point will be deleted.

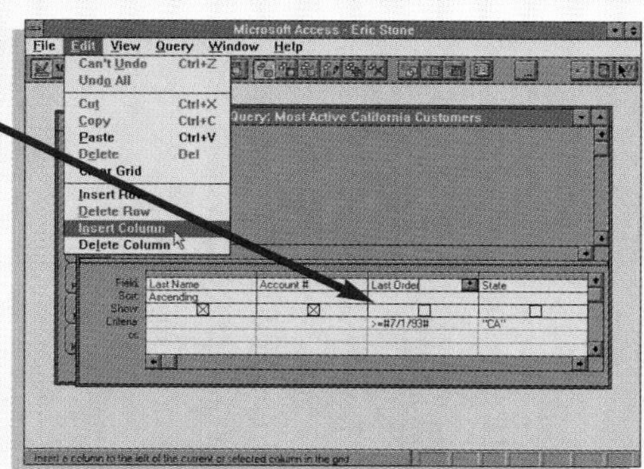

6 To remove a field from the query, click anywhere in the field, click on Edit in the menu bar, and then click on Delete Column.

7 To move a field to a new position, first select the whole field by pointing to the top of the field; the mouse pointer becomes a small, downward-pointing arrow. Then click.

Let me rephrase the question.

How to Perform a Calculation in a Query

All the queries discussed so far in this book have pulled ordinary fields from a table. But there's another kind of field called a *calculated field* that can turn a query into a great summarizing tool. A calculated field performs a calculation on other fields in the table and displays the results when you run the query. You simply tell Microsoft Access which fields to use in the calculation and what mathematical operations to perform.

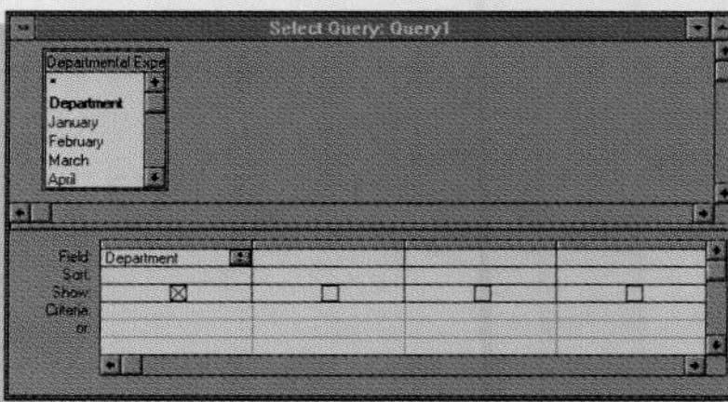

1. Start a new query or display an existing one in Design view (see preceding page or Chapter 8). Define all the fields except for the one(s) that will perform calculations.

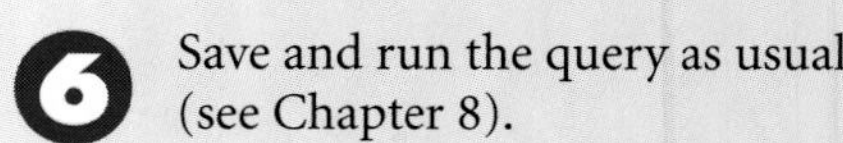

6. Save and run the query as usual (see Chapter 8).

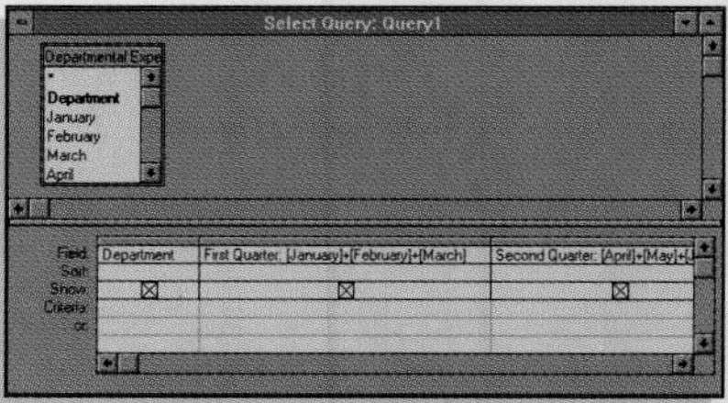

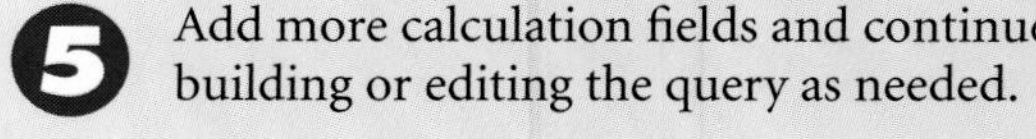

5. Add more calculation fields and continue building or editing the query as needed.

TIP SHEET

- **If you omit a name for the calculation field in step 3, Microsoft Access assigns it the name Expr1 (or Expr2 for the second calculation field, and so on). You can later replace this name with a name of your choice by editing the query (see preceding page).**
- **Most expressions are too wide to fit all at once in a query grid with the standard column widths. To widen a column so that it is just the right width to display its contents completely, double-click on the right column border just above the Field row.**
- **Although the sample query on this page contains no criteria—it summarizes the expenses of every department—there's no reason why it couldn't. For example, the query could summarize the expenses for only those departments that spent over $1,000 every month. Chapter 8 explains how to express criteria and how to specify whether the fields used in the criteria appear in the query results.**

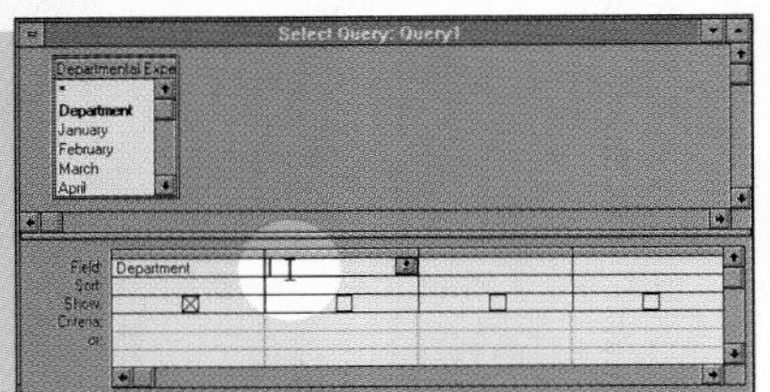

2 Click in an empty Field cell.

3 Type a name for the calculation field and follow it with a colon (:). This name will appear in the query results as the column heading for the calculation results.

First Quarter:

Departmental Expenses

Department	January	February	March	April	May	June	July	August	September	October	November	December
Accounting	$421.00	$499.00	$606.00	$586.00	$694.00	$498.00	$580.00	$722.00	$701.00	$584.00	$589.00	$823.00
Customer Service	$944.00	$1,024.00	$1,420.00	$1,243.00	$1,055.00	$959.00	$1,005.00	$1,293.00	$1,107.00	$885.00	$886.00	$1,018.00
Marketing	$1,724.00	$1,802.00	$942.00	$1,423.00	$1,393.00	$1,214.00	$1,190.00	$1,722.00	$1,217.00	$1,092.00	$1,345.00	$959.00
R&D	$4,103.00	$3,855.00	$2,955.00	$2,190.00	$2,804.00	$3,100.00	$2,995.00	$3,829.00	$3,644.00	$3,091.00	$2,987.00	$2,455.00
Sales	$5,150.00	$4,478.00	$5,100.00	$4,906.00	$4,871.00	$4,480.00	$5,054.00	$4,772.00	$4,711.00	$3,898.00	$4,417.00	$3,781.00
Warehouse	$480.00	$392.00	$355.00	$312.00	$410.00	$393.00	$442.00	$509.00	$465.00	$328.00	$367.00	$400.00

Quarterly Summary

Department	First Quarter	Second Quarter	Third Quarter	Fourth Quarter
Accounting	$1,526.00	$1,778.00	$2,003.00	$1,996.00
Customer Service	$3,388.00	$3,257.00	$3,405.00	$2,789.00
Marketing	$4,468.00	$4,030.00	$4,129.00	$3,396.00
R&D	$10,953.00	$8,094.00	$10,468.00	$8,533.00
Sales	$14,728.00	$14,257.00	$14,537.00	$12,096.00
Warehouse	$1,227.00	$1,115.00	$1,416.00	$1,095.00

First Quarter: [January]+[February]+[March]

"The contents of the January field plus the contents of the February field plus the contents of the March field."

4 Enter a mathematical expression for the query to carry out. Type field names in any letter case (upper or lower) and place them in brackets. The following standard mathematical operators are available: + (addition), – (subtraction), * (multiplication), and / (division). It does not matter whether you put spaces around the mathematical operators.

TRY IT!

Here's a chance to hone your querying skills on sample data before trying them out in the real world. Follow each step carefully at your computer. You will need to build a small table from which to pull data in a query. Steps 1 through 6 show you the table to create, but these steps assume you are familiar with basic table techniques. (Review Chapters 4 and 5 if necessary.) In addition, chapter numbers are included with most steps to point you to helpful information.

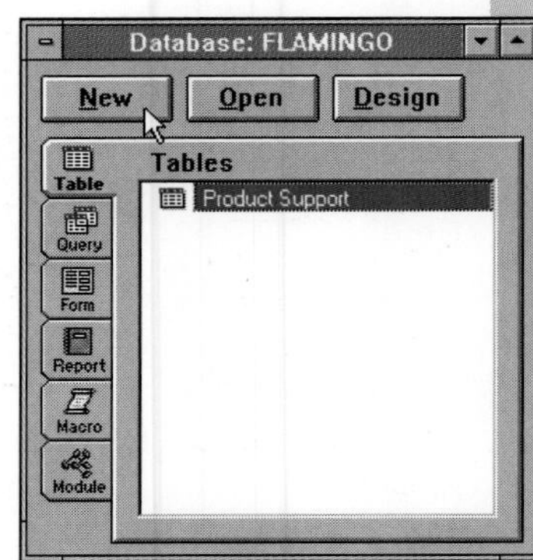

From the Database window, start a new table. You can put the table in any database, but you may wish to use the Flamingo database created in the Try It exercise after Chapter 7. That way, you'll keep sample data separate from your own work. *Chapter 4*

LawnBirds, Inc.

Vacation Accrual

Last Name	First Name	Emp #	Monthly Accrual	Carryover	Jan Accrue	Jan Use	Feb Accrue	Feb Use	Mar Accrue	Mar Use
Fuentes	Carla	1	1.25	9	1.25	0	1.25	-2	1.25	0
Rothstein	Jay	2	0.83	7	0.83	0	0.83	0	0.83	0
Eng	Stephanie	3	1.25	14	1.25	0	1.25	0	1.25	0
Tulanian	Doris	4	1.67	12	1.67	0	1.67	0	1.67	0
Lambert	Charles	5	1.67	2	1.67	-1	1.67	0	1.67	0
Jackson	Laura	6	1.67	14	1.67	0	1.67	-10	1.67	0
de la Hoz	Steven	7	1.25	11	1.25	0	1.25	0	1.25	0
Galante	Al	8	0.83	16	0.83	0	0.83	-1	0.83	0
Schwarzwald	Nanette	9	1.25	14	1.25	-2	1.25	0	1.25	0

Highest Vacation Accrual

Last Name	Monthly Accrual	Total Accrual
Eng	1.25	17.75
Galante	0.83	17.49
Schwarzwald	1.25	15.75
Tulanian	1.67	17.01

2

Define the fields in the table as shown here, setting the Emp # field as the primary key. *Chapter 4*

Table: Table1

Field Name	Data Type	Description
Last Name	Text	
First Name	Text	
Emp #	Number	
Monthly Accrual	Number	
Carryover	Number	
Jan Accrue	Number	
Jan Use	Number	
Feb Accrue	Number	
Feb Use	Number	
Mar Accrue	Number	
Mar Use	Number	

3

Close the table. When prompted, save the table as **Vacation Accrual**. *Chapter 4*

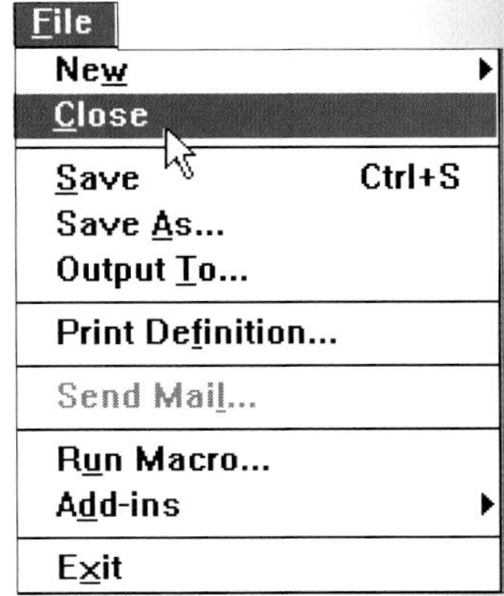

4

Open the table in Datasheet view. *Chapter 5*

Enter the data shown in the large table to the left. *Chapter 5*

Close the table, returning to the Database window. *Chapter 5*

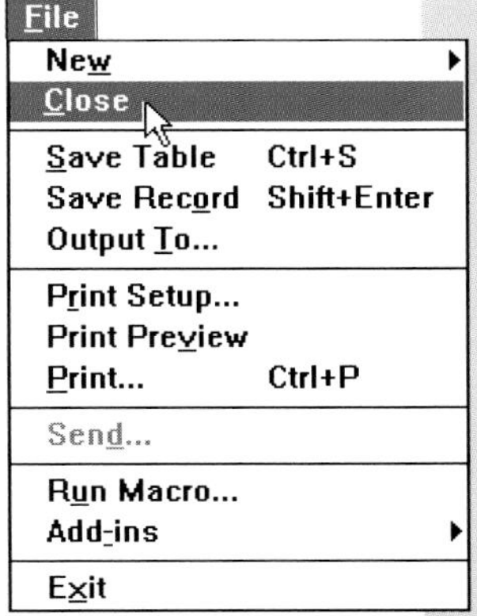

7

Click on the Query object button. *Chapter 8*

8

Click on the New button. *Chapter 8*

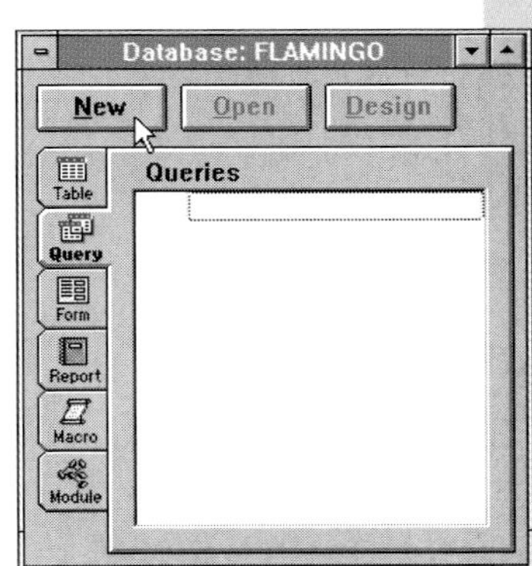

9

Click on New Query. *Chapter 8*

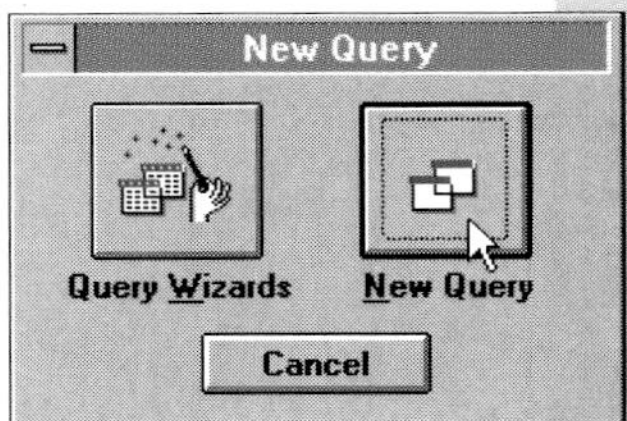

Continue to next page ▶

TRY IT!

Continue below

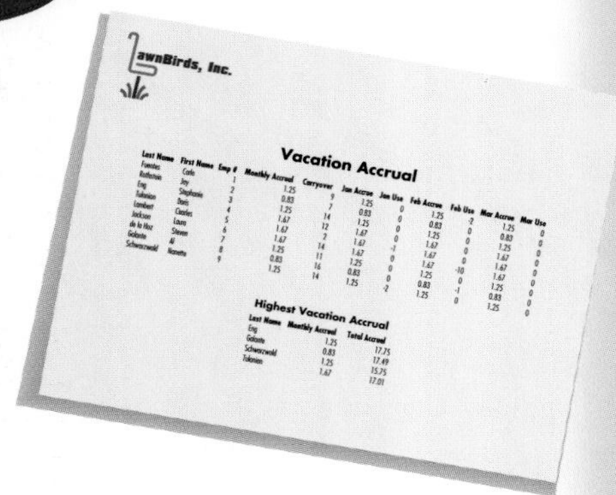

10

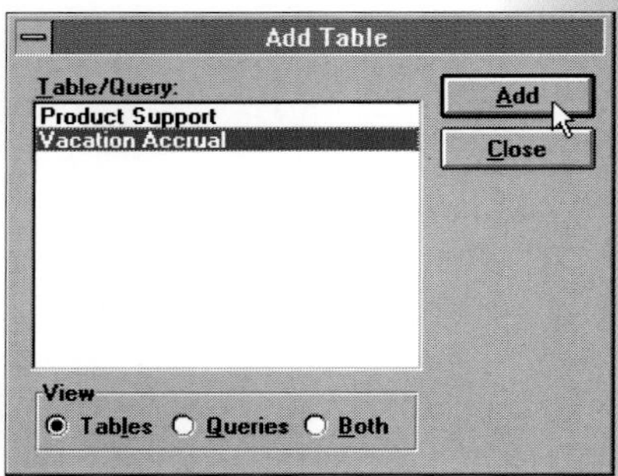

In the Add Table dialog box, click on Vacation Accrual, click on the Add button, and then click on the Close button. *Chapter 8*

11

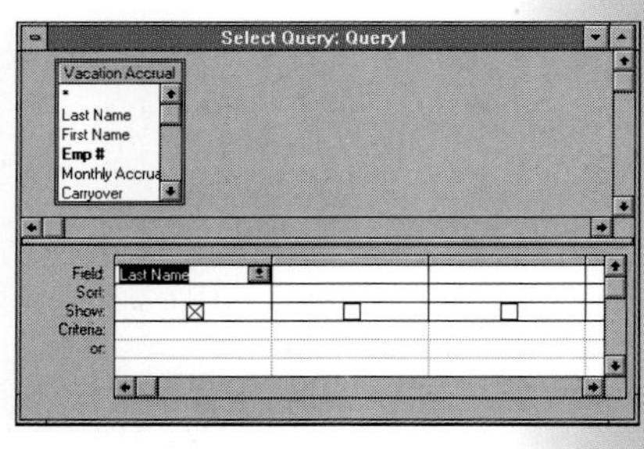

From the list of field names, drag the Last Name field into the top-left cell of the grid. *Chapter 8*

12

Click in the Sort cell for the Last Name field, click on the drop-down arrow, and then click on Ascending. *Chapter 8*

13

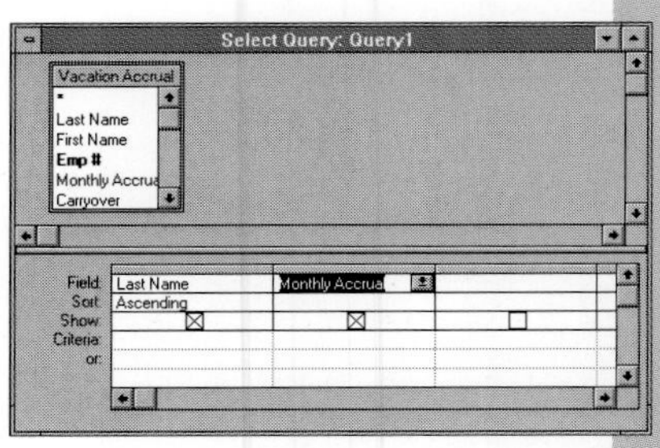

Drag the Monthly Accrual field into the top cell of the second column of the grid. *Chapter 8*

14

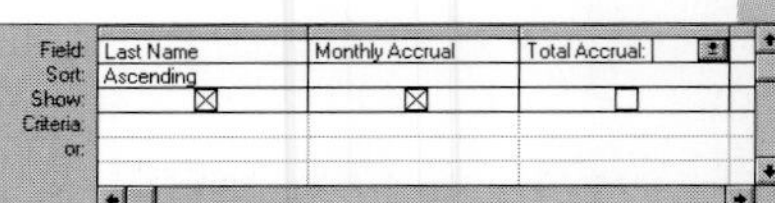

Click in the top cell of the third column and type **Total Accrual:** (including a space after the colon). This will be a calculated field. *Chapter 9*

15

Type [**Carryover**]+[**Jan Accrue**]+[**Jan Use**]+[**Feb Accrue**]+[**Feb Use**]+[**Mar Accrue**]+[**Mar Use**] as the calculation to perform. In the Vacation Accrual table the accrual numbers are positive and the usage numbers are negative, so this summation provides each employee's vacation reserve. *Chapter 9*

16

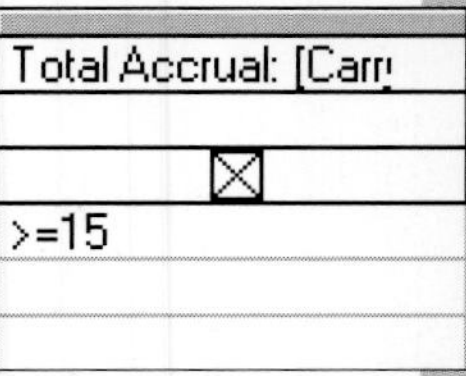

Click in the criteria cell for this calculated field and type **>=15** to pull the records of only those employees whose current accrual is 15 days or more. *Chapter 8*

Click on File in the menu bar and then click on the Save command. *Chapter 8*

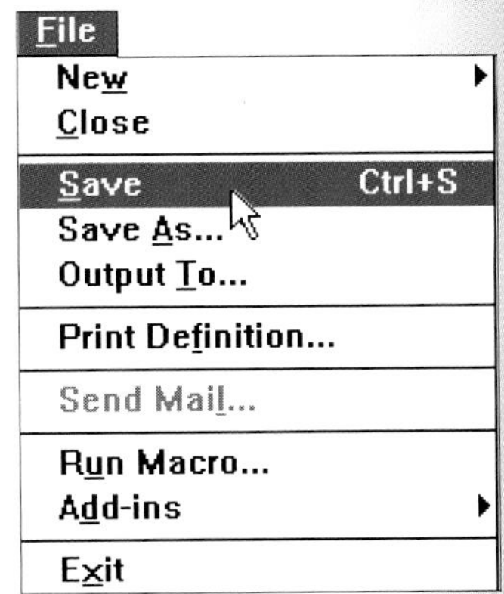

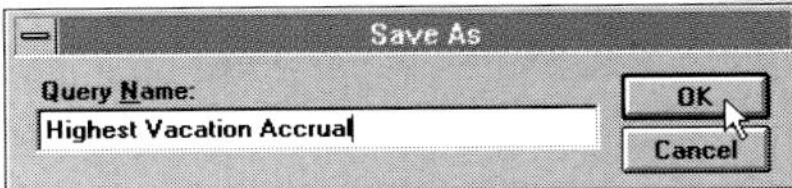

Type **Highest Vacation Accrual** and click on the OK button. *Chapter 8*

19

Click on View in the menu bar and then click on the Datasheet command to run the query. *Chapter 9*

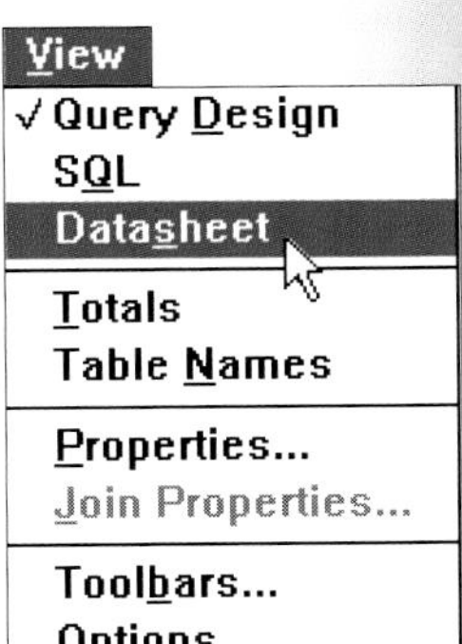

20

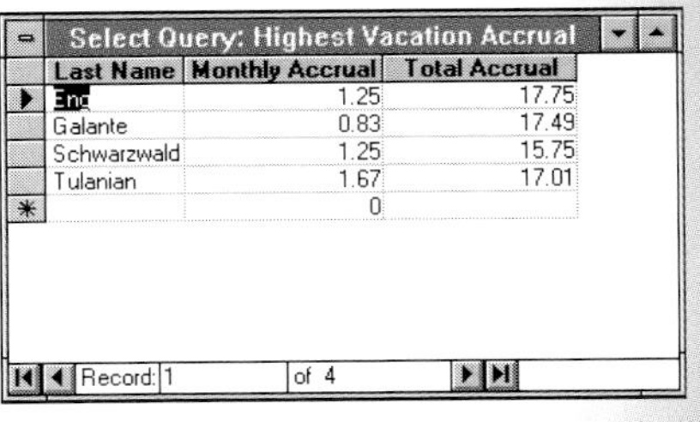
Select Query: Highest Vacation Accrual

Last Name	Monthly Accrual	Total Accrual
Eng	1.25	17.75
Galante	0.83	17.49
Schwarzwald	1.25	15.75
Tulanian	1.67	17.01
	0	

Record: 1 of 4

Observe that four records meet the criterion. That is, four employees have at least 15 days of vacation stored up. Now let's change the query to see how many employees have at least 10 days accrued. *Chapter 9*

Click on View in the menu bar and then click on the Query Design command. *Chapter 9*

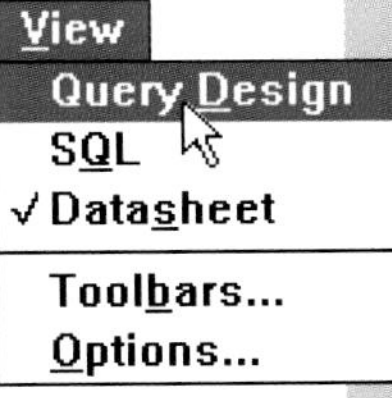

Click on the existing criterion and change *15* to **10**. *Chapter 9*

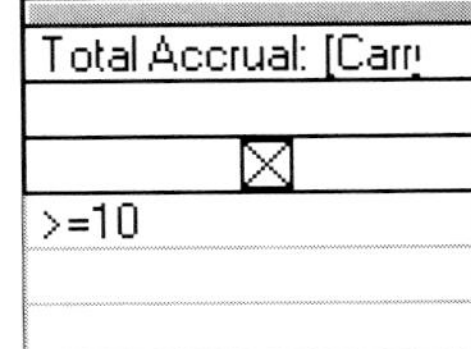

Click on View in the menu bar and then click on the Datasheet command. *Chapter 9.*

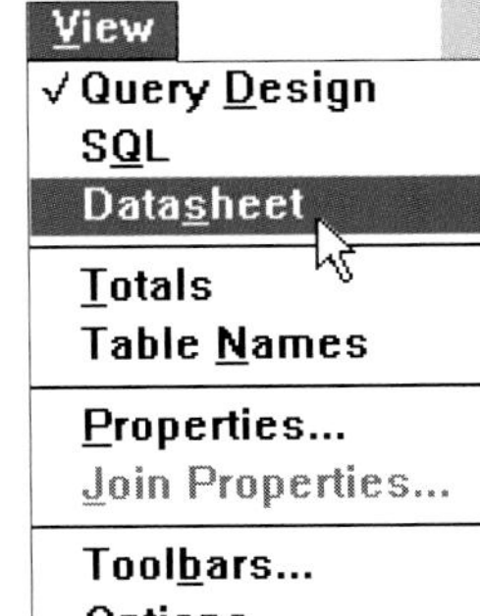

Observe that six employees meet the new criterion. *Chapter 8*

Select Query: Highest Vacation Accrual

Last Name	Monthly Accrual	Total Accrual
de la Hoz	1.25	14.75
Eng	1.25	17.75
Fuentes	1.25	10.75
Galante	0.83	17.49
Schwarzwald	1.25	15.75
Tulanian	1.67	17.01
	0	

Record: 1 of 6

25

Click on File in the menu bar and then click on the Close command. Answer Yes when asked whether to save your changes to the query. *Chapter 8*

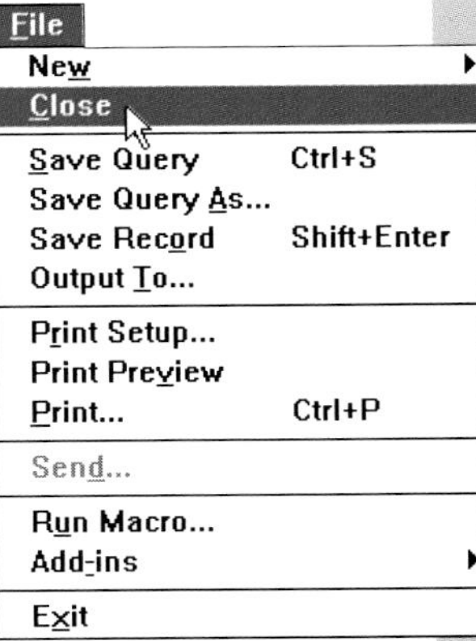

CHAPTER 10

Creating Forms

As a way to enter, edit, and view data, tables are no better than adequate. Their density and lack of visual relief can strain your eyes or bore you to tears. Many tables are too wide for the screen, forcing you to scroll the window. Focusing your attention on one record in a table can be difficult.

That's why Microsoft Access, like most database management programs, offers *forms,* an inviting way to work with data one record at a time. Forms are a lot like index cards. If your data were stored on index cards, each record would be on one card, and you would flip through the cards (which would probably be sorted in some logical way) to find the record you were interested in. Similarly, a form displays one record in the window, and you use the mouse and on-screen tools to move from one record to another—or to a blank form so that you can enter a new record.

All data in Microsoft Access is stored in a table. A form is merely an alternative way of manipulating the data. Whether you use forms or tables in a given situation is entirely your choice.

How to Start a New Form

In Microsoft Access, you can create forms easily with the help of a *Form Wizard,* a computerized interviewing tool that asks you a question or two and then does all the form designing for you. It takes mere seconds to create a perfectly passable form—not a work of art, mind you, but an easy-to-read data tool that can simplify your work life.

TIP SHEET

- **A form based on a table may be too large to fit in the window all at once. In this case, a vertical scroll bar appears so you can move to the out-of-view portions. Also, you can maximize the window to ensure that you are viewing as much of each record as possible. If the window is not already maximized, click on its Maximize button, the upward-pointing arrowhead in the top-right corner of the window. See Chapter 2 for more information on window operations.**
- **As you may have observed in step 4, you can base a form on a query rather than on a table. The form will include only those fields defined for the query and will display only those records that meet the query's criteria. Like a table-based form, a query-based form is merely an alternative way to view and manipulate data. To avoid confusion, you may wish to get some practice using forms based on tables before creating forms based on queries.**

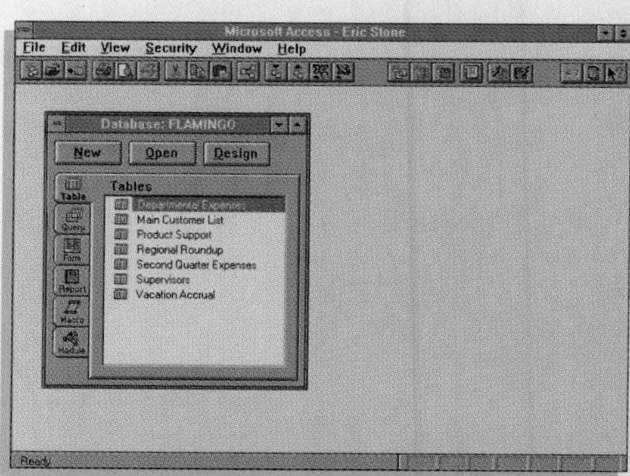

1 Open the database containing the table on which you will base your new form. Display the database window.

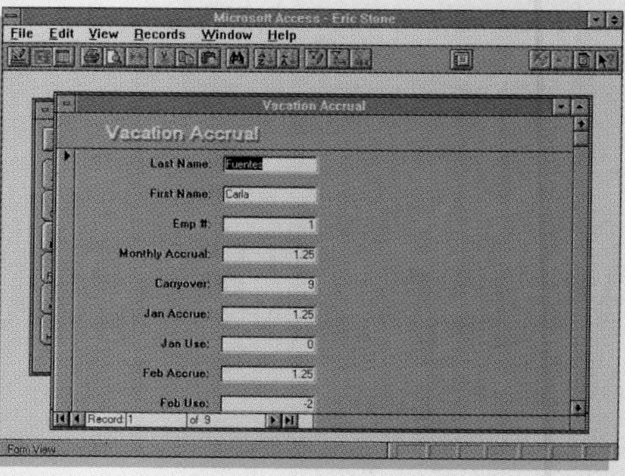

8 Microsoft Access creates the form and displays it on your screen. Observe that each entry in the form corresponds to a column heading (field name) in the table. You are now viewing the first record in the table. See the next page and the next chapter to learn how to work with your new form.

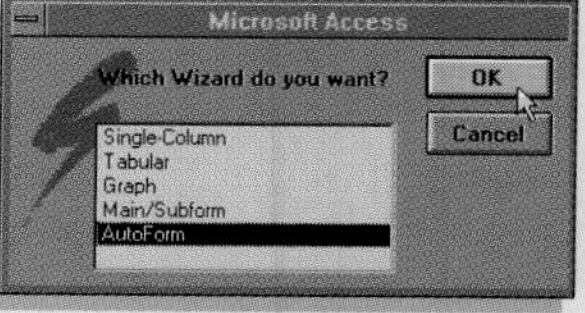

Click on the OK button.

2 Click on the Form object button.

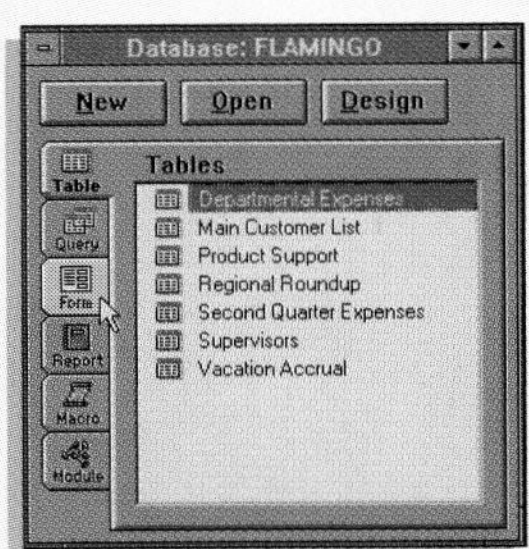

3 In the Database window, you see the forms already created for this database, if any. Click on the New button.

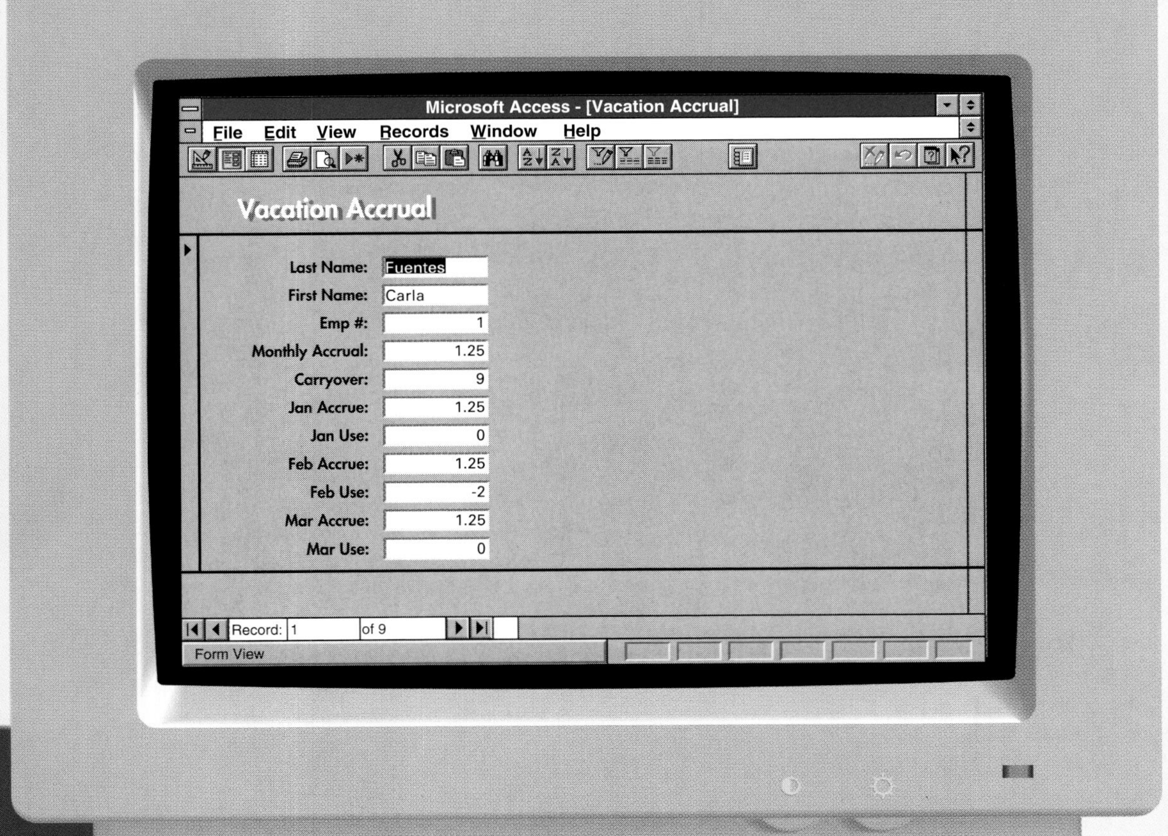

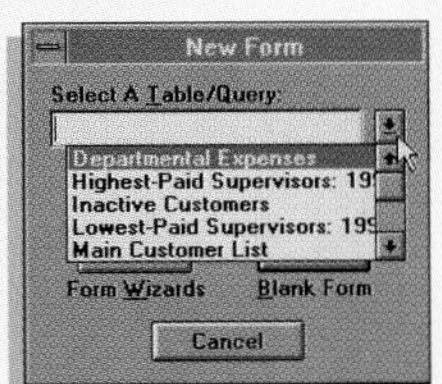

4 The New Form dialog box appears. Click on the Select A Table/Query drop-down arrow and then click on the name of the table on which to base the form.

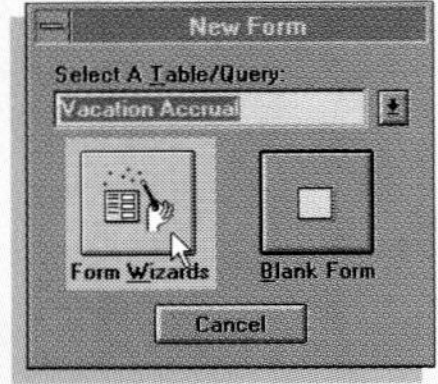

5 Click on Form Wizards.

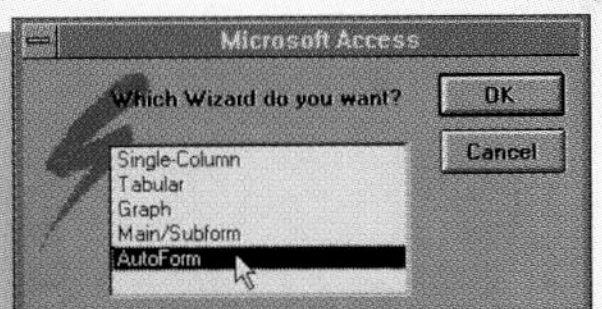

6 Microsoft Access asks, “Which Wizard do you want?” Click on AutoForm.

How to Name, Save, and Close a Form

Like tables and queries, forms are Microsoft Access objects. Thus, as you might expect, you must name and save a form upon creating it if you ever want to use it again.

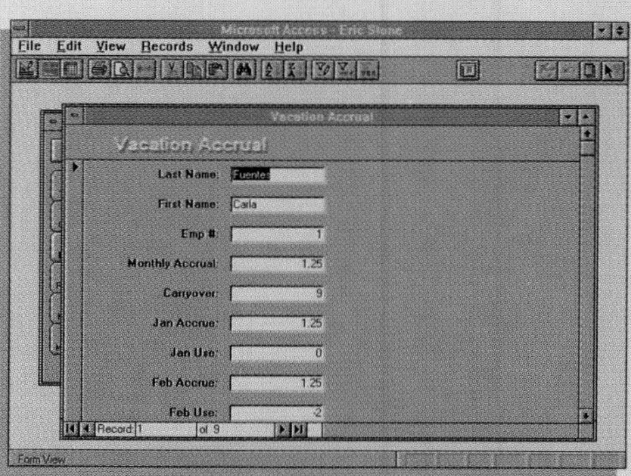

1 Create the form as explained on the preceding page.

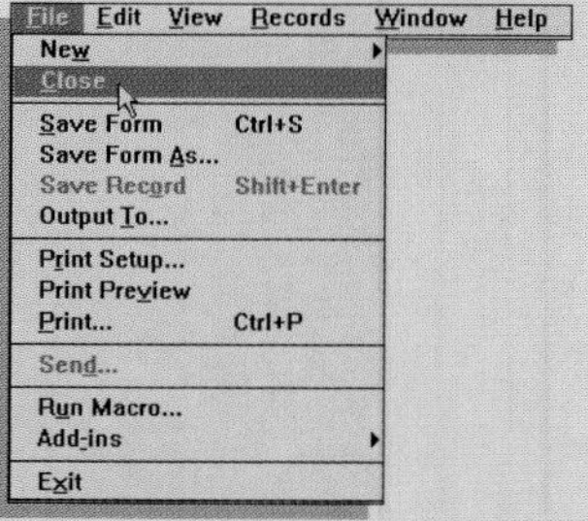

6 When done working with the form, click on File in the menu bar and then click on the Close command to return to the Database window. Of course, right now you probably are more interested in what you can do with a form that's still open! Read the next chapter to find out.

- **Some users assume that a form cannot have the same name as the table or query on which it is based. In fact, this is not just allowable but sometimes desirable—as long as it won't confuse you to have like-named objects in the Database window.**
- **Remembering to save your work is a good habit to form, but Microsoft recognizes that no one is perfect. If you have not yet saved the form when you issue the Close command (step 6), Microsoft Access prompts you to save it. If you answer Yes, you see the Save As dialog box, where you name and save the form as described in steps 3 and 4.**
- **Observe that after you save a form, the title bar continues to display the name of the table or query on which the form is based, not the form name. This does not mean that form names are useless. For example, you open a form (see the next chapter) by finding its name in the Database window.**

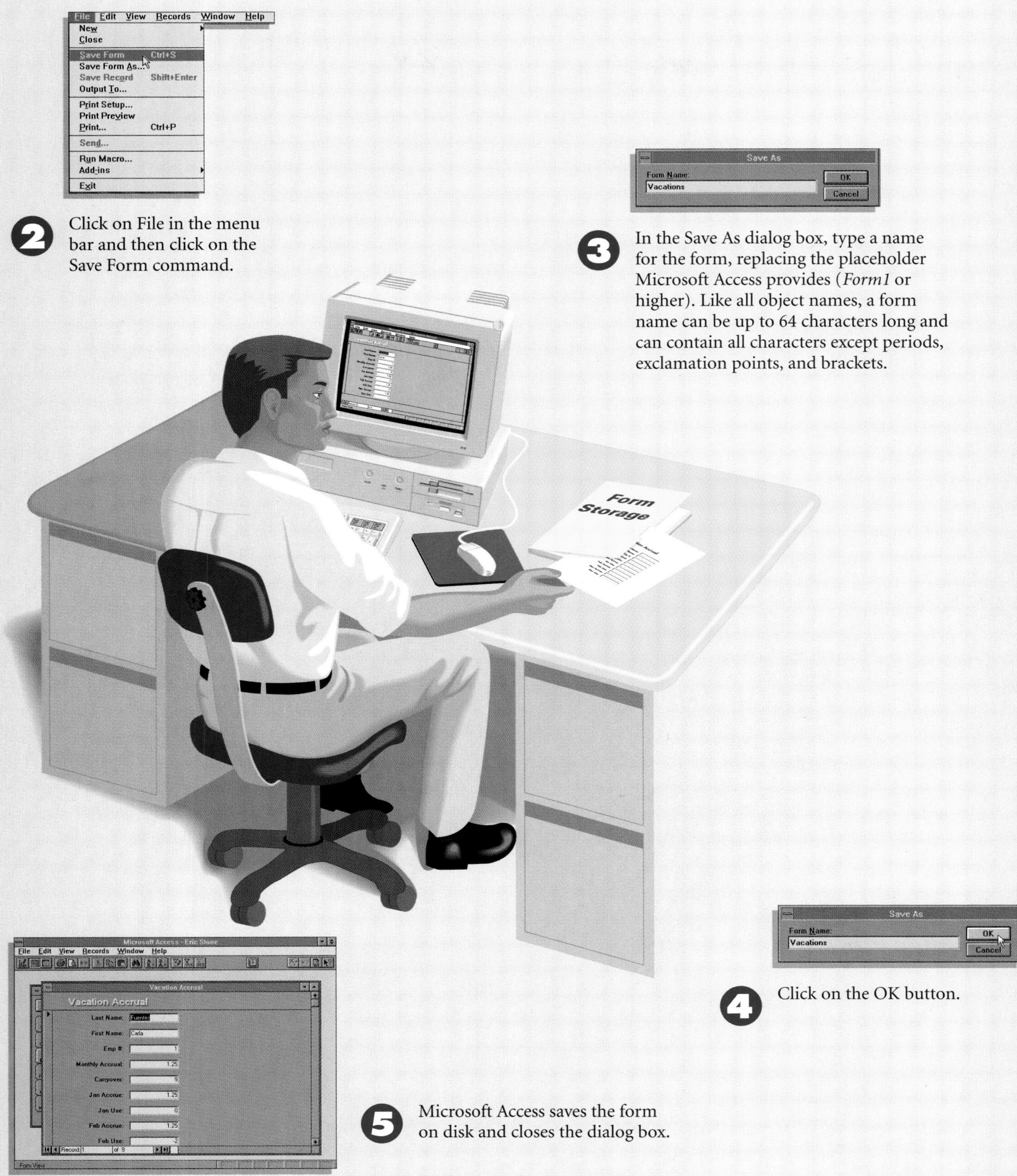

2 Click on File in the menu bar and then click on the Save Form command.

3 In the Save As dialog box, type a name for the form, replacing the placeholder Microsoft Access provides (*Form1* or higher). Like all object names, a form name can be up to 64 characters long and can contain all characters except periods, exclamation points, and brackets.

4 Click on the OK button.

5 Microsoft Access saves the form on disk and closes the dialog box.

CHAPTER 11

Using Forms

Chapter 10 sure left you hanging, didn't it? You know how to create a form, but you can't do a thing with it. This chapter is here to "fill in the blanks."

What can you do with forms? Well, you can do pretty much the same things you learned to do with tables in Chapters 5 and 6: view, enter, and edit data. Working with forms is just an attractive and often convenient alternative to manipulating data in Datasheet view. In fact, forms and tables are inextricably linked. If you change data in a form that is based on a table, you will see the change reflected in the table next time you open it. Likewise, editing data in a query-based form will in turn change the table from which the query pulls its data.

This chapter helps you work not only with forms you created yourself but also with forms that a manager, consultant, or advanced user at your office may have created for you and your colleagues. If you use such forms, you may observe that they are formatted more elaborately than the ones you learned to create in Chapter 10. Don't let this throw you off balance. No matter how fancy, a form is a form, and you work with all forms as described in this chapter.

How to View Records in a Form

The major benefit of forms is that they enable you to view your data one record at a time in a visually appealing format. But when viewing one record at a time in forms, you need a way to "flip" from one record to another on the screen the way you might if the records were written on index cards. This page explains how to open a form and view the record you need.

TIP SHEET

- As in a table, Microsoft Access sorts records in table-based forms according to the primary key, if any. If no primary key is defined, records appear in the order in which they were entered. In a query-based form, records appear according to the sort order, if any, defined for the underlying query; otherwise, they follow the same sort rules as tables. See "How to Sort Records in a Form" later in this chapter to learn how to display records in a more convenient sequence.
- Microsoft Access offers some form types that display more than one record at a time. You may encounter these if you are using forms created by others. Don't worry. All techniques described in this chapter apply to both form types. In forms that display multiple records, you have the added benefit of a vertical scroll bar; you can scroll through the form until the record you need is in view.
- There's an easy way to jump to a specific record if you know its position within the underlying table or query. Select (drag across) the active record number at the bottom of the window in Form view, type the number of the record you want (that is, its position within the table or query), and press Enter. Say you want to view the 19th record. Just select the existing record number, type 19, and press Enter.

1 Open the database and click on the Form object button in the Database window.

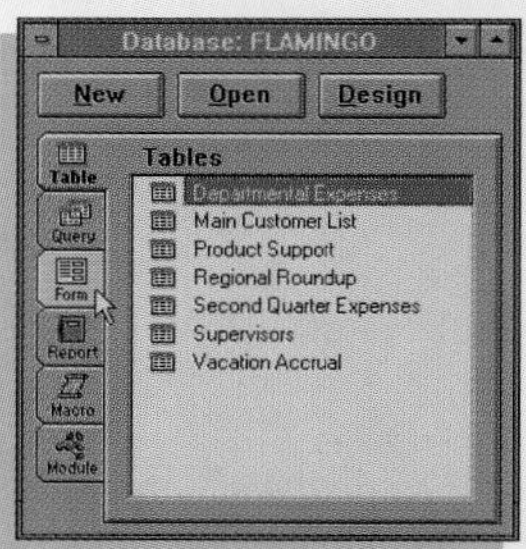

2 Click on the form you want to open, and then click on the Open button.

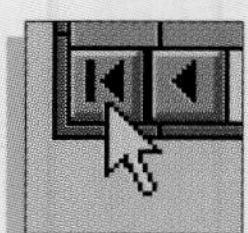

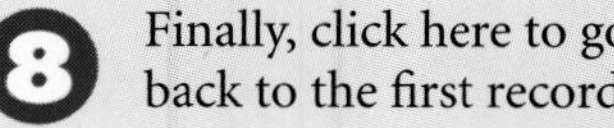

8 Finally, click here to go back to the first record.

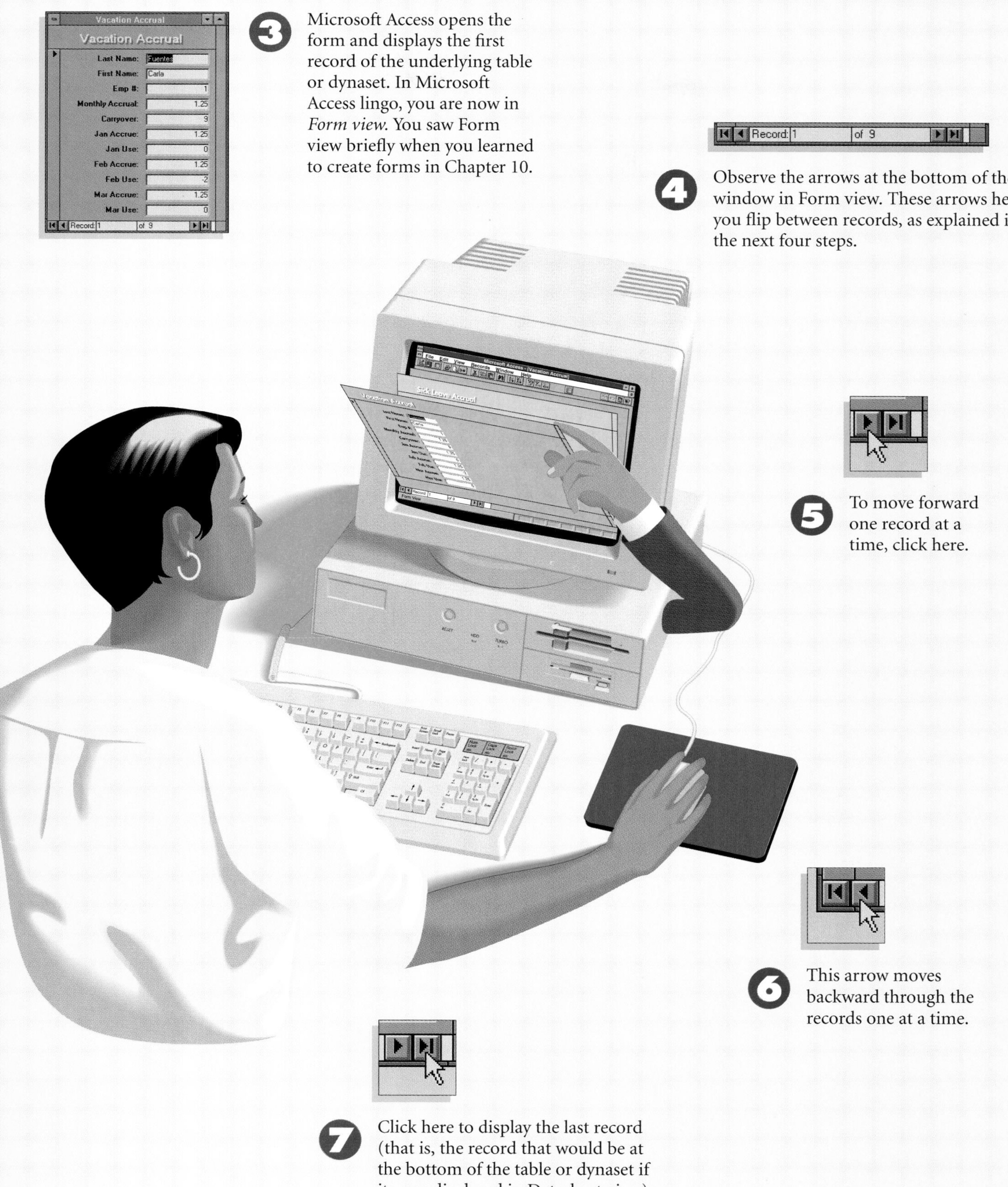

3. Microsoft Access opens the form and displays the first record of the underlying table or dynaset. In Microsoft Access lingo, you are now in *Form view.* You saw Form view briefly when you learned to create forms in Chapter 10.

4. Observe the arrows at the bottom of the window in Form view. These arrows help you flip between records, as explained in the next four steps.

5. To move forward one record at a time, click here.

6. This arrow moves backward through the records one at a time.

7. Click here to display the last record (that is, the record that would be at the bottom of the table or dynaset if it were displayed in Datasheet view).

How to Edit Data in a Form

The data you see in Form view sits in text boxes. That means that you are free to edit it. Editing data in Form view has the exact same result as editing it in Datasheet view. Try it for yourself on some sample data: Edit data in a form as described on this page, close the form, and open the form's underlying table or dynaset in Datasheet view (see Chapter 5 or 8). The changes you made in the form will be reflected in the table or dynaset.

TIP SHEET

- **As when editing in Datasheet view, you need not take any special action to save your changes when editing in Form view. Microsoft Access saves your data automatically.**
- **If you prefer to keep your hands on the keyboard when editing data, you can press Tab to move forward from field to field within a record. Press Shift+Tab to move backward. When you move to a field by pressing Tab or Shift+Tab, the field contents are selected. To deselect the data and activate the insertion point for editing press F2. Then edit the data as described in steps 4 through 6.**
- **Pressing Tab when the insertion point is in the last field of a record displays the next record. Pressing Shift+Tab when in the first field displays the previous record.**
- **Forms are a great way to focus on one record, but sometimes you need the broader perspective offered by Datasheet view. You need not close the form and reopen the table or query to get the big picture. Instead, simply click on View in the menu bar and then click on the Datasheet command. When done working with your data in Datasheet view, click on View and then click on Form to return to Form view.**

1 Open the form.

Display the record you want to edit, as described on the preceding page.

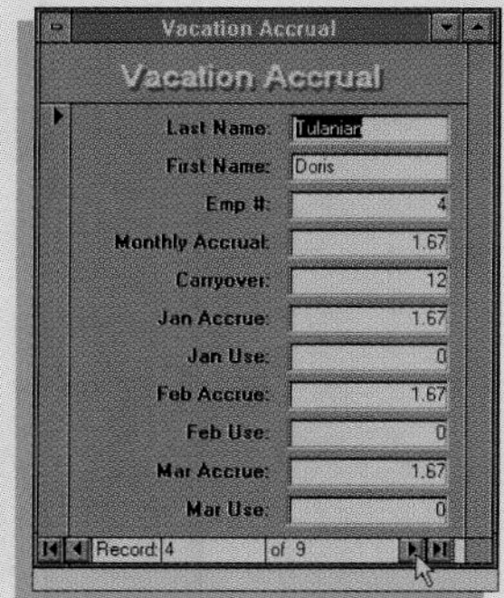

If the contents of a text box are too long to fit in the allotted space, use the left or right arrow key to bring the out-of-view portion into sight. Press Home to move the insertion point to the beginning of the field, or press End to move to the end of the field.

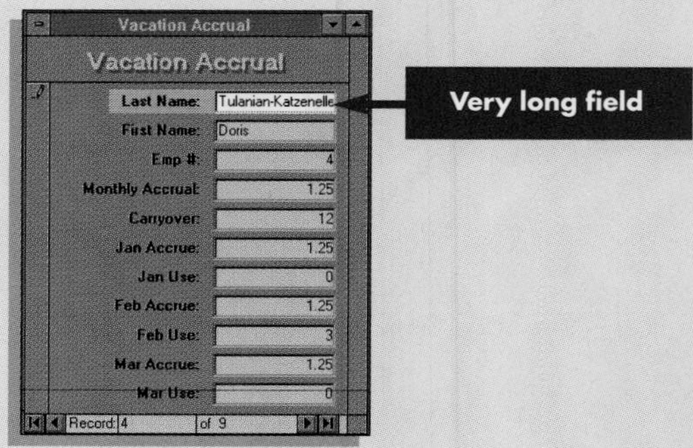

Repeat steps 3 through 6 to edit data in other fields of the same record, or steps 2 through 6 to edit data in other records.

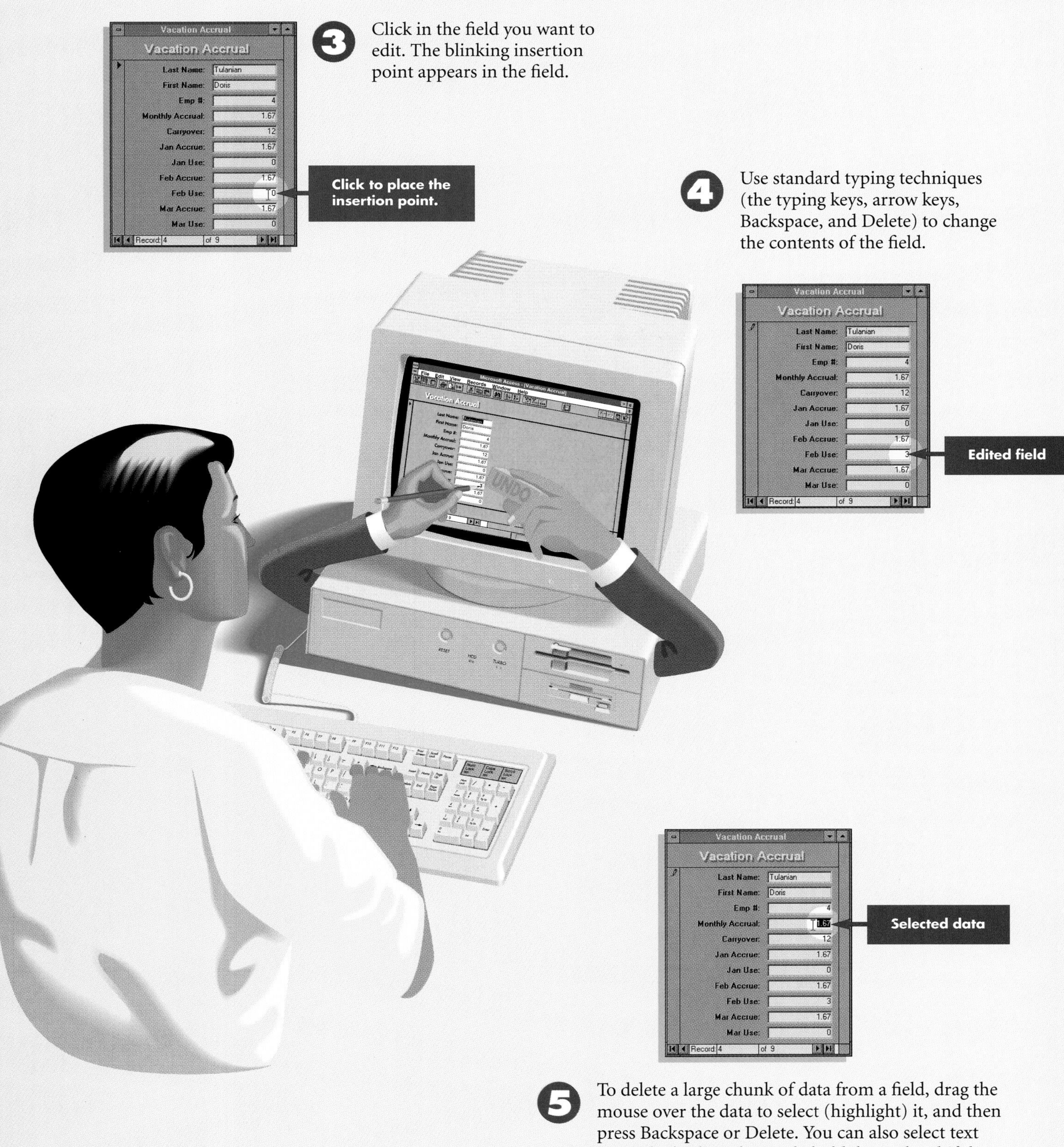

3 Click in the field you want to edit. The blinking insertion point appears in the field.

4 Use standard typing techniques (the typing keys, arrow keys, Backspace, and Delete) to change the contents of the field.

5 To delete a large chunk of data from a field, drag the mouse over the data to select (highlight) it, and then press Backspace or Delete. You can also select text using the keyboard. Simply hold down the Shift key while pressing the left or right arrow key. Reminder: If you delete data by mistake and you notice the error immediately, click on Edit and then on Undo.

How to Enter Records in a Form

Why are forms called forms? Because entering data records in them is like filling in a form on paper. As a vantage point for data entry, Form view is generally more appealing than Datasheet view. It places each field name right next to the place where you enter the data for that field. Form view also minimizes distraction by displaying only the record you are entering. This page helps you enter data through the Data Entry command, which presents a blank form in which to enter data and makes it impossible to overwrite data in an existing record accidentally.

1 Open the form.

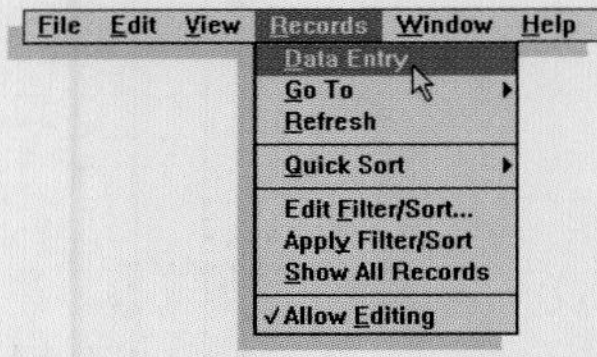

2 Click on Records in the menu bar and then click on the Data Entry command.

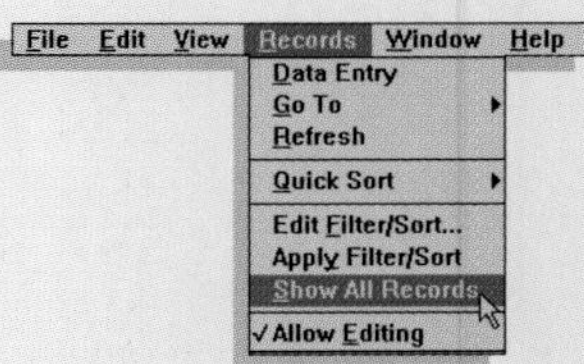

6 When done entering data, click on Records in the menu bar and then click on the Show All Records command. Now you can view all the records in the form's underlying table or dynaset, including the records you just entered.

TIP SHEET

- **Forms are ideal when you need to enter complete or nearly complete records. If instead you need to enter data here and there in several records throughout a table or dynaset, choose Datasheet view as described in Chapters 5 and 8. In Datasheet view, it is easier to find and jump to different records.**
- **There is no need to save your data as you enter it in Form view. Microsoft Access saves it for you automatically.**
- **Microsoft Access sorts records entered in Form view the same way it sorts records entered in Datasheet view. That is, it sorts on the primary key if there is one. Otherwise, it keeps records in the order in which you entered them.**

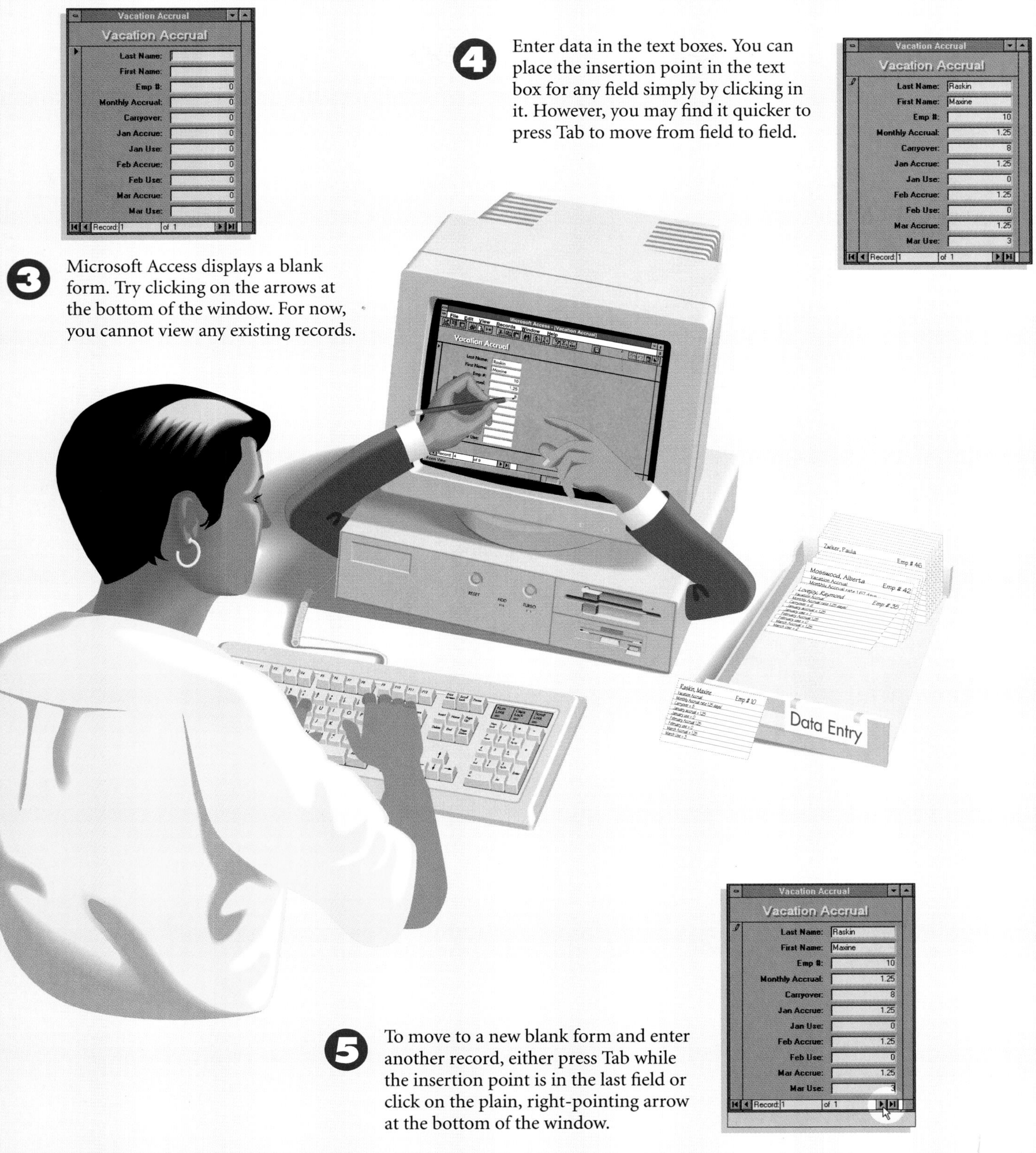

3 Microsoft Access displays a blank form. Try clicking on the arrows at the bottom of the window. For now, you cannot view any existing records.

4 Enter data in the text boxes. You can place the insertion point in the text box for any field simply by clicking in it. However, you may find it quicker to press Tab to move from field to field.

5 To move to a new blank form and enter another record, either press Tab while the insertion point is in the last field or click on the plain, right-pointing arrow at the bottom of the window.

How to Sort Records in a Form

Before you flip through records in a form, it can be convenient to arrange them according to the field that is of greatest interest. Say you want to see which of your employees have large amounts of vacation time saved up from last year. You can sort the records from highest to lowest vacation accrual and flip through them in that sequence. If you read about sorting tables in Datasheet view (Chapter 6), the steps in this procedure will be very familiar to you. Recall too that the *sort key* is the field whose content serves as the basis for the sort.

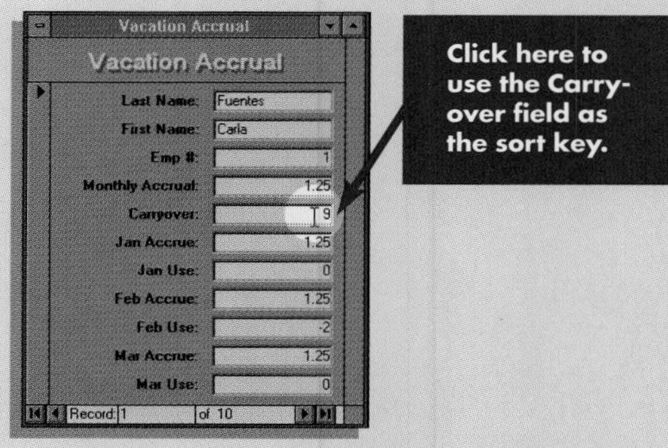

2 Click anywhere in the field you want to use as the sort key.

1 Open the form.

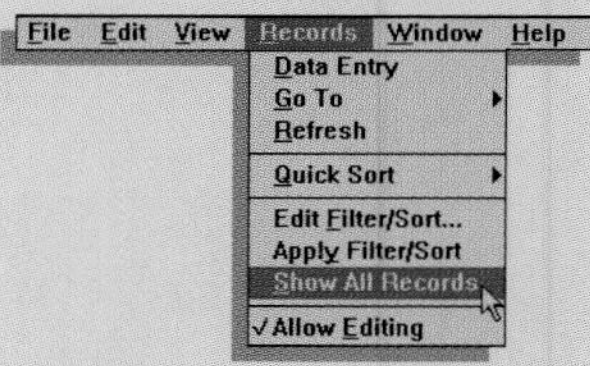

6 If you wish to cancel the sort and see records in their natural order again, click on Records in the menu bar and then click on the Show All Records command.

TIP SHEET

- **The Quick Sort command does not sort records permanently. Next time you open the form, table, or query, it will revert to the old sequence, which is based on the primary key (if any), the order of data entry, or the sort sequence defined in the underlying query (for query-based forms).**

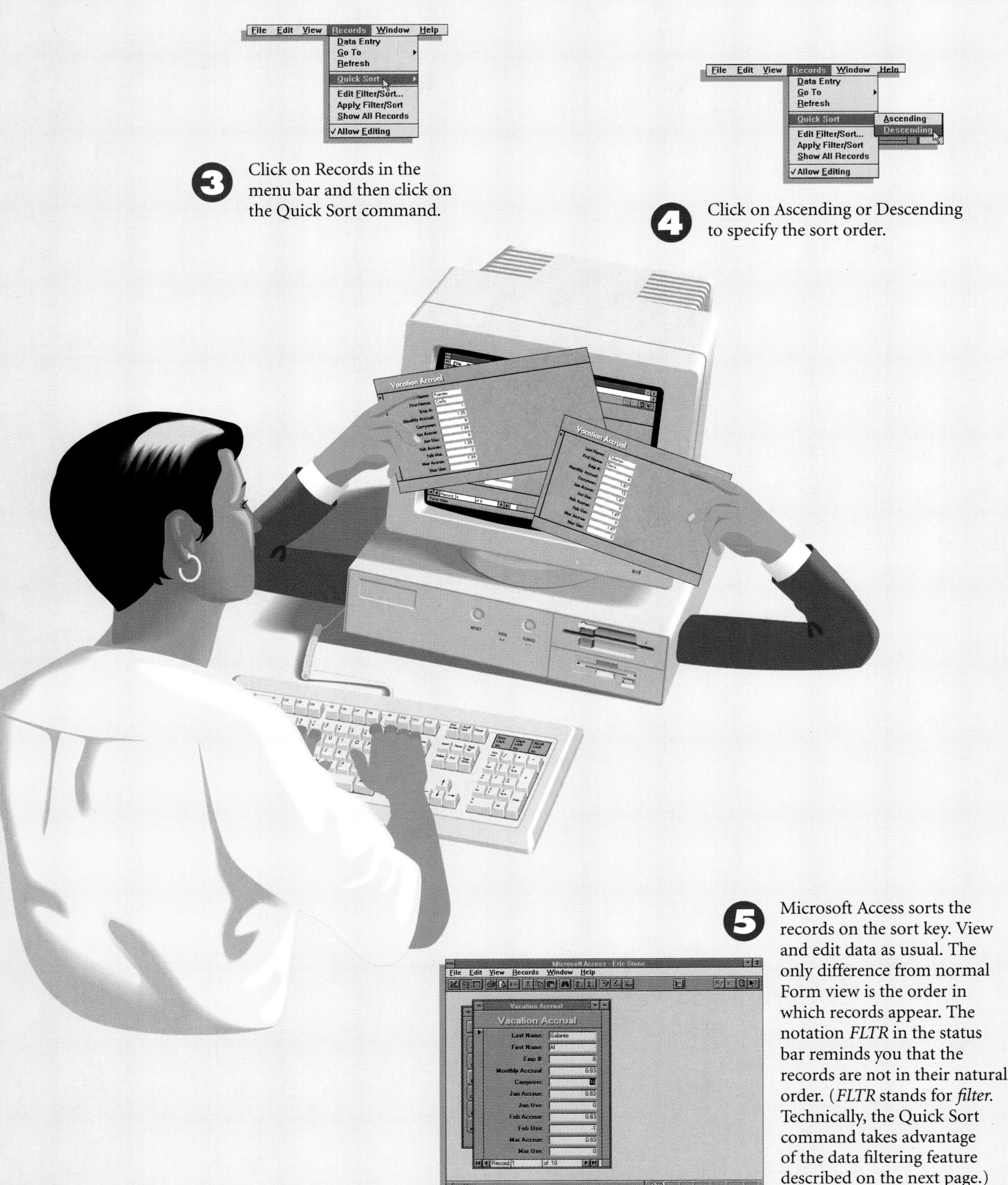

3 Click on Records in the menu bar and then click on the Quick Sort command.

4 Click on Ascending or Descending to specify the sort order.

5 Microsoft Access sorts the records on the sort key. View and edit data as usual. The only difference from normal Form view is the order in which records appear. The notation *FLTR* in the status bar reminds you that the records are not in their natural order. (*FLTR* stands for *filter.* Technically, the Quick Sort command takes advantage of the data filtering feature described on the next page.)

How to Display Only Selected Records in a Form

Through a capability called filtering, Microsoft Access can temporarily hide ("filter out") all records except those that meet your criteria. That way, you can flip through a form and see only those records that are of special interest at the moment. If this sounds familiar, it's because filtering a form is a lot like running a query. The major difference is that filtering lasts only until you close the form; it does not produce a Microsoft Access object. Another notable difference is that filtering forces you to show complete records, whereas queries let you limit the number of fields displayed. Though not as powerful and flexible as building and running a query, filtering is so easy that it's worth learning about.

TIP SHEET

- **Recall that filtering does not delete records but merely hides them temporarily. You can unfilter a form at any time and regain access to every record. Simply click on Records in the menu bar and then click on the Show All Records command. Moreover, you can freely close a form while it is filtered; next time you open the form the filtering will be gone and you will have access to every record. There is no way to lose data inadvertently through filtering.**
- **Microsoft Access remembers your filter definition even after you issue the Show All Records command. To reapply the filter, simply click on Edit and then on Apply Filter/Sort. However, when you close the form, the filter definition is lost.**

1 Open the form.

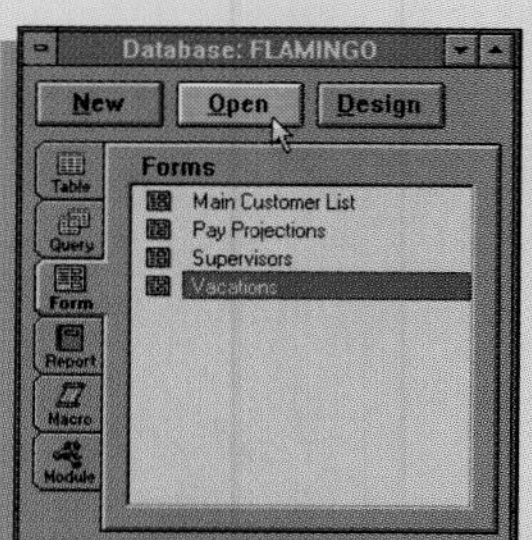

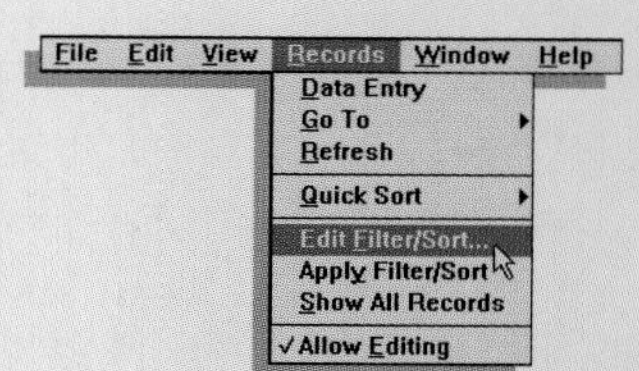

2 Click on Records in the menu bar and then click on the Edit Filter/Sort command.

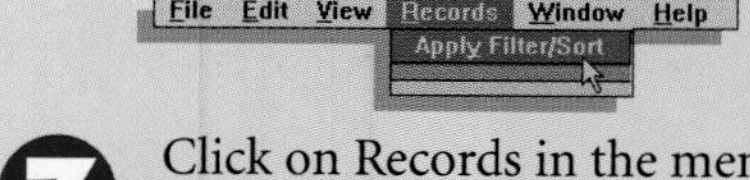

Click on Records in the menu bar and then click on the Apply Filter/Sort command.

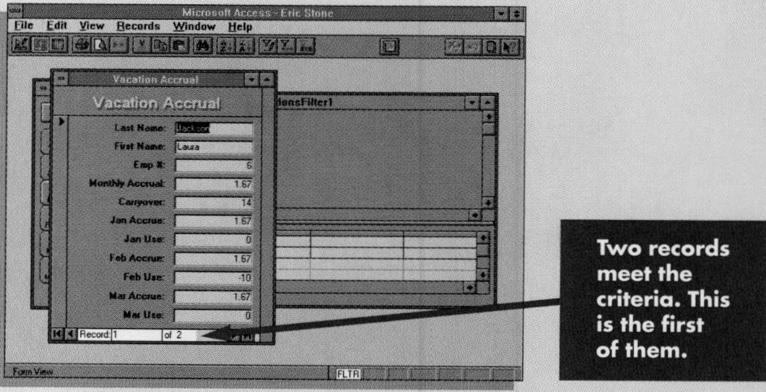

8 Microsoft Access processes the filter and displays the first record that meets your criteria. Work with the filtered form the same way you work with an unfiltered form, as described throughout this chapter. At the bottom of the window, you can see how many records passed the test. The notation *FLTR* in the status bar is a reminder that you are working with a filtered form.

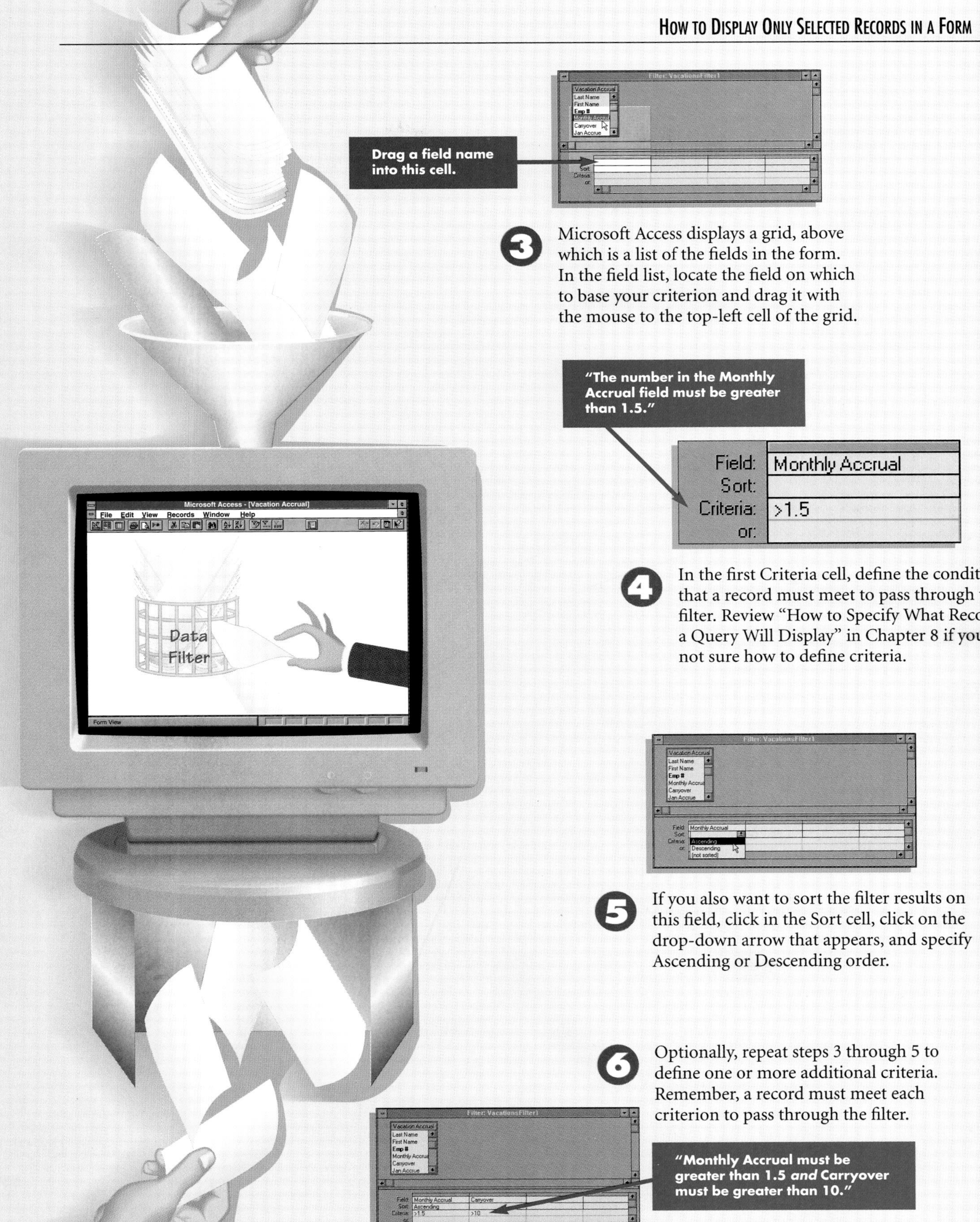

3 Microsoft Access displays a grid, above which is a list of the fields in the form. In the field list, locate the field on which to base your criterion and drag it with the mouse to the top-left cell of the grid.

4 In the first Criteria cell, define the condition that a record must meet to pass through the filter. Review "How to Specify What Records a Query Will Display" in Chapter 8 if you're not sure how to define criteria.

5 If you also want to sort the filter results on this field, click in the Sort cell, click on the drop-down arrow that appears, and specify Ascending or Descending order.

6 Optionally, repeat steps 3 through 5 to define one or more additional criteria. Remember, a record must meet each criterion to pass through the filter.

CHAPTER 12

Creating Reports

Earlier in this book you learned how to print tables and query results. The results, however, were not too impressive.

To produce appealing, easy-to-read printouts of your Microsoft Access data, you create *reports.* A report is like a template or framework into which Microsoft Access plugs the data from a table or dynaset. The template can feature a wide array of special effects that you might not expect a database program to offer, including a variety of fonts (type styles), type sizes, text attributes such as italics, and even graphics. Presenting data in a well-designed report is a great strategy for bolstering your message or softening the blow of bad news.

For some expert users, report design is a discipline all its own—a discipline not so different from desktop publishing. But you don't need any special skills to create nice-looking reports. That's because Microsoft Access comes with several professionally designed report styles, which you can choose among with the help of *Report Wizards.* This chapter explains how to take advantage of Report Wizards and create reports in just a few steps.

Despite the convenience of Report Wizards, report creation is perhaps the most elaborate operation you'll perform as a Microsoft Access beginner. Therefore, this chapter breaks up the process into four very manageable chunks. To master report creation, be sure to read this chapter in sequence from start to finish.

How to Start a Report

Reports are Microsoft Access objects, just like tables, queries, and forms. Therefore, the way you start a new report will be quite familiar.

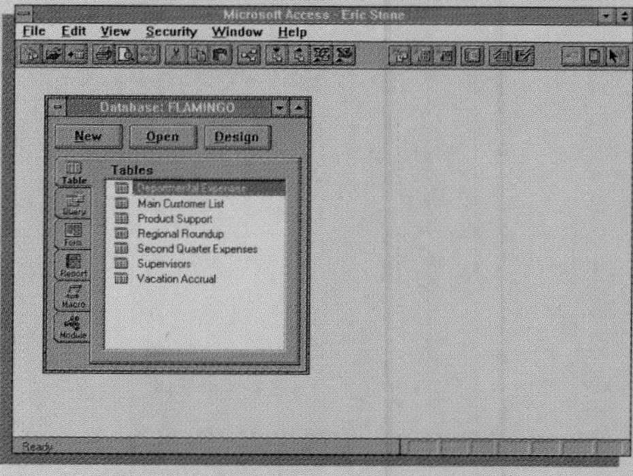

1. Open the database containing the data you want to express in a report. Close any open objects to display the Database window.

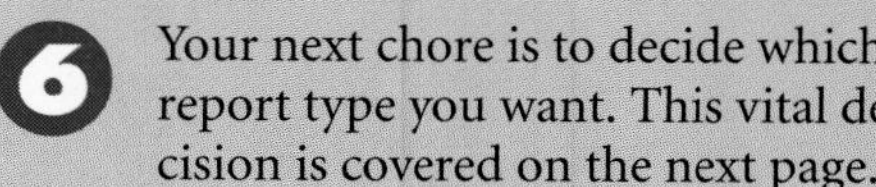

6. Your next chore is to decide which report type you want. This vital decision is covered on the next page.

TIP SHEET

- **Don't be intimidated by the many steps in the report creation process. Reports simply display data; they do not change it. Therefore, no mistake you make while creating a report can affect your underlying data. The worst that can happen is you'll be dissatisfied with your report and you'll have to start over.**

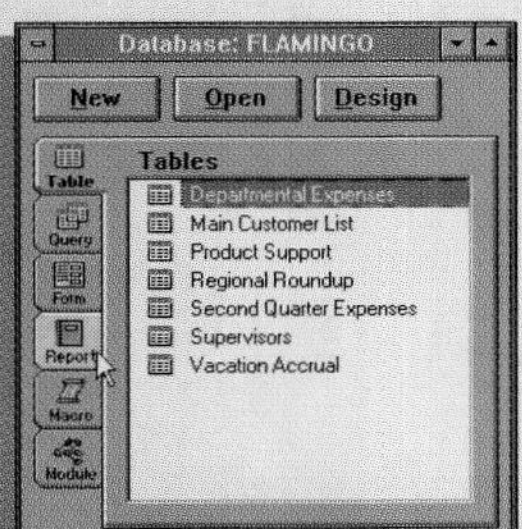

2 Click on the Report object button.

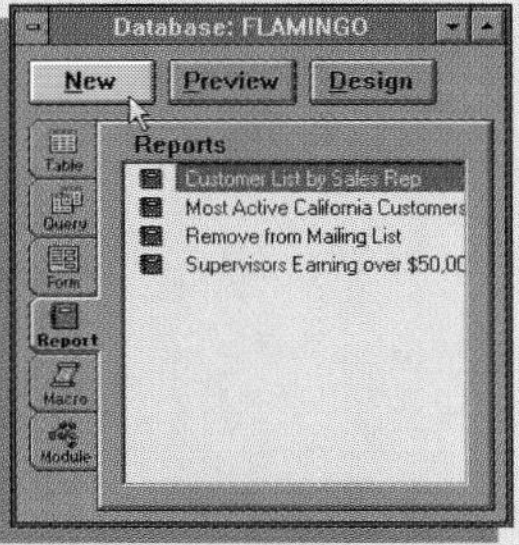

3 The window now lists any reports already created for this database. To create a new report, click on the New button.

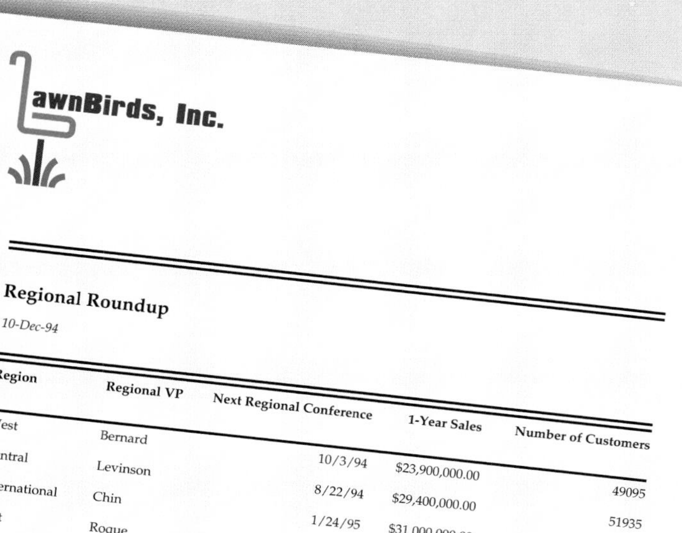
LawnBirds, Inc.

Regional Roundup

10-Dec-94

Region	Regional VP	Next Regional Conference	1-Year Sales	Number of Customers
West	Bernard	10/3/94	$23,900,000.00	49095
Central	Levinson	8/22/94	$29,400,000.00	51935
International	Chin	1/24/95	$31,000,000.00	18005
East	Roque	9/26/94	$38,500,000.00	55885
			$122,800,000.00	**174920**

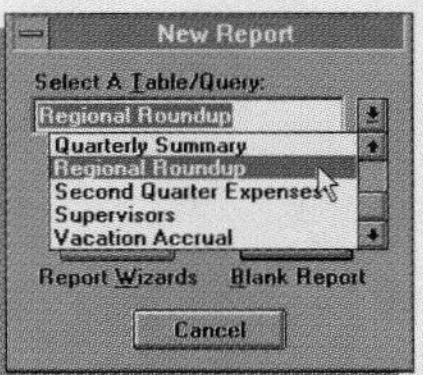

4 The New Report dialog box appears. First, Microsoft Access needs to know the table or query (dynaset) on which the report will be based. Click on the Select A Table/Query drop-down arrow and then click on a table or query name.

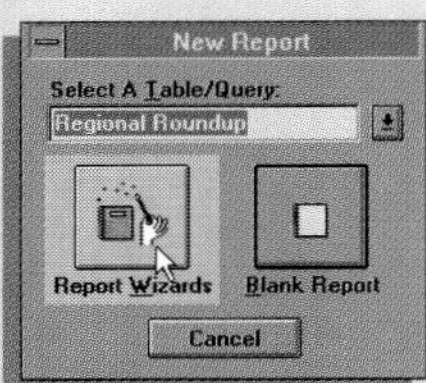

5 Click on Report Wizards.

How to Select a Report Type

Microsoft Access offers several report types, one of which is likely to meet your needs. After you select a report type, a Report Wizard will ask you for more information, as explained on the next page. There is also a special report type called AutoReport. If you select Auto-Report, Microsoft Access immediately builds and displays a report based on its best assumptions of what you want. This page and the next cover the report types of greatest interest to beginning users. Once you gain experience with Microsoft Access, feel free to experiment will all of the report types offered.

TIP SHEET

- **Except in an AutoReport, you need not show every field in a report if only certain fields are of interest. Limiting the number of fields is an efficient way to shorten or simplify a report (except in an AutoReport). The next page explains how.**
- **When you select AutoReport (step 3), Microsoft Access immediately shows you the report on the screen, just as it will appear when printed. The last page of this chapter and all of Chapter 13 show you what you can do with a report once you've created it. What if you find the report inadequate? Simply abandon it and start over, this time selecting another report type. To abandon the report, click on File, click on Close, and answer No when asked whether you want to save the report. You will return to the database window, where you can start a new report as described throughout this chapter.**
- **The Mailing Label report type is not just for names and addresses. For example, if you keep a manual folder (as well as an electronic database record) for each of your clients, you can use the Mailing Labels report to print labels for the folders. Each label might contain the client's name and account number.**

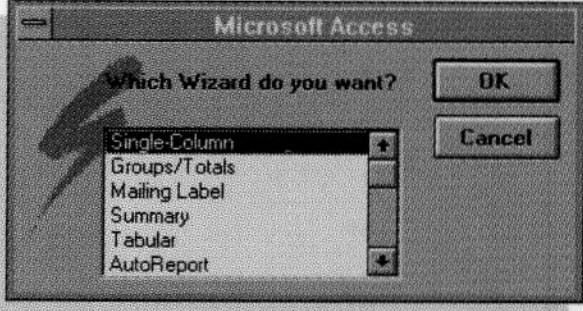

1 Follow the steps on the preceding page. You should then see a dialog box that asks, "Which Wizard do you want?"

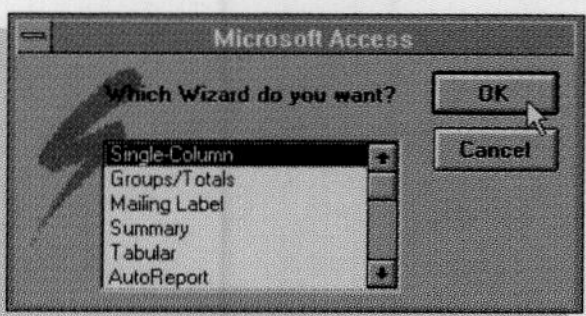

2 Click on the report type you want, and then click on the OK button. The upcoming steps provide more information on your choices.

6 As you might guess, a Mailing Label report formats your data so you can print it on mailing labels. You must tell Microsoft Access how to format the addresses (or other data) and what type of labels you will be printing on (see the next page for details).

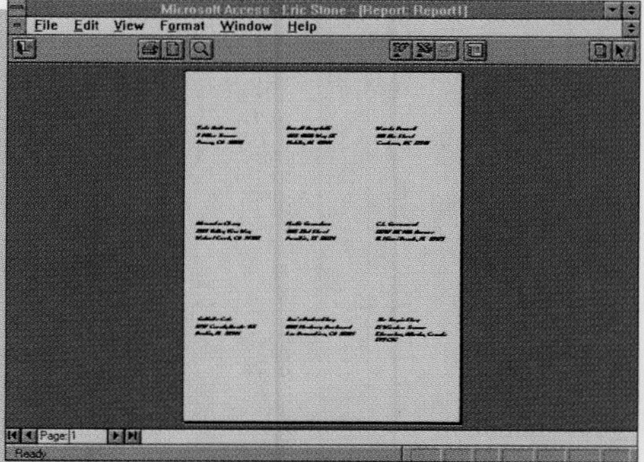

7 After you select a report type (except for Auto-Report), a Report Wizard opens and starts asking you questions about the contents and appearance of the form. These questions vary according to the report type. The next page prepares you for the questions you may encounter.

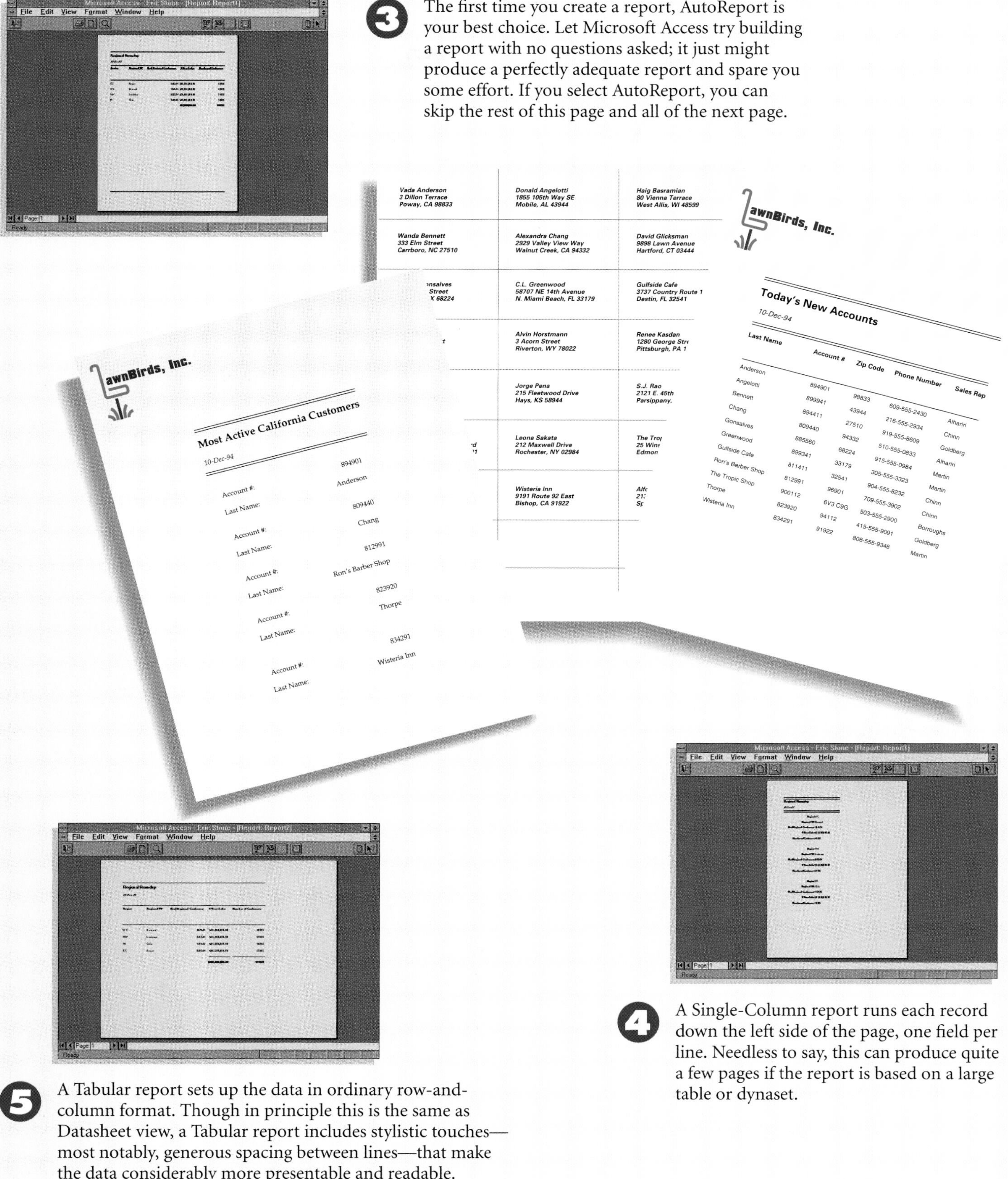

3 The first time you create a report, AutoReport is your best choice. Let Microsoft Access try building a report with no questions asked; it just might produce a perfectly adequate report and spare you some effort. If you select AutoReport, you can skip the rest of this page and all of the next page.

4 A Single-Column report runs each record down the left side of the page, one field per line. Needless to say, this can produce quite a few pages if the report is based on a large table or dynaset.

5 A Tabular report sets up the data in ordinary row-and-column format. Though in principle this is the same as Datasheet view, a Tabular report includes stylistic touches—most notably, generous spacing between lines—that make the data considerably more presentable and readable.

How to Specify the Contents and Look of a Report

As noted on the preceding page, a Report Wizard will ask you different questions depending on which report type you choose. Generally, you need to state what fields to include in the report, how to sort the records, and how you want the report to look. This page helps you decipher the questions you are likely to encounter. It assumes that you have already started a new report and specified the report type as explained on the two preceding pages.

TIP SHEET

- **Fields in a report can appear in any sequence you choose, regardless of their sequence in the underlying table or dynaset. Simply place the fields in the list in the order in which you want them to appear (step 1 or 2).**
- **Reminder: Reports merely display data; they do not change it. No matter what fields you omit from a report or what sequence you assign to fields and records in a report, the next time you open the underlying table or dynaset, it will look the same as it did before.**
- **When using a Report Wizard, you can click on the < Back button in any dialog box to return to the previous dialog box and make different selections. Or click on Cancel to abandon the report completely.**
- **If your labels are not Avery brand, check the label packaging; an Avery equivalent may be listed.**

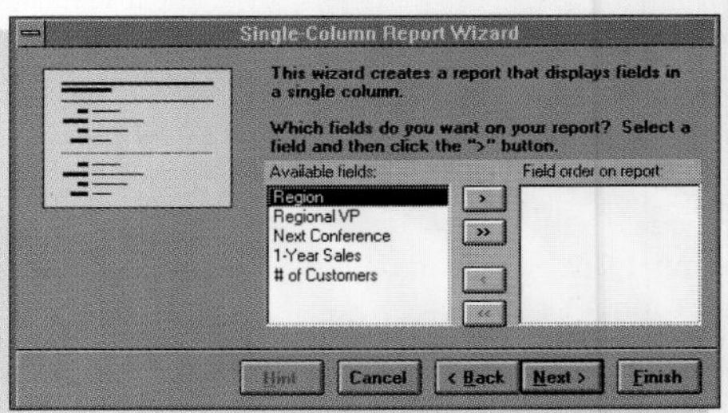

1 This dialog box appears if you selected a Single-Column or Tabular report. (Only the title and the sample report vary.) You tell the Report Wizard to include a field in the report by moving the field name from the list on the left ("Available fields") to the list on the right ("Field order on report"). To do so, double-click on the field name. As a shortcut, you can include every field by clicking on the >> button. If you change your mind about including a field in the report, double-click on the field name again to move it back to the list of available fields. When done making your selections, click on the Next > button.

7 Finally, the Report Wizard asks you what you want to do now that you have made your choices. Optionally, for Single-Column and Tabular reports, change or delete the report title, which by default is the same as the title of the table or dynaset on which the report is based. Otherwise, stick with the default settings by clicking on the Finish button. Microsoft Access displays your report.

6 For Single-Column and Tabular reports, the Report Wizard offers some general choices for the appearance of the report. These considerations are practical as well as aesthetic. For example, in a Tabular report, printing in landscape (sideways) rather than portrait orientation may enable Microsoft Access to fit all fields on one page. When done making your selections, click on the Next > button.

2 This dialog box appears if you selected a Mailing Label report. You need to tell the Report Wizard not only what fields to include on each label but also where to place punctuation characters, spaces, and line breaks. In the list of available fields, double-click on the first field that is to appear on each label. The field name now appears in the "Label appearance" box. Next, click on the formatting button representing what should come after that field (typically a space, a comma, or a new line). Continue double-clicking on field names and clicking on formatting buttons until you have set up a model of the complete label. If you make a mistake, click on the < button one or more times to remove items from the "Label appearance" box. When done, click on the Next > button.

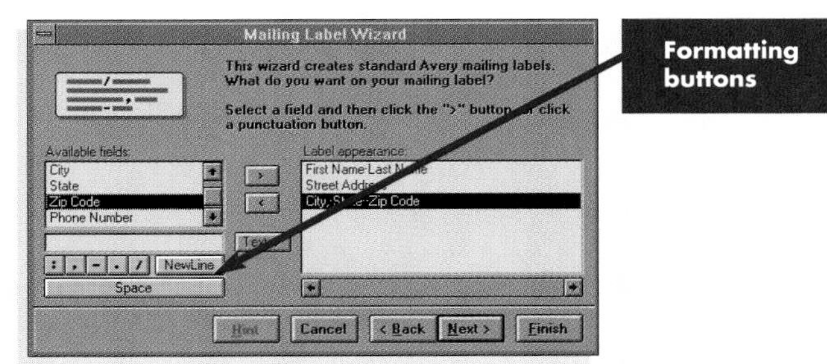

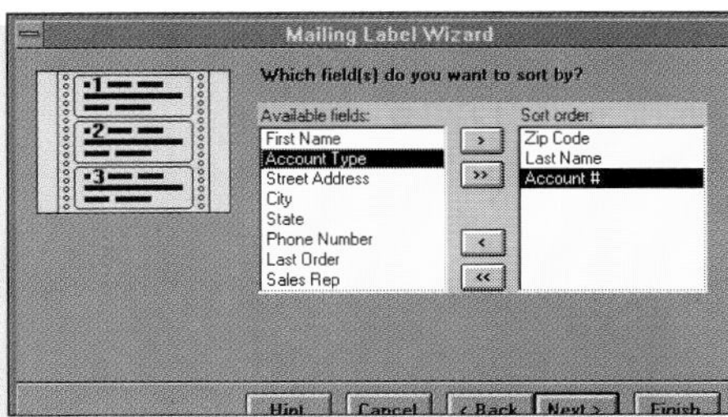

3 In this dialog box, you can select a field to use as the sort key by double-clicking on it. You can also add up to nine additional sort keys that kick in when the preceding key results in a tie. For example, you could sort your client list first by zip code, then by last name (for clients with the same zip code), and finally by account number (for clients with the same zip code and last name). When done specifying a sort order, click on the Next > button.

4 For a Mailing Label report, you must tell the Report Wizard the type of labels you plan to use. This affects the number of records per page and their layout on the page. First, check and, if necessary, change the Label Type and Unit of Measure settings to reflect the labels you're using. Then click on the correct product number and finally, click on the Next > button.

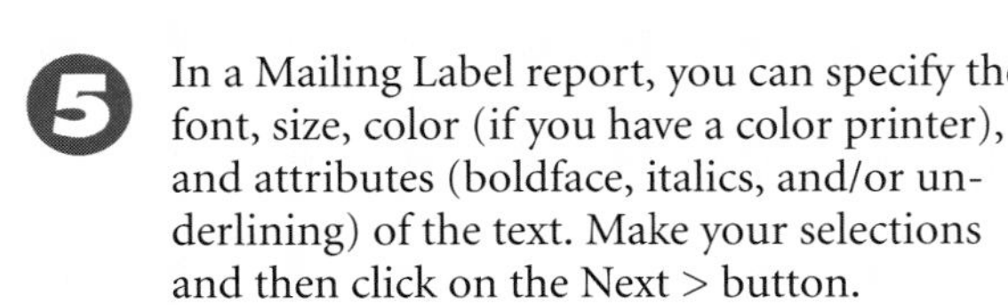

5 In a Mailing Label report, you can specify the font, size, color (if you have a color printer), and attributes (boldface, italics, and/or underlining) of the text. Make your selections and then click on the Next > button.

How to Name, Save, and Close a Report

Since a report is a Microsoft Access object, you name, save, and close it much the same as you do for a table, query, or form. These steps should all be quite familiar by now.

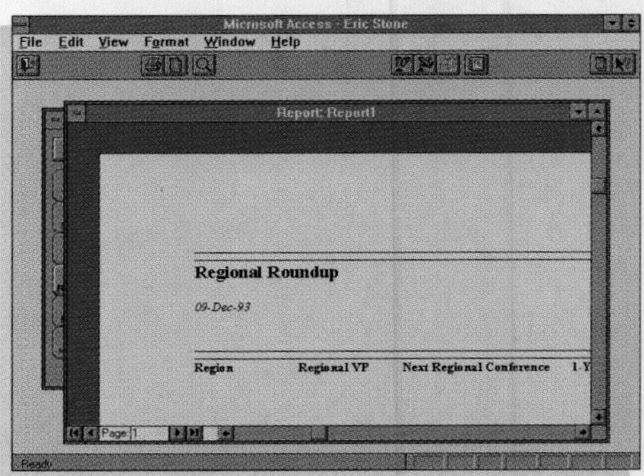

1 Create the report as described on the preceding pages.

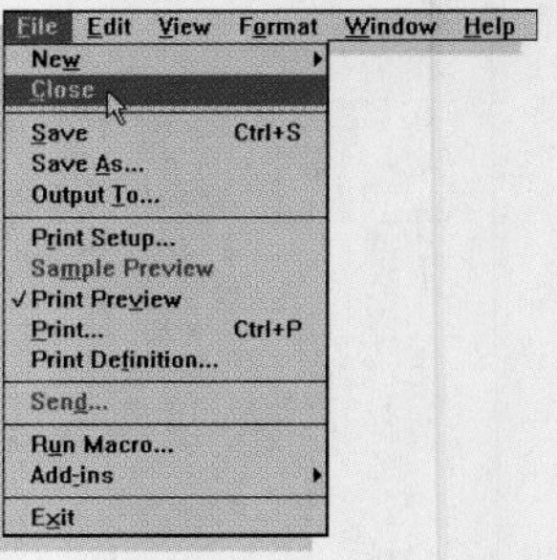

6 When you want to close the report and return to the Database window, click on File in the menu bar and then click on the Close command. (Of course, you've yet to learn what you can do with a report once it's created and open. Read the next chapter to find out.)

TIP SHEET

- **The report *name* you assigned in step 3 serves a different function from the report *title* (see step 7 on the preceding page). The report name appears in the Database window along with other objects, enabling you to reopen and print the report later. The report title appears on the printed report. However, there is no reason why the report name and the report title can't be the same.**
- **In Chapter 13, you will learn how to make certain small-scale improvements to a report. But what if you're so dissatisfied with a report that you want to abandon it and start over? Instead of following the steps on this page, simply click on File, click on Close, and answer No when asked whether you want to save the report.**

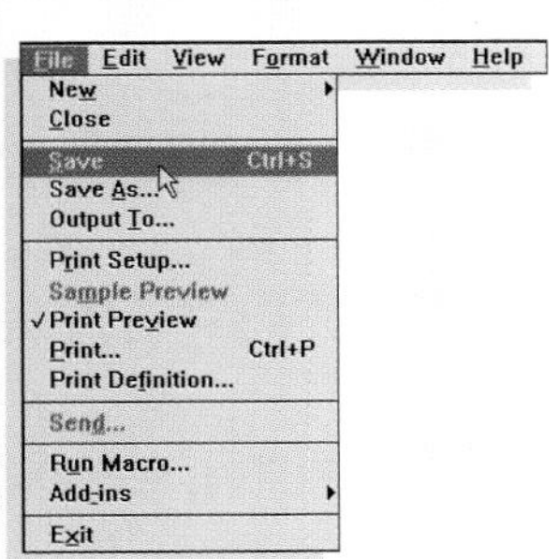

2 Click on File in the menu bar and then click on the Save command.

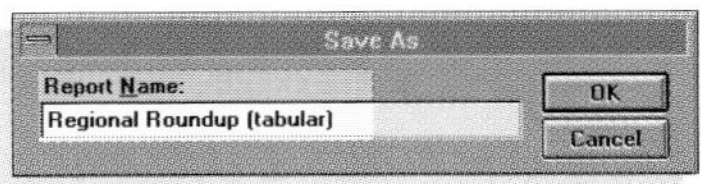

3 Type a name for the report, replacing the placeholder provided (*Report1* or higher). Like all object names, a report name can be up to 64 characters long and can contain all characters except periods, exclamation points, and brackets.

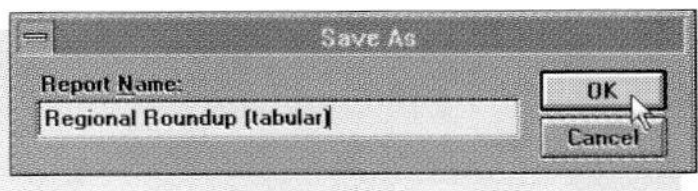

4 Click on the OK button.

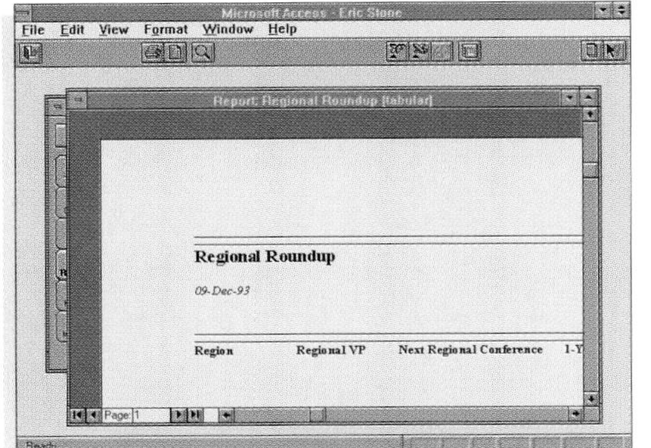

5 Microsoft Access saves the report on disk and closes the dialog box. The new report name appears in the title bar.

CHAPTER 13

Using and Improving Reports

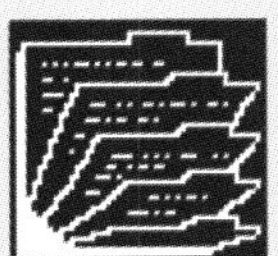

Reports don't do very much. In Microsoft Access, you perform all of your data management through tables, forms, and queries. Reports can do only one thing: display data.

But when you need to show your data to others, reports are priceless. That's because reports perform their one function (the display of data) remarkably well. Printouts of reports far surpass stodgy, crowded printouts of tables and dynasets in effectively conveying information.

Chapter 12 introduced reports but did not take you as far as actually printing them, which undoubtedly is your goal. That's the job of this chapter. You will learn how to display a report on your screen much as it will appear when printed, and then, of course, you will learn how to print it out.

In addition, this chapter lists a few ways to improve a report by changing its appearance or contents. On this topic, a few candid words of warning are in order: Changing a report is not easy—not even for Microsoft Access experts. That's because the software offers a dazzling array of options for placing data, headlines, and graphics in a report. Don't let all these options concern you. The second half of this chapter will show you several techniques that any Microsoft Access user can master easily. Once you reach the status of an advanced user, you'll be well equipped to experiment with the other available report options.

How to Preview a Report

Microsoft Access can *preview* a report on your screen, displaying the report almost exactly as it will look when printed. In fact, as you may have observed in Chapter 12, the Report Wizards preview your reports on the screen as the last stage of the report creation process. Whenever you preview a report, Microsoft Access inserts data in it based on the current contents of the underlying table or dynaset. Previewing a report let's you know immediately whether it meets your needs, so that you can opt to change the report (or the table or dynaset) before wasting time and paper on a printout.

1 Open the database, display the Database window, and click on the Report object button.

2 Click on the name of the report you want to preview.

8 When done previewing the report, you can either press Escape to return to the Database window or print the report as described on the next page.

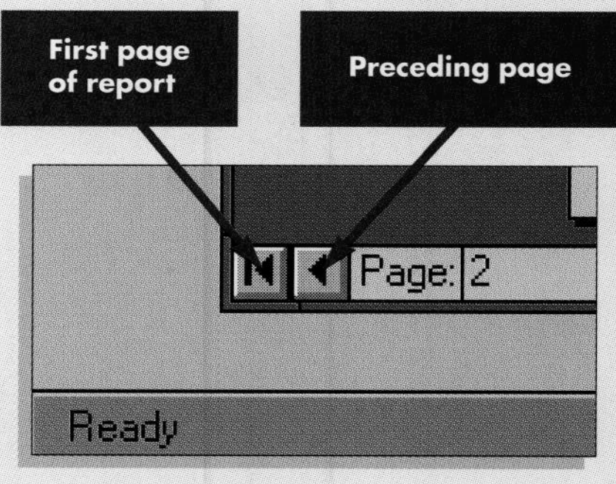

7 Click here to move backward through a multipage report.

TIP SHEET

- **Instead of clicking on a report name and then clicking on Preview (steps 2 and 3), you can simply double-click on a report name to preview the report.**
- **You cannot edit data or field names within a report. If previewing a report indicates that editing is necessary, press Escape to return to the Database window and then edit the data or field names through a table, query, or form as described in earlier chapters.**

3 Click on Preview.

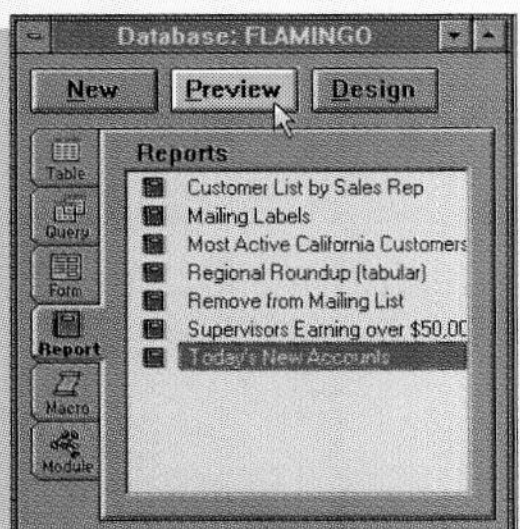

4 Microsoft Access displays the first page of the report. Use the scroll bars if necessary to see out-of-view parts of the page.

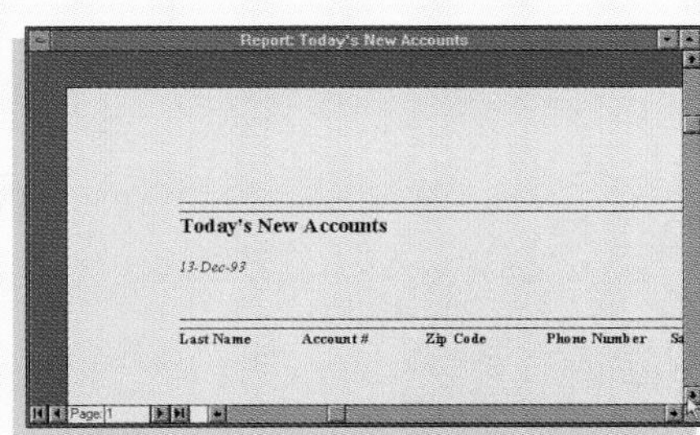

6 Click on these arrows to move forward through a multipage report.

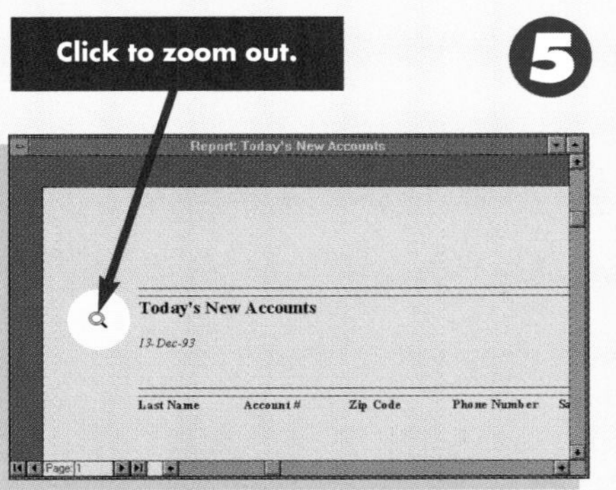

5 Observe that the mouse pointer becomes a magnifying glass when it is over the previewed page. At this point you can click on the page to "zoom out," gaining a better perspective on the overall page layout but losing readability of the text. Click on the page again to zoom back in.

How to Print a Report

A printed report is the fanciest output you'll ever get from Microsoft Access. Yet printing a report is a cinch. You can print the whole report or just specific pages. Microsoft Access updates your reports before printing them, so you are always sure that your printout reflects the current contents of the underlying table or dynaset.

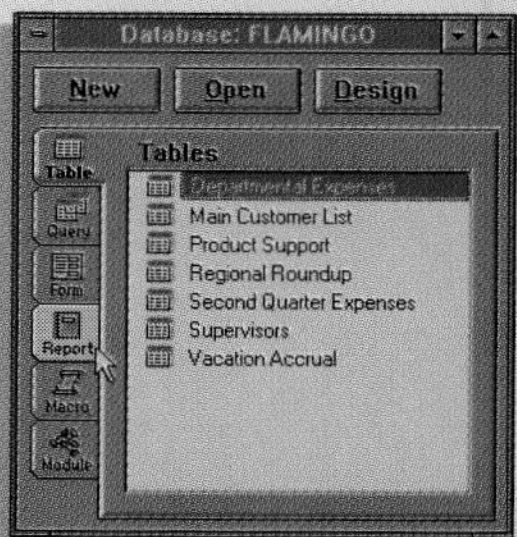

1. Open the database, display the Database window, and click on the Report object button.

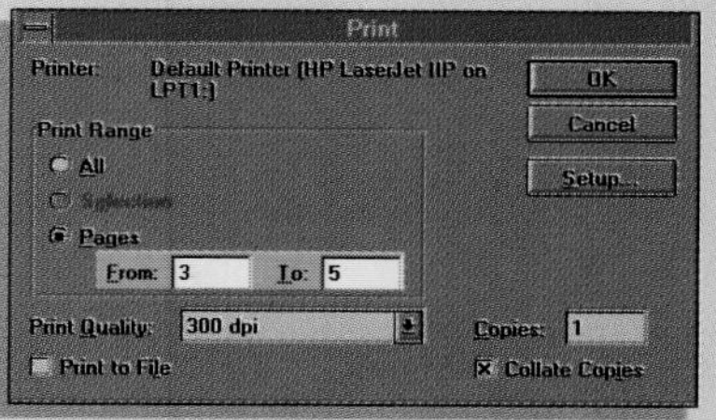

5. If you want to print only a certain range of pages, click in the From text box, type the first page to print, click in the To text box, and type the last page to print.

6. Click on OK.

- **If you are already previewing a report (see preceding page), you can print it without returning to the Database window. Just start with step 3 on this page.**
- **Observe in step 5 that you need not click on the Pages radio button to specify that you want to print a page range. Microsoft Access marks this radio button for you when you enter page numbers in the From and To text boxes.**
- **To print just one page of your report, enter the page number in both the From and To text boxes in step 5.**

2 Click on the name of the report you want to print.

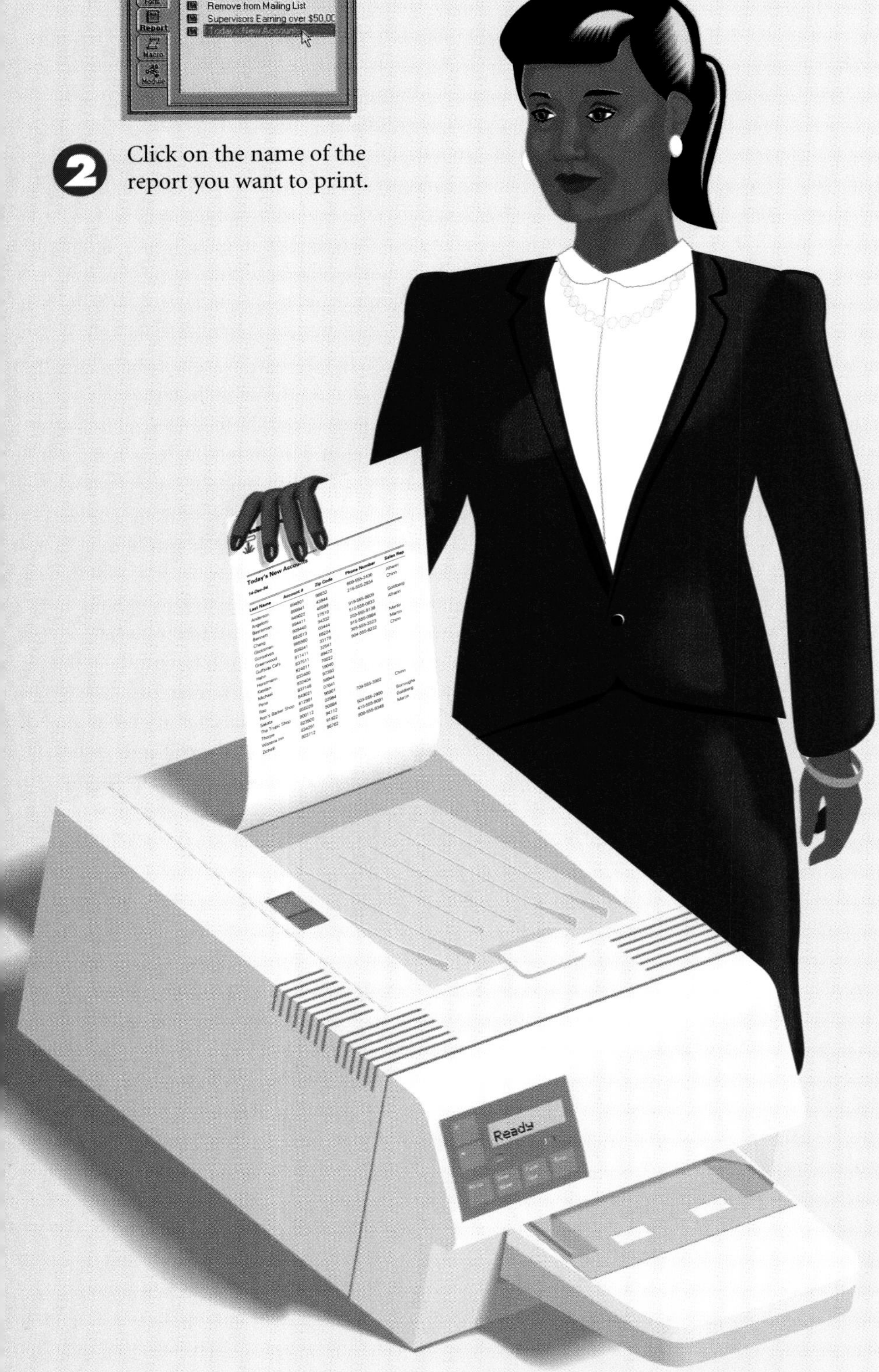

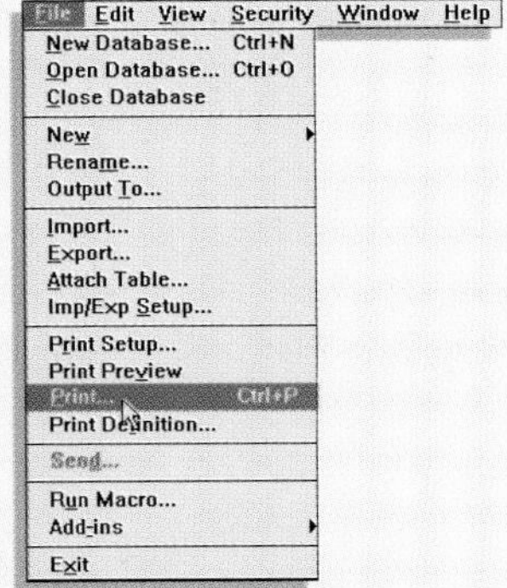

3 Click on File and then click on Print.

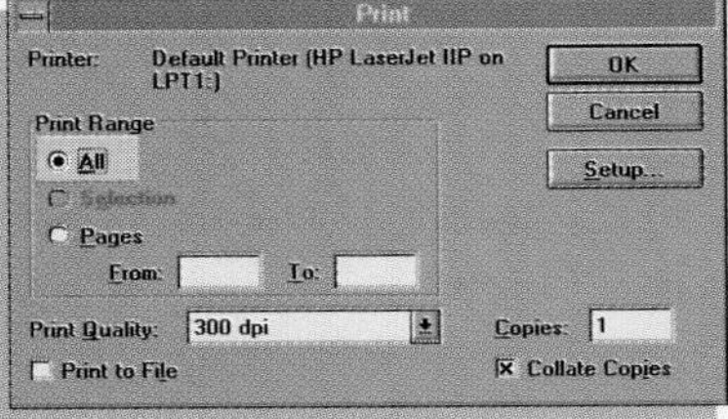

4 Observe in the Print dialog box that Microsoft Access is preset to print the entire report. If that is what you want, skip to step 6.

How to Change the Appearance of a Report

Behind the scenes, Microsoft Access puts a lot of work into designing your reports, deciding what main heading to use, where to place the various fields, what fonts and type sizes to use, and so on. On this page, you will learn how to display a report in Design view and control the most important aesthetic considerations. Beware: Only an expert user can take full advantage of the options in Design view. This page covers only the basics. If you are really interested in report design, consult an advanced-level Microsoft Access book for further help.

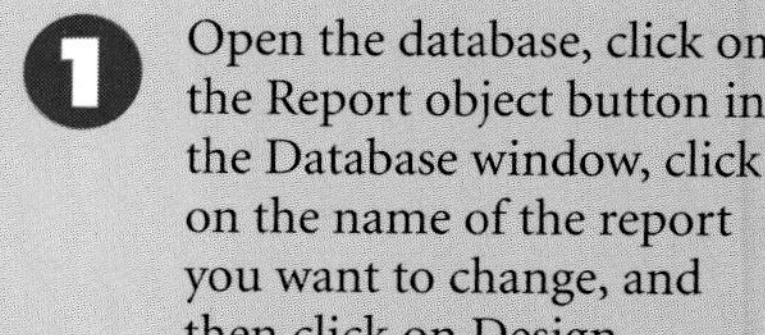

1 Open the database, click on the Report object button in the Database window, click on the name of the report you want to change, and then click on Design.

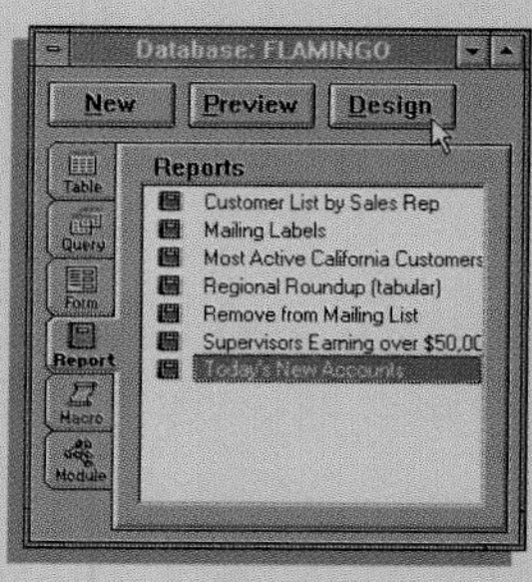

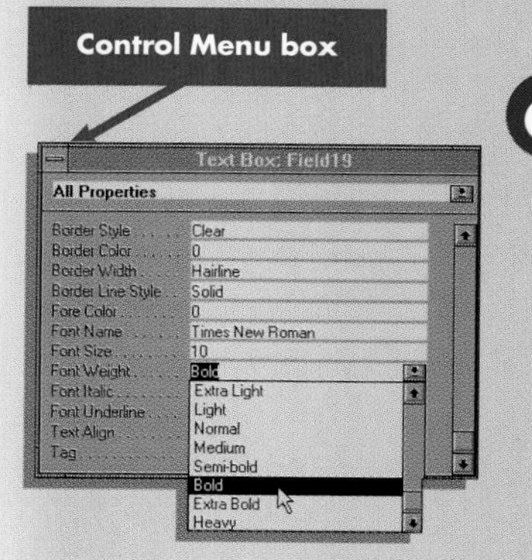

6 In the Properties list, locate the property you want to change, such as Font Name, Font Size, Font Weight, or Text Align. Click on the property, click on the drop-down arrow that appears, and then click on the appropriate option. Double-click on the Control Menu box when you're done.

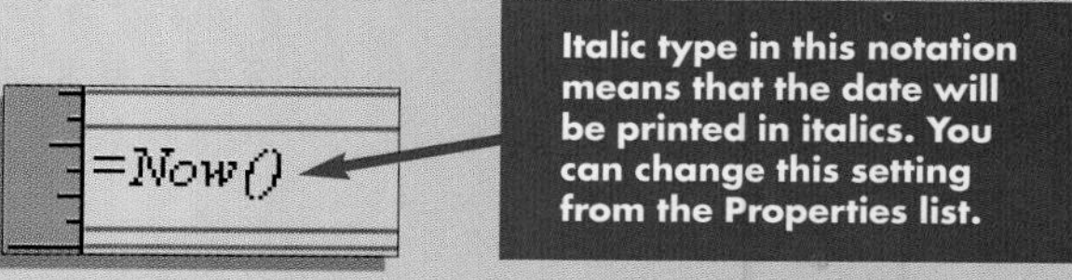

7 Most reports contain the notations *=Now()* and *=Page*. *=Now()* means that whenever you print the report, the date will change to reflect the date stored by your computer's clock; it will be printed at that position. *=Page* shows where the page number will be printed. You can move, realign, and reformat these controls just as you would other controls.

8 Click on File and then click on Save to store any changes you've made to the report design. Then at your discretion, click on File and then on Close to return to the Database window, click on File and then on Print Preview to preview the modified report, or click on File and then on Print to print the report.

TIP SHEET

- **Another way to open the Properties list for a control is to double-click on the control. However, this works only if the control was *not* already selected (that is, if its handles were not already displayed). You can remove the handles from a control by clicking elsewhere on the report.**
- **Don't let the considerable length of the Properties list intimidate you. Many of the options are only for the truly finicky. Just concentrate on finding and changing the settings that interest you.**
- **Beginners have little use for the Toolbox that appears when you open a report in Design view. To hide the Toolbox, click on its Control Menu box.**
- **The Undo command is active in Design view. To reverse your most recent change, click on Edit and then click on Undo.**

2 Microsoft Access displays your report in Design view. Most report designs contain the following sections from top to bottom: Report Header (text that will appear at the top of the report), Page Header (text for the top of every page in the report), Detail (the fields that will appear for each record in the underlying table or dynaset), Page Footer (text for the bottom of every page), and Report Footer (text for the bottom of the report). Use the scroll arrows to see out-of-view parts of the report design.

3 Each element of the report design—each headline, field name, and so on—is called a *control.* Click on a control, and it acquires eight *handles,* solid boxes along the perimeter of the control that help you manipulate it. To move a control, drag its upper-left handle. For example, to lower the main heading within the area reserved for the report header, drag it downward by its upper-left handle.

Observe the shape of the mouse pointer.

Handles

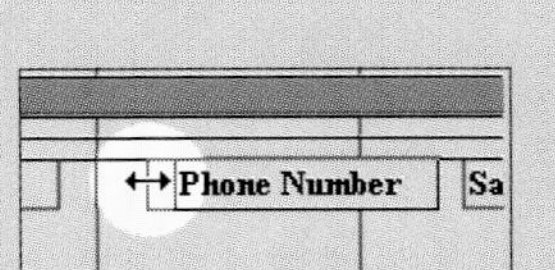

4 To widen a control (so it can fully display its contents) or to narrow an unnecessarily wide control, drag one of its two side handles in or out. A helpful space-saving technique: Shorten the contents of a control (as explained on the next page) and then narrow the control itself, since it no longer needs all the space originally devoted to it.

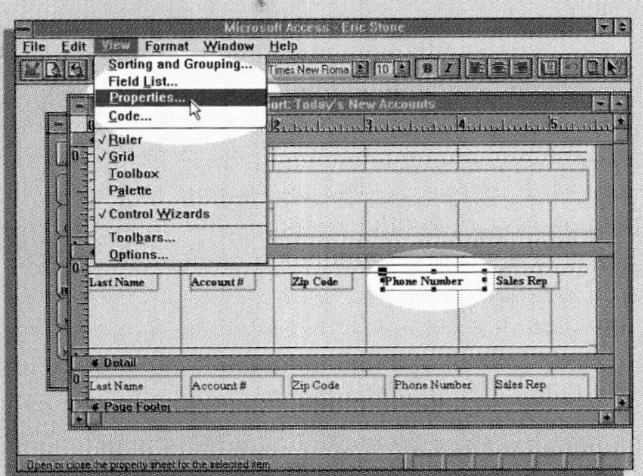

5 You can change the format or alignment of text within a control by editing its *Properties* list. Click on the control to display its handles, click on View, and then click on Properties.

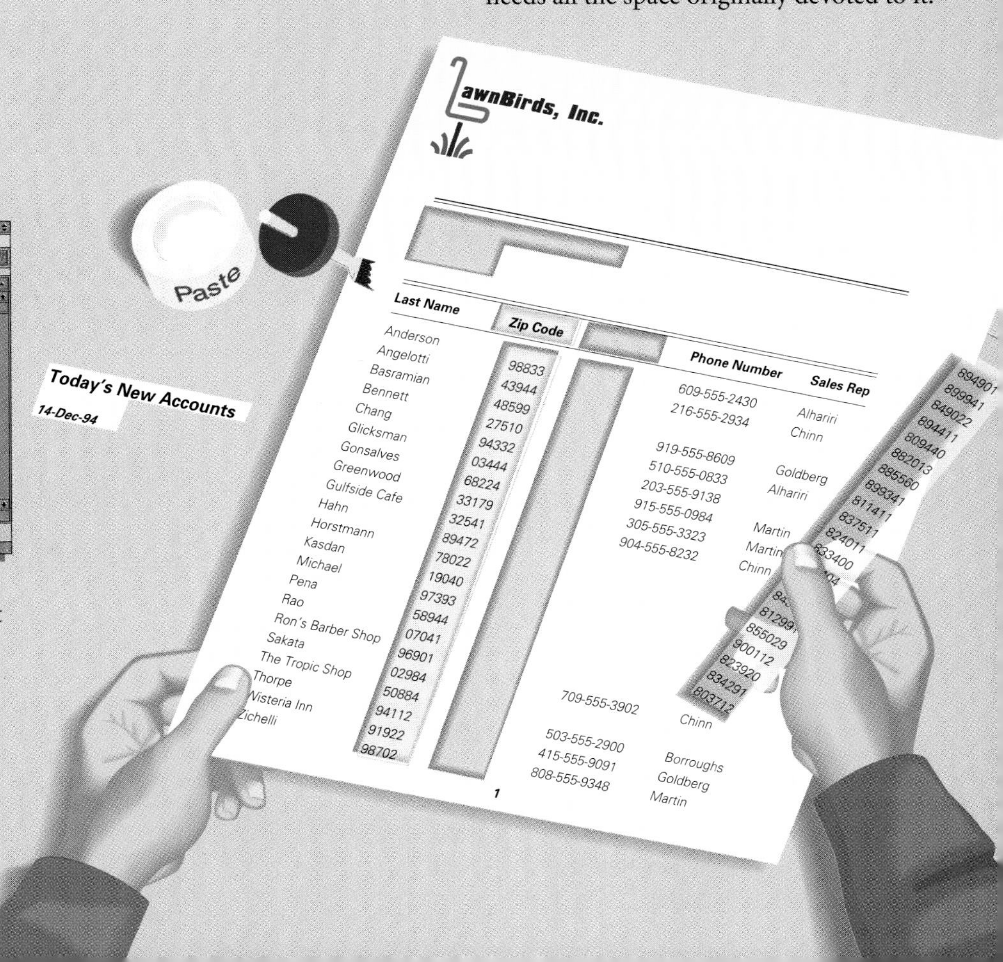

How to Change the Contents of a Report

No doubt you have observed that reports often include text other than your data. For example, Single-Column and Tabular reports also contain field names and a main heading. In your report design, you can edit all such nondata text. Moreover, you can delete any control—even a control that supplies data from the underlying table or dynaset. For example, if a personnel report in the Tabular format is too wide to fit on one page, you can save space by deleting a control that inserts less important data, such as the employee's middle name.

1 Open the database, click on the Report object button in the Database window, click on the name of the report you want to change, and then click on Design.

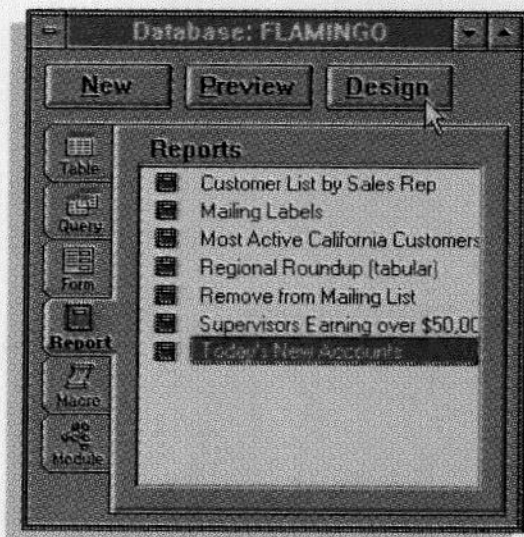

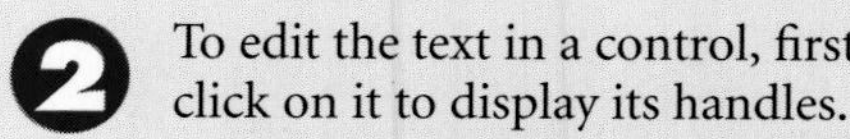

2 To edit the text in a control, first click on it to display its handles.

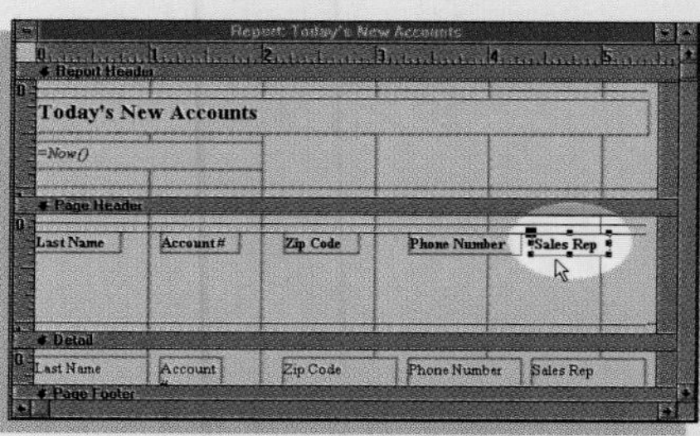

6 To delete a control, first click on it to display its handles.

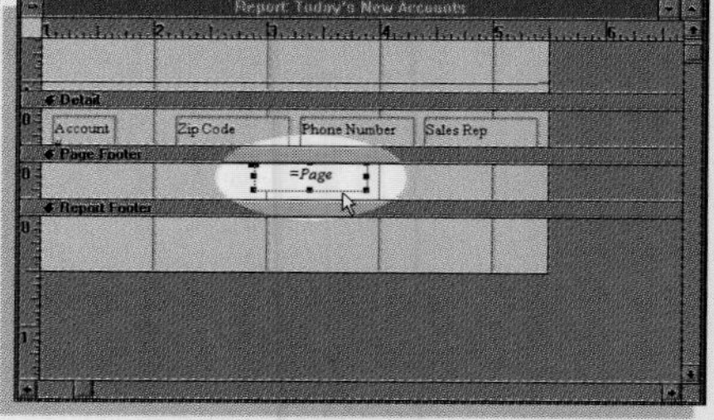

7 Press the Delete key.

8 As you edit a report, remember to click on File and then on Save occasionally to store the revisions. When done editing, click on File and then on Close.

TIP SHEET

- **In a report, you may wish to clarify, abbreviate, or otherwise edit field names where they are used in controls as identifiers such as column headings. You are free to do so, as described on this page. However, you are *not* free to edit field names in controls that supply data to the report. Doing so will make Microsoft Access unable to find the required data. In Design view, you can determine whether a field name is subject to editing by displaying its Properties list (see preceding page). If the title bar of the list begins *Text Box,* do not edit the field name. You are free to delete field names under all circumstances.**
- **If you delete a control that supplies data to the report, be sure to delete the corresponding heading as well. Otherwise, you'll have a heading that points to blank space.**
- **Deleting a nonessential control is a good way to save space on a report. After deleting a control, you can move another control wholly or partially into the vacated space by dragging its upper-left handle.**

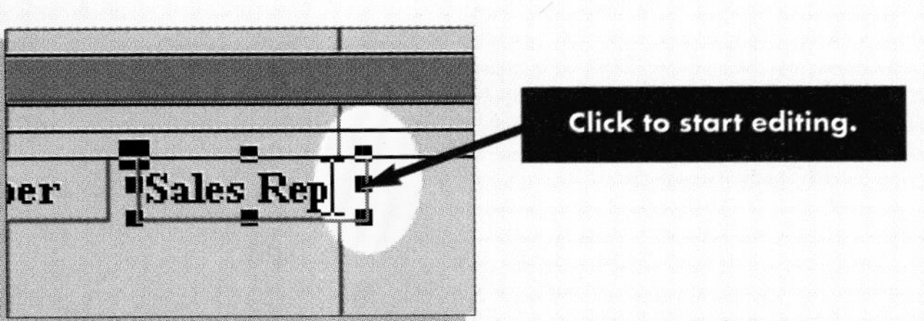

3. Observe that the mouse pointer becomes an I beam when you move it over the active control. This indicates that you can click in the control to place the insertion point there and then edit the text.

4. Use ordinary editing techniques (the typing keys, the arrow keys, Backspace, and Delete) to change the contents of the control.

5. Press the Enter key to indicate that you're done editing the text. (Do not press Escape; this will cancel your changes.)

LawnBirds, Inc.

Today's New Accounts

14-Dec-94

Last Name	Zip Code	Account #	Phone Number	Rep
Anderson	98833	894901	609-555-2430	Alhariri
Angelotti	43944	899941	216-555-2934	Chinn
Basramian	48599	849022		
Bennett	27510	894411	919-555-8609	Goldberg
Chang	94332	809440	510-555-0833	Alhariri
Glicksman	03444	882013	203-555-9138	
Gonsalves	68224	885560	915-555-0984	Martin
Greenwood	33179	899341	305-555-3323	Martin
Gulfside Cafe	32541	811411	904-555-8232	Chinn
Hahn	89472	837511		
Horstmann	78022	824011		
Kasdan	19040	833400		
Michael	97393	832404		
Pena	58944	837148		
Rao	07041	849021		
Ron's Barber Shop	96901	812991		
Sakata	02984	855029	709-555-3902	Chinn
The Tropic Shop	50884	900112		
Thorpe	94112	823920	503-555-2900	Borroughs
Wisteria Inn	91922	834291	415-555-9091	Goldberg
Zichelli	98702	803712	808-555-9348	Martin

TRY IT!

This is an opportunity to bolster your skills at your own pace before creating that all-important report on the job. Follow each step carefully at your computer to produce the report shown below. Chapter numbers cited with most steps direct you to background information on related skills. You will need to create a table on which to base the report. Steps 1 through 5 show you the table, but they assume you are familiar with the basic table techniques explain

and 5.

1

From the Database window, start a new table. *Chapter 4*

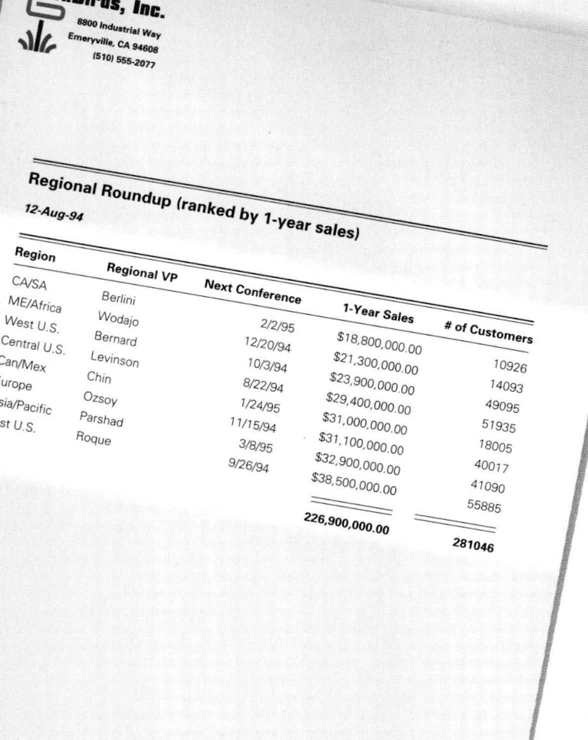

LawnBirds, Inc.
8800 Industrial Way
Emeryville, CA 94608
(510) 555-2077

Henry Bernard
1000 Green Street No. 4
San Francisco, CA 94109

Regional Roundup (ranked by 1-year sales)

12-Aug-94

Region	Regional VP	Next Conference	1-Year Sales	# of Customers
CA/SA	Berlini	2/2/95	$18,800,000.00	10926
ME/Africa	Wodajo	12/20/94	$21,300,000.00	14093
West U.S.	Bernard	10/3/94	$23,900,000.00	49095
Central U.S.	Levinson	8/22/94	$29,400,000.00	51935
Can/Mex	Chin	1/24/95	$31,000,000.00	18005
Europe	Ozsoy	11/15/94	$31,100,000.00	40017
Asia/Pacific	Parshad	3/8/95	$32,900,000.00	41090
East U.S.	Roque	9/26/94	$38,500,000.00	55885
			226,900,000.00	**281046**

2

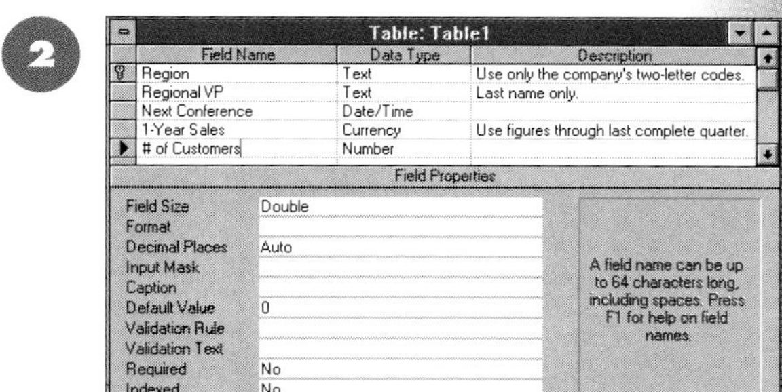

Define the five fields in the table as shown here, setting the Region field as the primary key. *Chapter 4*

Close the table, saving it as **Regional Roundup**. *Chapter 4*

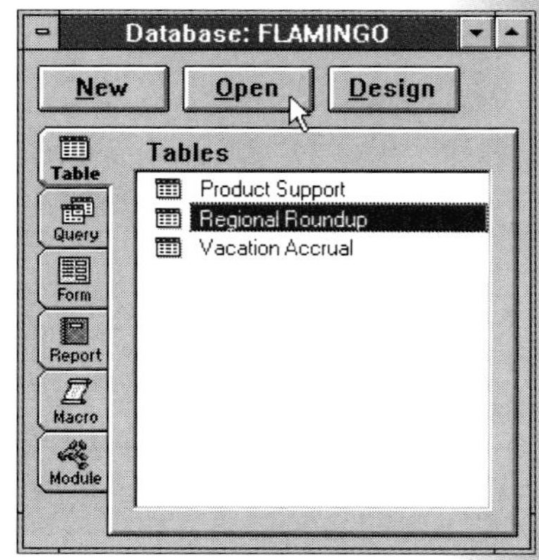

Open the table in Datasheet view. *Chapter 5*

Table: Regional Roundup

Region	Regional VP	Next Conference	1-Year Sales	# of Customers
Asia/Pacific	Parshad	3/8/95	$32,900,000.00	41090
CA/SA	Berlini	2/2/95	$18,800,000.00	10926
Can/Mex	Chin	1/24/95	$31,000,000.00	18005
Central U.S.	Levinson	8/22/94	$29,400,000.00	51935
East U.S.	Roque	9/26/94	$38,500,000.00	55885
Europe	Ozsoy	11/15/94	$31,100,000.00	40017
ME/Africa	Wodajo	12/20/94	$21,300,000.00	14093
West U.S.	Bernard	10/3/94	$23,900,000.00	49095

Record: 8 of 8

Enter the eight records shown here and then close the table, returning to the Database window. *Chapter 5*

Click on the Report object button.

7

Click on New.

8

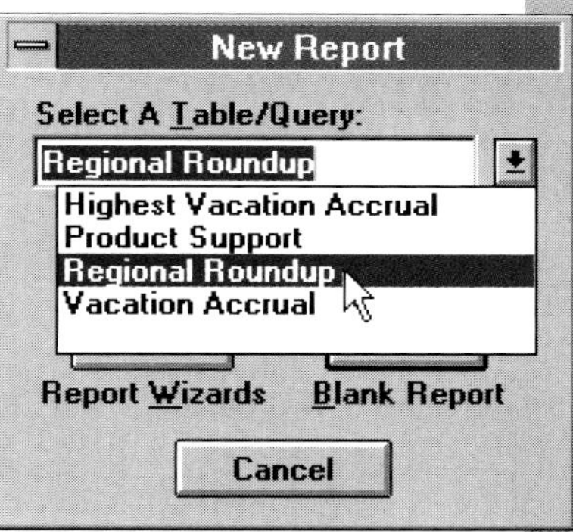

Click on the Select a Table/Query drop-down arrow and then click on Regional Roundup. *Chapter 12*

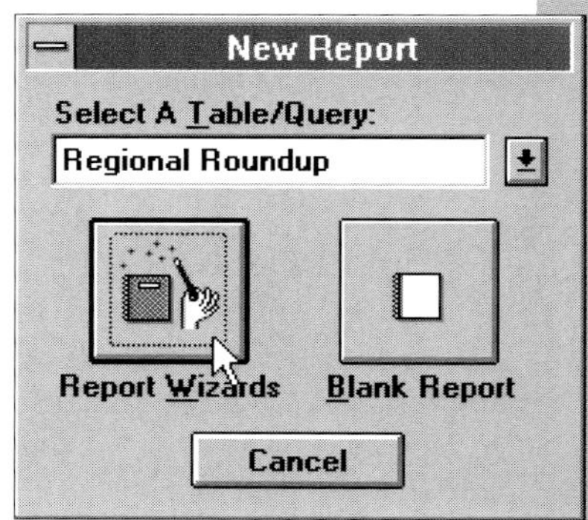

Click on Report Wizards. *Chapter 12*

Continue to next page ▶

TRY IT!

Continue below

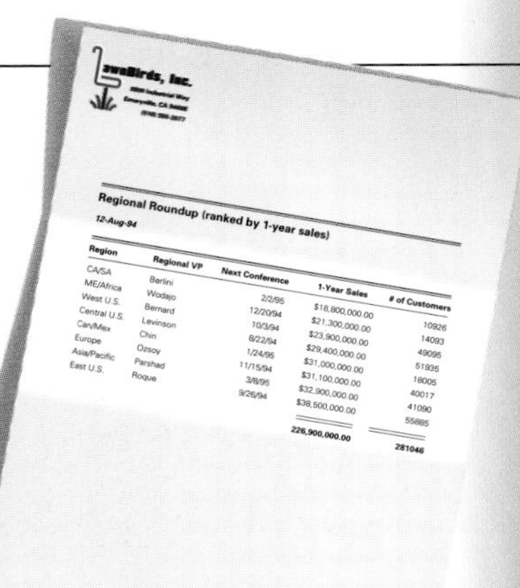

10

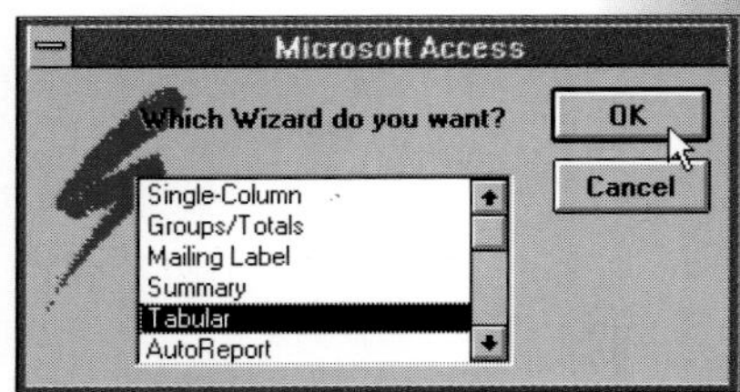

Click on Tabular and then click on OK. *Chapter 12*

11

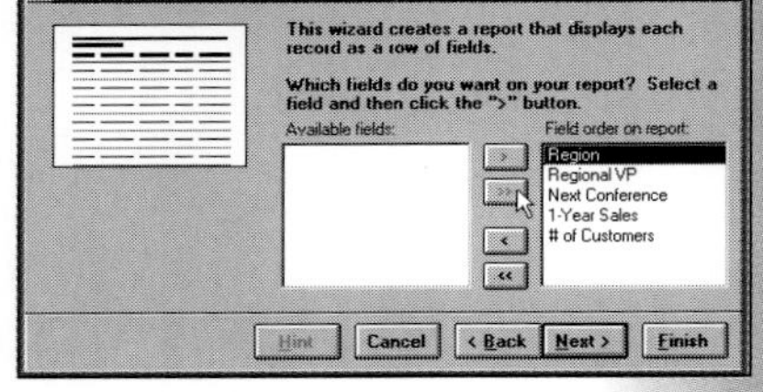

Click on the >> button to include all fields in the report. Then click on Next >. *Chapter 12*

12

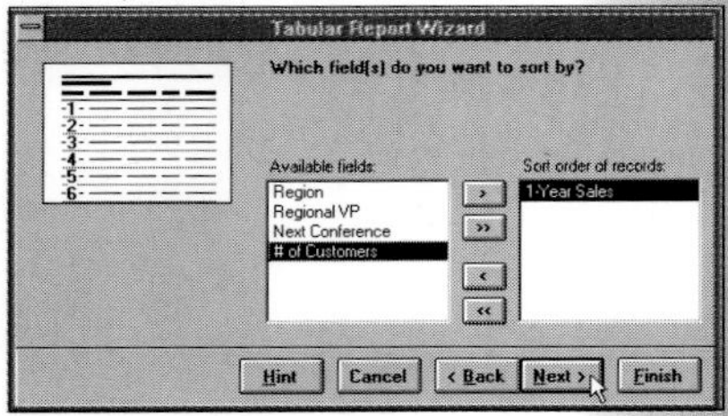

Double-click on 1-Year Sales to use this field as the sort key. Then click on Next >. *Chapter 12*

13

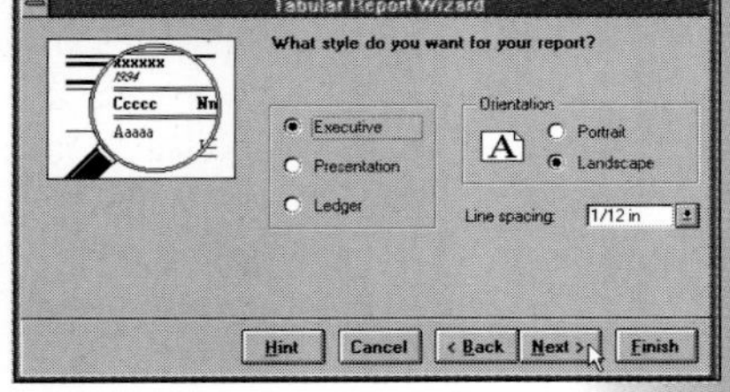

Click on Next > again to bypass this set of questions from the Report Wizard. *Chapter 12*

14

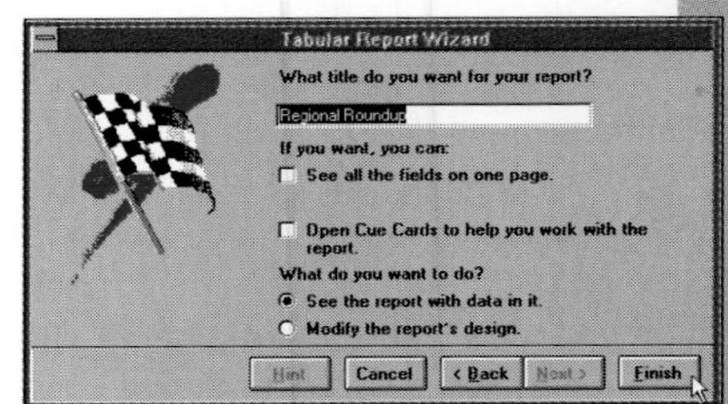

Click on Finish. *Chapter 12*

15

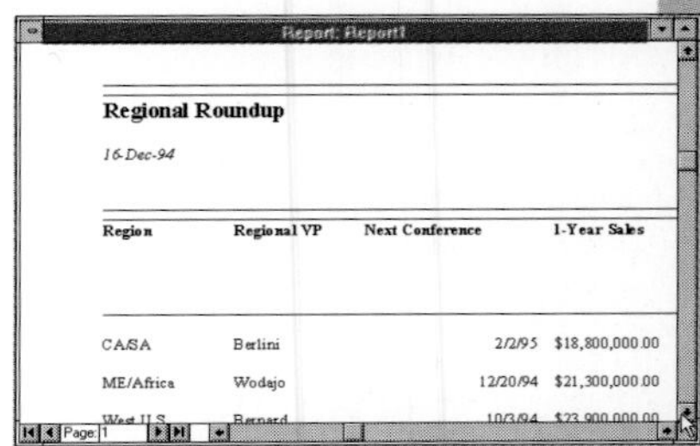

Use the scroll bars to browse through the preview of the report on your screen. You can click on the report to zoom out for a different perspective. *Chapter 13*

16

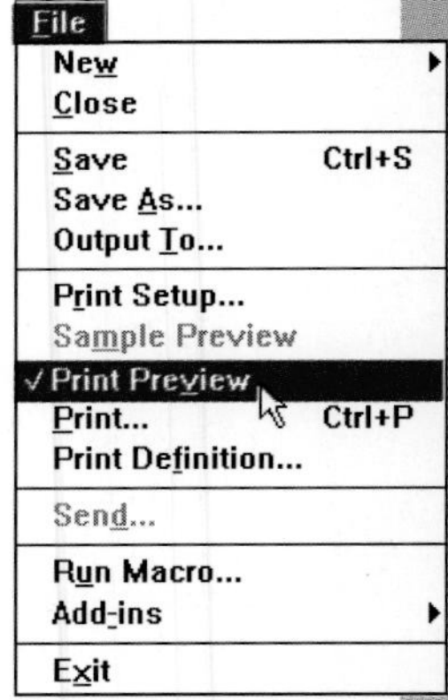

Click on File and then click on Print Preview to end the preview and see the report in Design view. *Chapter 13*

17

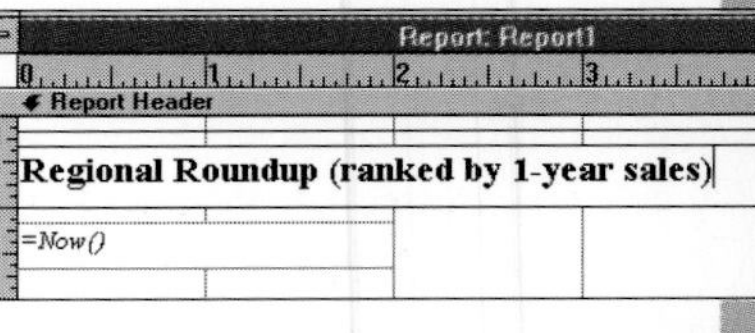

Click on the main report title (Regional Roundup) to display its handles. Click on it again to activate the insertion point, and then add (**ranked by 1-year sales**) to the end of the title. *Chapter 13*

18

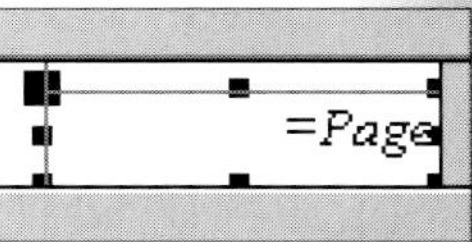

In the Page Footer area, click on =*Page* to display its handles, and then press the Delete key to delete this control. (Why print a page number on a one-page report?) *Chapter 13*

19

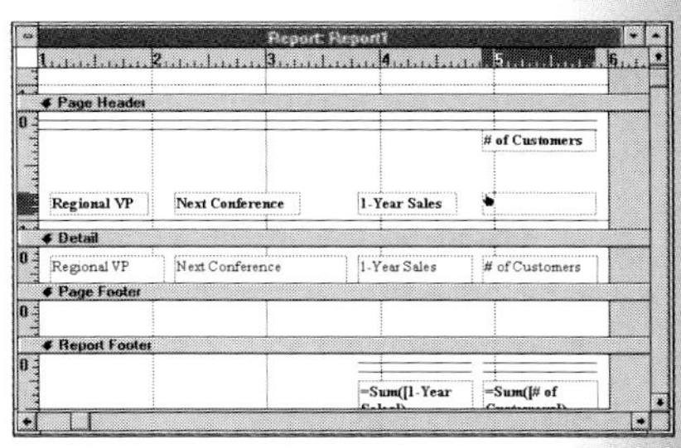

Move each column heading lower within the Page Header section. To do so, click on each heading and drag the control downward by its top-left handle. *Chapter 13*

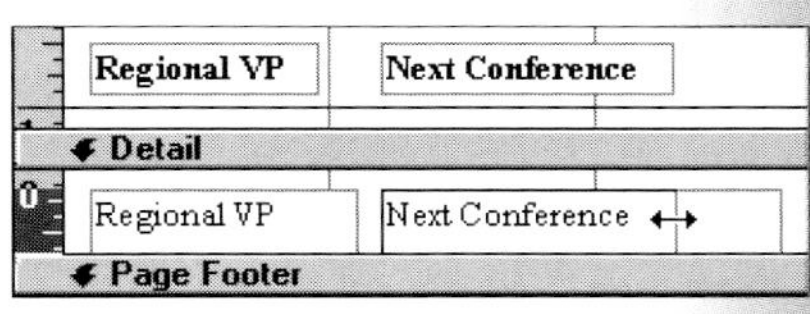

In the Detail area, narrow the Next Conference control by dragging the right side-handle to the left. Make this control as wide as the like-named label above it. *Chapter 13*

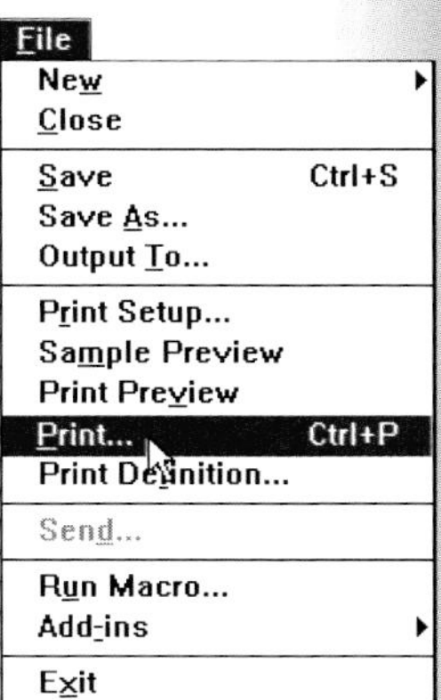

Click on File and then click on Print. *Chapter 13*

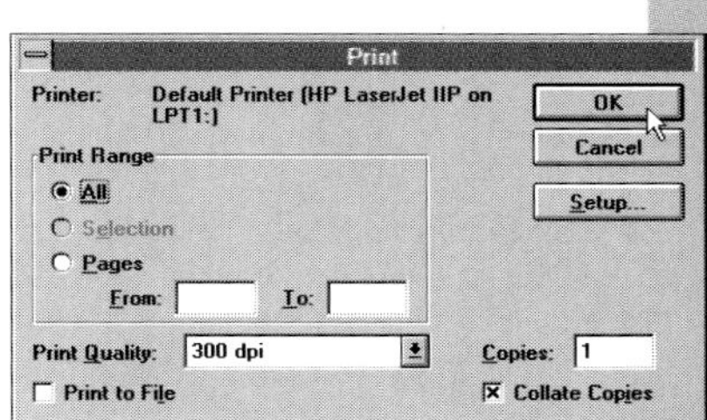

Click on OK to print one copy of the report. *Chapter 13*

23

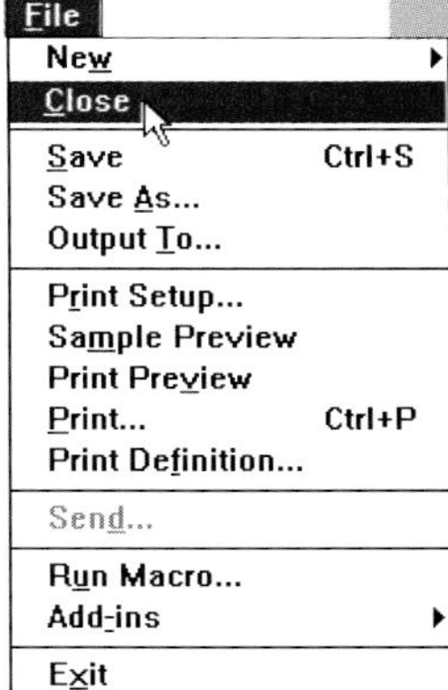

Click on File and then click on Close. *Chapter 12*

24

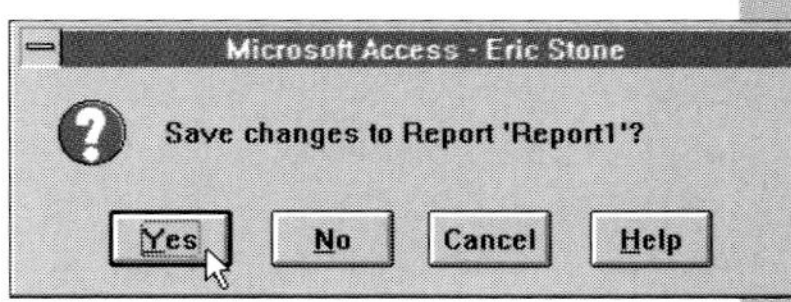

When asked whether to save the report, click on Yes. *Chapter 12*

Type **Regional Roundup (tabular)** as the report name and then click on OK to save and close the report. Observe your newly created report object in the Database window. *Chapter 12*

CHAPTER 14

Shortcuts

Have you ever asked for driving directions in an unfamiliar city? The less familiar you were with the territory, the more likely you wanted to know the easiest, least confusing way to go—even if it wasn't the fastest. Only when you are comfortable with the general layout of a city do you become interested in shortcuts.

Learning to use software is a similar experience. That's why this book really is not about shortcuts. Since you started out as an inexperienced user, this book has assumed that you want to know one way—the most straightforward way—to get the job done.

But now that you are comfortable with Microsoft Access, you are ready to explore the many convenient shortcuts available from the toolbars and the keyboard. Some of these shortcuts can save you considerable effort over the long run and certainly are worth the time it takes to learn them. However, you may want to skip the ones that address tasks you perform infrequently. All techniques explained in this chapter are entirely optional.

The Toolbars

A *toolbar* is a row of buttons ("tools") that sits below the menu bar. The tools substitute for commands that you would otherwise issue from the menu bar and from dialog boxes. To use a tool, simply click on it. Microsoft Access has a toolbar tailored to each situation. For example, it displays one toolbar when you are designing a query and another when you are previewing a report. However, many tools appear in more than one toolbar. This page introduces the best of the tools available from the various toolbars.

TIP SHEET

- **What if you want to use the toolbar but it does not appear in some or all situations? To see a list of available toolbars, click on View in the menu bar and then click on Toolbars. In the dialog box that appears, click on the toolbar appropriate to your situation; for example, if you are at the Database window, click on Database. Click on Show, and then click on Close.**
- **A colleague may have customized one or more of your toolbars, replacing tools that you're unlikely to need with tools more appropriate to your work environment. If your toolbars differ from the ones shown here, try to track down whoever customized your toolbars so you can learn what each tool does. Failing that, you can point to a tool and read the brief description of it on the status bar. Alternatively, click on the Help tool (if it appears on the customized toolbar) and then click on a tool in question to display a Help window for that tool.**

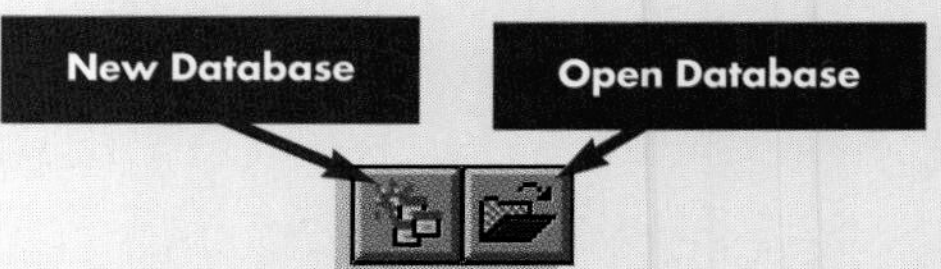

1. From the Database window, click on the New Database tool to start a new database. Click on the Open Database tool to display the Open Database dialog box.

2. When you want to print the active table, query, form, or report, click on the Print tool to display the Print dialog box. This tool is not available when you are in Design view.

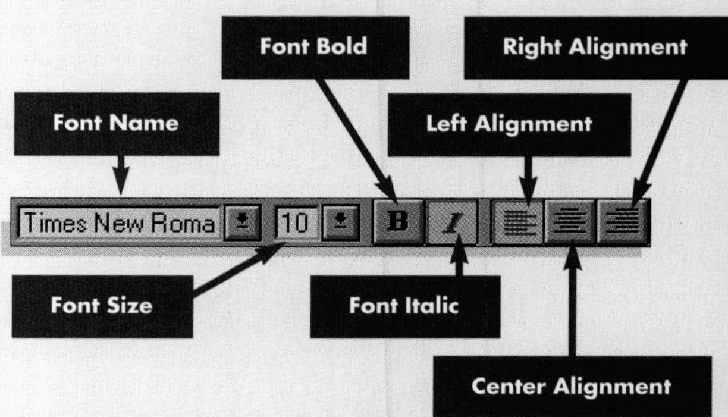

7. When editing a report in Design view, click on a control to display its handles and then use these tools to format the contents of the control, bypassing the Properties list. Click on the Font Name or Font Size drop-down arrow, and choose a font or size by clicking on it. To boldface or italicize the text in the active control, click on the Font Bold or Font Italic tool; do the same to remove boldface or italics. The Left, Center, and Right Alignment tools change the alignment of text with respect to the left and right borders of the control.

3 Available from every toolbar, the Database Window tool activates the Database window, deactivating but not closing the window you were viewing. To reactivate the original window, simply click on it. As you might expect, clicking on the Database Window tool has no effect when the Database window is already active.

4 The Undo tool is available in most toolbars. Clicking on it reverses your most recent action, just like clicking on Edit in the menu bar and then on Undo. You may recall from Chapter 7 that the Undo command is unavailable when your most recent action is not of the type that Microsoft Access can reverse. In this situation, the Undo tool is visible but dimmed, and clicking on it has no effect.

DATABASE TOOLBAR

TABLE DATASHEET TOOLBAR

TABLE DESIGN TOOLBAR

QUERY DATASHEET TOOLBAR

QUERY DESIGN TOOLBAR

FORM VIEW TOOLBAR

PRINT PREVIEW TOOLBAR (REPORTS)

REPORT DESIGN TOOLBAR

5 When you click on the Help tool, the mouse pointer acquires a question mark. Point to anything on your screen—such as a mysterious tool on the toolbar—and click on it to open the help system and display information about the mystery item. Once the help system is open, you work with it as described in Chapter 7.

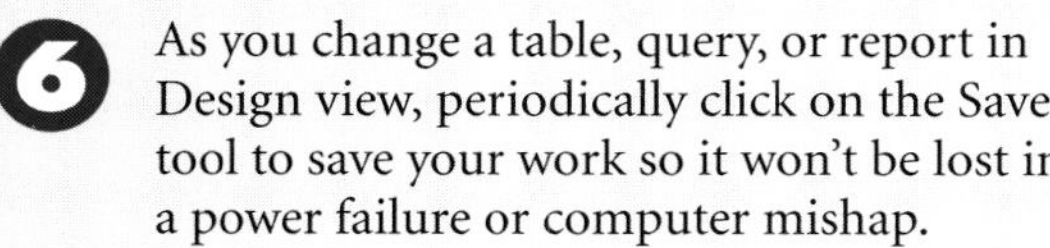

6 As you change a table, query, or report in Design view, periodically click on the Save tool to save your work so it won't be lost in a power failure or computer mishap.

The Most Useful Keyboard Techniques

The mouse is quite an intuitive input device, but a decent typist can work much faster in Microsoft Access by using keyboard shortcuts for certain tasks. The drawback is that to effectively take advantage of a keyboard shortcut, you have to memorize it. This page lists a few particularly helpful keyboard shortcuts. Consider memorizing the ones that appeal to you most.

2 Press Ctrl+Z to issue the Undo command, reversing your most recent action.

1 In Design view, press Ctrl+S to save your work. It's equivalent to clicking on File and then on Save, or to clicking on the Save tool in the toolbar.

7 Press Alt+F4 at any time to exit Microsoft Access. If you have not saved all your work, Microsoft Access will ask you whether you want to save it before closing the program.

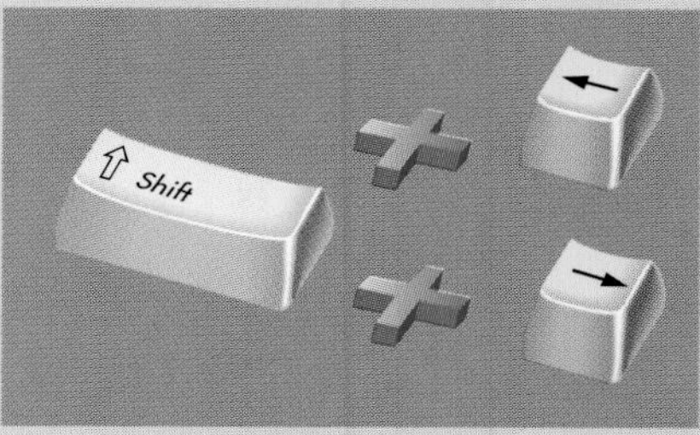

6 To select text for editing within a cell, hold down the Shift key and press the left or right arrow key. For example, you can select a word this way and then press Backspace to delete it.

TIP SHEET

- **See "How to Use the Keyboard in Windows" in Chapter 2 for a general overview of keyboard techniques that work not just in Microsoft Access but in all Windows-based programs.**
- **No doubt you've observed that it takes a few seconds to start Microsoft Access from Program Manager. With keyboard techniques, you can use this time effectively by issuing your first command or two while Microsoft Access loads into your computer's memory. For example, recall that Microsoft Access places your four most recently edited databases near the bottom of the File menu; thus, you can press Alt, f, 1 to open the database you worked with most recently. Then you might press Alt, v, q to display query objects in the Database window—all before Microsoft Access is done loading.**

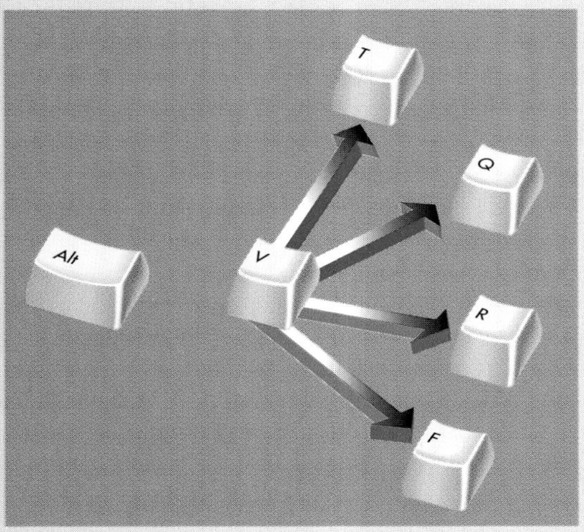

3 Instead of clicking on an object button in the Database window, you can select it from the View menu using your keyboard. Each object type is a command on the View menu. Press Alt to activate the menu bar, type **v** to pull down the View menu, and then type the first letter of the object type, such as **r** for reports.

4 When performing intensive data entry in a table or form, press Tab to move to the next field. Press Shift+Tab to move back one field.

5 Moving into an occupied field with Tab or Shift+Tab selects the entire field contents. To deselect the contents and activate the insertion point for editing, press F2.

APPENDIX

Installation

Software is not built into your computer. It is a separate product that someone has to buy and install. In many office situations, an administrator is responsible for installing software on users' machines or making it available over a network of linked computers. Likewise, computers purchased from stores and mail-order firms often come with software such as Microsoft Access already installed. Thus, there is a good chance that someone has prepared Microsoft Access for you, and you can skip this appendix.

If you are not sure whether Microsoft Access is installed on your computer, follow the steps in "How to Get Started in Microsoft Access" in Chapter 3 of this book. If you can start Microsoft Access, then, plainly, it has been installed.

Microsoft provides clear, complete installation instructions in a printed manual that comes with Microsoft Access. Those instructions are more than sufficient for most computer users. Plus, once you start the installation process, on-screen messages will tell you what to do.

This appendix clarifies some of the installation issues that can slow down people who have little computer experience. It gives you the extra knowledge you may need to follow a generally straightforward procedure.

Tips on Installing Microsoft Access

The basic installation procedure is simple: You place a floppy disk in a disk drive, and your computer copies information from the floppy disk onto your computer's hard disk. Then you place another floppy disk in the disk drive, the computer copies more information, and so on until the hard disk holds the entire Microsoft Access program. There are quite a few variables in the installation process—so many that this book could not possibly discuss them all. Rest assured, however, that for most users in most situations, installation proceeds very smoothly. And the absolute worst thing that can happen if you make a mistake during installation is that you'll have to start over.

TIP SHEET

- **Even if you received a shrink-wrapped copy of Microsoft Access with your computer, the program may already be installed. That's because it is more convenient—and perfectly legal—for retailers to install software using an already open copy rather than the copy they give you.**
- **Your computer may be set to start Windows as soon as it is switched on. In this case, you will see *Program Manager* somewhere on your screen. Instead of exiting Windows to display the DOS prompt and perform step 4, you can click on File in the Program Manager menu bar, click on the Run command, type** a:\setup **or** b:\setup **depending on what floppy-disk drive holds the Setup disk, and click on the OK button.**
- **You can start and use Microsoft Access as soon as installation is finished. See Chapter 3 of this book—or read Chapters 1 and 2 for some background information on DOS, Windows, and databases in general.**

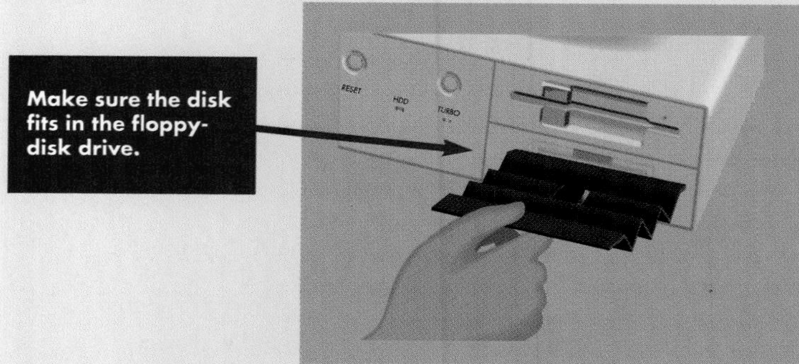

1 Your copy of Microsoft Access is on either 3.5-inch hard-cased disks or 5.25-inch soft-cased disks. To hold these disks during installation, your computer may have one 3.5-inch floppy-disk drive, two drives of the same size, or—the most convenient arrangement—one drive of each size. Contact your software retailer if you don't have a floppy-disk drive of the correct size to accommodate your Microsoft Access disks.

8 It can take awhile for your computer to read information from the floppy disks. When it's time to remove the disk and put in another, your computer will beep at you and tell you what disk it needs. After putting in the next disk, you must click on the OK button.

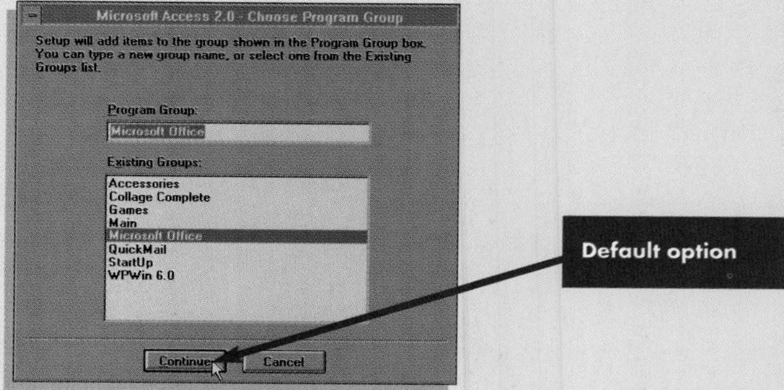

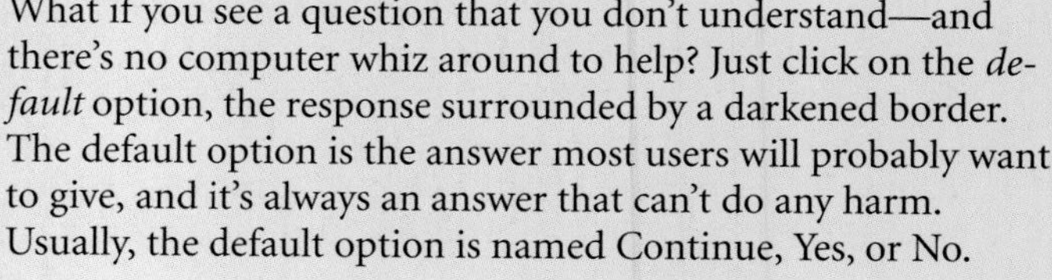

7 What if you see a question that you don't understand—and there's no computer whiz around to help? Just click on the *default* option, the response surrounded by a darkened border. The default option is the answer most users will probably want to give, and it's always an answer that can't do any harm. Usually, the default option is named Continue, Yes, or No.

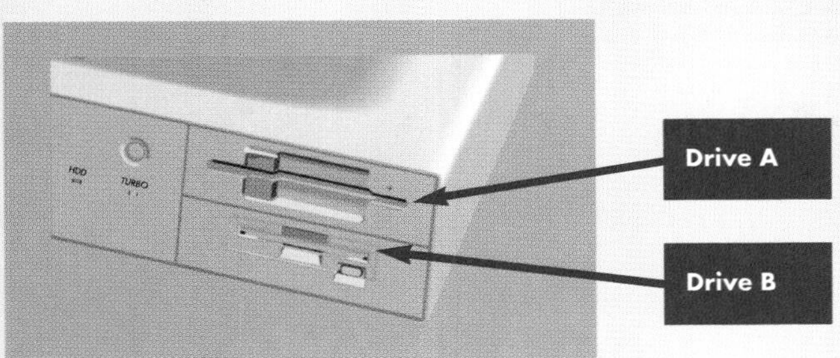

2 To start the installation, you will need to know the *drive letter* of the floppy-disk drive you'll be using to install Microsoft Access. If your computer has only one floppy-disk drive, it is drive A. If your computer has two floppy-disk drives, the top or left drive is drive A, and the bottom or right drive is drive B.

3 One of your Microsoft Access disks is labeled, among other things, *Setup*. To start the installation process, switch on your computer and wait until it is done warming up. Then insert the Setup disk in a floppy-disk drive. During installation, on-screen instructions will tell you when to take out one disk and insert another.

4 With the DOS prompt displayed on your computer screen, type **win a:\setup** if the Setup disk is in drive A, or **win b:\setup** if the Setup disk is in drive B. Then press the Enter key.

5 Wait as information is copied from the floppy disk to your computer's hard disk. Periodically, you will be asked questions about how you want to install Microsoft Access. The questions vary according to such factors as your computer equipment and the amount of empty space on your hard disk. Find the answer on the screen and *click* on it. To click on an item means to roll the mouse so that the *mouse pointer* is over the item and then press and immediately release the left mouse button.

6 When you see this window, click on the button next to "Typical." This means that you want to install the Microsoft Access components that most users need. Microsoft Access will alert you if there is not enough room on your hard disk for all these components and will redisplay this window. If that happens, click on the button next to Complete/Custom and follow the on-screen instructions to omit nonessential components. To perform every task covered in this book, you can omit any component except Microsoft Access (obviously), Wizards, and Help and Cue Cards.

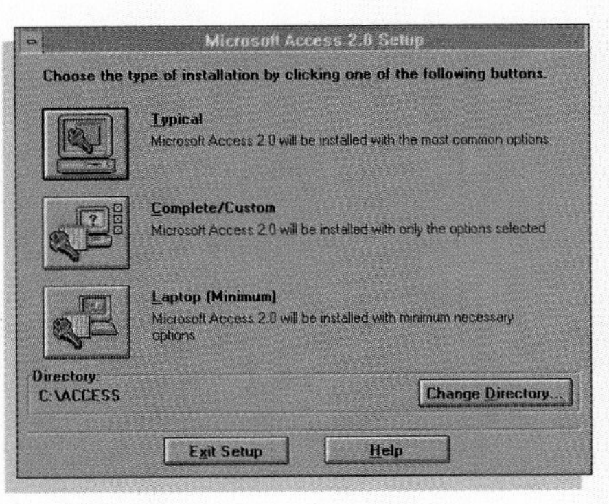

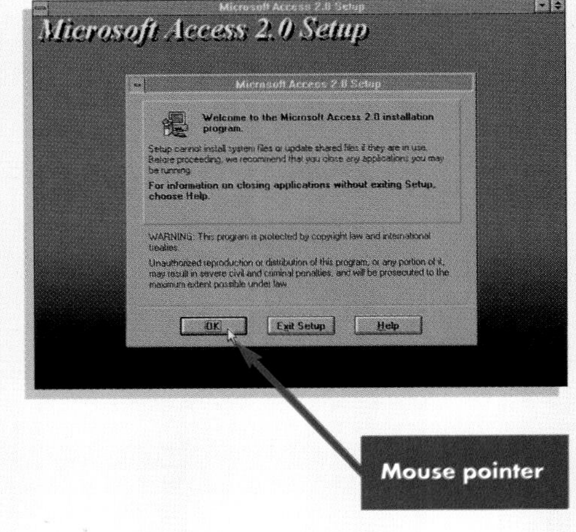

INDEX

A

Access. *See* Microsoft Access
Alt+Esc (switching between Windows programs), 36
Alt+F4 (closing a program), 15
application window, 10
  title bar in, 11
arrow, drop-down, 17
arrow keys, 15
asterisk (*), end of table marker, 42
AutoReport, Report Wizard, 111
Avery labels, 112

B

Backspace key, 42
Bad command or file name message, 9

C

calculated field, 82
cell, 32-33
  activating for data entry, 43
check boxes, marking and clearing, 17
click on, 13
closing
  a dialog box, 16
  a program, 15
  a table, 34-35
columns, changing width of, 40
commands, 8
  issuing using keyboard, 14–15
computer, starting, 8-9
context-sensitive help, 57
control handles, 123
Control Menu
  box, 20-21
  opening, 15
controls
  changing report design with, 123
  editing format and alignment of Properties list with, 122-123
criteria, query
  adding and deleting, 80-81
  separating multiple with AND or OR, 73
Ctrl+End (moving to bottomof window), 14
Ctrl+Home (moving to top of window), 14
Ctrl+S (saving work in Design view), 134
Ctrl+Z (Undo command), 44, 134

D

data
  delteting, 124–125
  displaying in reports, 117–125
  editing in forms, 98–99
  finding in large tables, 52–53
database, 23
  naming a new, 25
  opening from disk, 24–25
  opening with Form object button, 91
  starting a new, 24–25
database management system, 1–5
Database toolbar, 20–21, *20*, 133
Database window, 30
  New Database tool, 132
  object buttons in, 31
  Query object button in, 68
  tool, 133
datasheet cell, 32–33
Datasheet view, 23
  opening and viewing tables in, 40–41
  working with large tables in, 51–55
Data Type, specifying, 33
date, setting for reports, 122
Delete key (Del), 42
Delete Row command, 47
deleting
  data from reports, 124–125
  records from a table, 44–45
Design view, 23
  changing report appearance in, 122–123
  changing table design in, 46–47
  controls, 123
  hiding Toolbox in, 122
  viewing blank table in, 30
dialog boxes, 16–17
directories, 25
disk drives, 24–25
  changing, 27
disk operating system (DOS), 7
document windows, 10–11
DOS (disk operating system), 7
  starting Windows from, 8–9
DOS prompt, 8–9
DOS Shell, 8
double-click, 10, 13
dragging the mouse, 13
drop-down arrow, 17
dynaset, 76–77

E

Edit, Find command, 53
editing
  data in forms, 98–99
  reports, 124–125
  reports using toolbar, 133
Enter key, 9

error correction, using Undo, 58–59
Escape (Esc) key, 14
exiting Microsoft Access, 36–37
  using Alt+F4, 134

F

field names, entering, 32
Field Properties area, 33, 46
fields, 3
  adding to queries, 81
  calculated, 82
  defining in a new table, 32–33
  inserting, 46–47
  moving, 81
  moving between, 135
file name, extensions and specifications, 24–25
files, opening, 26–27
filter (FLTR), 54, 103
Find dialog box, 52–53
F1 key (Help command), 60–61
footers, 123
Form object button, 91
  opening databases with, 96
forms definition, 2, 89
  displaying only selected records in, 104–105
  editing data in, 98–99
  entering records in, 100–101
  naming, saving, and closing, 92–93
  sorting records in, 102–103
  starting new, 90–91
  using, 95
  viewing records in, 96–97
Form view, 93, 97
  navigating in, 96–97
Form View toolbar, 133
Form Wizards, 91
function keys, 15

H

handles, control, 123
hand symbol, in Help screen, 61
headers, 123
Help command, 57
  issuing with F1, 60–61
  issuing from toolbar, 133
horizontal scroll bar, 13

I

icons, program group, 11
inserting, new fields in tables, 46–47
insertion point, 32
Insert Row command, 47
installing Microsoft Access, 137–139

K

keyboard
  alternatives to mouse, 14–15
  shortcuts, 134–135
  starting programs with, 10

L

Labels, 112–113
List Files of Type, 26

M

macros, 23
Mailing Label, Report Wizard, 110
  dialog box, 113
  Label Type, 112–113
  Unit of Measure setting, 113
Maximize button, 12
menu bar, 20–21
  in application window, 11
Microsoft Access, 1
  exiting, 36–37
  features, 5
  getting started in, 20–21
  installing, 137–139
  interface, 4
  opening a database in, 26–27
  program icon, 20
  starting a new database in, 24–25
  terms and concepts, 22–23
Microsoft Windows. *See* Windows
Minimize button, 12, 21
modules, 23
mouse
  dragging, 13
  starting programs with, 10
  using in Windows, 12–13
mouse pointer, 12–13, 20–21
  as I beam, 125
moving
  a dialog box, 16
  between fields, 135

N

naming tables, 34–35
network, 24
New Database dialog box, 25
New Database tool, in Database window, 132
New Form dialog box, 91
New Table button, 31
New Table dialog box, 31
Num Lock key, 15

O

object buttons, in Database window, 31
on-line help, 57, 61
Open Database dialog box, 26–27
  opening from toolbar, 132
opening files, 25–26

P

Page Footer, 123
Page Header, 123
page layout, previewing before printing, 119
paper orientation, print setup, 49
Print dialog box, 49, 121
printing, 48–49
  previewing before, 118–121
  query results, 76–77
  reports, 120–121
  selected pages only, 120
  setup for, 49, 121
Print Preview toolbar (Reports), 133
Print Setup dialog box, 49, 121
Print tool, 132
program group icons, 11
program items, 11
Program Manager, 9
  starting a program from, 10–11
programs, 1. *See also* database management system
  starting, 10–11
Properties list, 122, 123

Q

queries, 3
  adding criteria to, 80–81
  adding sort key to, 81
  choosing records to display, 72–73
  correcting and improving, 80–81
  naming, saving, and closing, 74–75
  performing calculations in, 82–83
  printing results of, 76–77
  running, 76–77
  specifying fields for, 70–71
  starting new, 68–69
Query Datasheet toolbar, 133
Query Design toolbar, 133
Query object button, in Database window, 68
Quick Sort command, 54–55
  sorting form records with, 102–103

R

radio buttons, selecting, 17
RAM (random access memory), 7
record, 3
report design, changing, 122–123
Report Design toolbar, 133
Report Footer, 123
Report Header, 123
Report object button, 120, 122, 124
reports, 3
  changing appearance of, 122–123
  changing contents of, 124–125
  creating, 107
  date in, 122
  displaying data in, 117–125
  editing with toolbar, 133
  naming, saving, and closing, 114–115
  previewing, 118–119
  printing, 120–121
  specifying fields in, 112–113
  starting, 108–109
  types of (in Report Wizard), 110–111
  using and improving, 117
Report Wizards, 107
Restore button, 12, 21

S

Save As dialog box, 34
Save tool, 133
saving tables, 34–35, 133
scroll arrow, 13
scroll button, dragging, 13
scrolling a window, 14
Set Primary Key command, 34
shortcuts, keyboard, 134–135
Single-Column, Report Wizard, 111
  dialog box, 112
sorting
  records in forms, 102–103
  tables, 54–55
sort key, adding to a query, 81
sort order, specifying, 55, 72
starting your computer, 8–9
status bar, 20–21
subdirectory, 25

T

Tab key, moving between fields with, 33, 43
Table Datasheet toolbar, 133
Table Design toolbar, 133
Table object button, 31
tables
  building and improving, 39
  changing contents of, 44–45
  changing design of, 46–47

closing, 34–35
designing, 29–37
editing within a dynaset, 77
entering data in, 42–43
finding data in, 51–53
naming, 34–35
opening and viewing, 40–41
printing, 48–49
saving, 34–35
sorting, 54–55
starting new, 30–31
storing and changing data in, 34–35
Tabular Report Wizard, 111
dialog box, 112
text boxes, changing entries in, 16
title bar, 21
in application window, 11
toolbars, *132–133*
toolbar shortcuts, 132–133
Toolbox, in Design View, 122

U

Undo command (Ctrl+Z), 44
correcting errors with, 58–59
in Design view, 122
Undo tool, 133

V

validation rule, changing, 46
Validation Rule text box, limiting field values with, 33
vertical scroll bar, 13
views, 22–23

W

window elements, 20–21
Windows, 7
starting from DOS, 8–9
Wizards, 30
Form, 91
Report, 107

Z

Zoom feature, previewing page layout with, 119

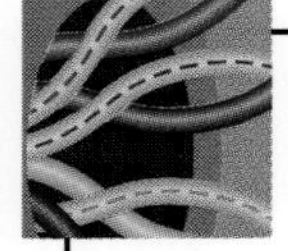

Imagination. Innovation. Insight.

The How It Works Series from Ziff-Davis Press

"... a magnificently seamless integration of text and graphics ..."

Larry Blasko, The Associated Press, reviewing *PC/Computing How Computers Work*

No other books bring computer technology to life like the *How It Works* series from Ziff-Davis Press. Lavish, full-color illustrations and lucid text from some of the world's top computer commentators make *How It Works* books an exciting way to explore the inner workings of PC technology.

ISBN: 094-7 Price: $22.95

PC/Computing How Computers Work

A worldwide blockbuster that hit the general trade bestseller lists! *PC/Computing* magazine executive editor Ron White dismantles the PC and reveals what really makes it tick.

How Networks Work

Two of the most respected names in connectivity showcase the PC network, illustrating and explaining how each component does its magic and how they all fit together.

ISBN: 129-3 Price: $24.95

ISBN: 184-6 Price: $17.95

How Macs Work

A fun and fascinating voyage to the heart of the Macintosh! Two noted *MacUser* contributors cover the spectrum of Macintosh operations from startup to shutdown.

ISBN: 146-3 Price: $24.95

How Software Works

This dazzlingly illustrated volume from Ron White peeks inside the PC to show in full-color how software breathes life into the PC. Covers Windows™ and all major software categories.

ISBN: 133-1 Price: $24.95

How to Use Your Computer

Conquer computerphobia and see how this intricate machine truly makes life easier. Dozens of full-color graphics showcase the components of the PC and explain how to interact with them.

ISBN: 155-2 Price: $22.95

All About Computers

This one-of-a-kind visual guide for kids features numerous full-color illustrations and photos on every page, combined with dozens of interactive projects that reinforce computer basics, making this an exciting way to learn all about the world of computers.

ISBN: 166-8 Price: $15.95

How To Use Word

Make Word 6.0 for Windows Work for You!

A uniquely visual approach puts the basics of Microsoft's latest Windows-based word processor right before the reader's eyes. Colorful examples invite them to begin producing a variety of documents, quickly and easily. Truly innovative!

How To Use Excel

Make Excel 5.0 for Windows Work for You!

Covering the latest version of Excel, this visually impressive resource guides beginners to spreadsheet fluency through a full-color graphical approach that makes powerful techniques seem plain as day. Hands-on "Try It" sections give new users a chance to sharpen newfound skills.

ISBN: 185-4 Price: $17.95

Available at all fine bookstores or by calling 1-800-688-0448, ext. 100. Call for more information on the Instructor's Supplement, including transparencies for each book in the *How It Works* Series.

Cut Here

Cut Here

Ziff-Davis Press Survey of Readers

Please help us in our effort to produce the best books on personal computing. For your assistance, we would be pleased to send you a FREE catalog featuring the complete line of Ziff-Davis Press books.

1. How did you first learn about this book?

- Recommended by a friend . . . . ☐ -1 (5)
- Recommended by store personnel . . . . ☐ -2
- Saw in Ziff-Davis Press catalog . . . . ☐ -3
- Received advertisement in the mail . . . . ☐ -4
- Saw the book on bookshelf at store . . . . ☐ -5
- Read book review in: ________________ ☐ -6
- Saw an advertisement in: ______________ ☐ -7
- Other (Please specify): ________________ ☐ -8

2. Which THREE of the following factors most influenced your decision to purchase this book? (Please check up to THREE.)

- Front or back cover information on book . . . ☐ -1 (6)
- Logo of magazine affiliated with book . . . . . ☐ -2
- Special approach to the content . . . . ☐ -3
- Completeness of content . . . . ☐ -4
- Author's reputation . . . . ☐ -5
- Publisher's reputation . . . . ☐ -6
- Book cover design or layout . . . . ☐ -7
- Index or table of contents of book . . . . ☐ -8
- Price of book . . . . ☐ -9
- Special effects, graphics, illustrations . . . . ☐ -0
- Other (Please specify): ________________ ☐ -x

3. How many computer books have you purchased in the last six months? _____ (7-10)

4. On a scale of 1 to 5, where 5 is excellent, 4 is above average, 3 is average, 2 is below average, and 1 is poor, please rate each of the following aspects of this book below. (Please circle your answer.)

Depth/completeness of coverage	5	4	3	2	1	(11)
Organization of material	5	4	3	2	1	(12)
Ease of finding topic	5	4	3	2	1	(13)
Special features/time saving tips	5	4	3	2	1	(14)
Appropriate level of writing	5	4	3	2	1	(15)
Usefulness of table of contents	5	4	3	2	1	(16)
Usefulness of index	5	4	3	2	1	(17)
Usefulness of accompanying disk	5	4	3	2	1	(18)
Usefulness of illustrations/graphics	5	4	3	2	1	(19)
Cover design and attractiveness	5	4	3	2	1	(20)
Overall design and layout of book	5	4	3	2	1	(21)
Overall satisfaction with book	5	4	3	2	1	(22)

5. Which of the following computer publications do you read regularly; that is, 3 out of 4 issues?

- Byte . . . . ☐ -1 (23)
- Computer Shopper . . . . ☐ -2
- Corporate Computing . . . . ☐ -3
- Dr. Dobb's Journal . . . . ☐ -4
- LAN Magazine . . . . ☐ -5
- MacWEEK . . . . ☐ -6
- MacUser . . . . ☐ -7
- PC Computing . . . . ☐ -8
- PC Magazine . . . . ☐ -9
- PC WEEK . . . . ☐ -0
- Windows Sources . . . . ☐ -x
- Other (Please specify): ________________ ☐ -y

Please turn page.

Cut Here

Cut Here

PLEASE TAPE HERE ONLY—DO NOT STAPLE

6. What is your level of experience with personal computers? With the subject of this book?

	With PCs		With subject of book	
Beginner	☐	-1 (24)	☐	-1 (25)
Intermediate	☐	-2	☐	-2
Advanced	☐	-3	☐	-3

7. Which of the following best describes your job title?

Officer (CEO/President/VP/owner)	☐	-1 (26)
Director/head	☐	-2
Manager/supervisor	☐	-3
Administration/staff	☐	-4
Teacher/educator/trainer	☐	-5
Lawyer/doctor/medical professional	☐	-6
Engineer/technician	☐	-7
Consultant	☐	-8
Not employed/student/retired	☐	-9
Other (Please specify): ________________	☐	-0

8. What is your age?

Under 20	☐	-1 (27)
21-29	☐	-2
30-39	☐	-3
40-49	☐	-4
50-59	☐	-5
60 or over	☐	-6

9. Are you:

Male	☐	-1 (28)
Female	☐	-2

Thank you for your assistance with this important information! Please write your address below to receive our free catalog.

Name: ________________________________

Address: ________________________________

City/State/Zip: ________________________________

Fold here to mail.

2230-13-15

NO POSTAGE NECESSARY IF MAILED IN THE UNITED STATES

BUSINESS REPLY MAIL

FIRST CLASS MAIL PERMIT NO. 1612 OAKLAND, CA

POSTAGE WILL BE PAID BY ADDRESSEE

Ziff-Davis Press
5903 Christie Avenue
Emeryville, CA 94608-1925
Attn: Marketing